KNIGHT'S MICROSOFT® BUSINESS INTELLIGENCE 24-HOUR TRAINER

Knight's Microsoft® Business Intelligence 24-Hour Trainer

Knight's Microsoft® Business Intelligence 24-Hour Trainer

LEVERAGING MICROSOFT SQL SERVER® INTEGRATION, ANALYSIS, AND REPORTING SERVICES WITH EXCEL® AND SHAREPOINT®

Brian Knight, Devin Knight, Adam Jorgensen, Patrick LeBlanc, Mike Davis

WILEY

Wiley Publishing, Inc.

Knight's Microsoft® Business Intelligence 24-Hour Trainer: Leveraging Microsoft SQL Server® Integration, Analysis, and Reporting Services with Excel® and SharePoint®

Published by
Wiley Publishing, Inc.
10475 Crosspoint Boulevard
Indianapolis, IN 46256
www.wiley.com

Copyright © 2010 by Wiley Publishing, Inc., Indianapolis, Indiana

Published simultaneously in Canada

ISBN: 978-0-470-88963-3

Manufactured in the United States of America

10 9 8 7 6 5 4 3 2 1

For general information on our other products and services please contact our Customer Care Department within the United States at (877) 762-2974, outside the United States at (317) 572-3993 or fax (317) 572-4002.

Wiley also publishes its books in a variety of electronic formats. Some content that appears in print may not be available in electronic books.

Library of Congress Control Number: 2010932417

To my best friend and wife, Jennifer

— BRIAN KNIGHT

Psalm 115:1

— DEVIN KNIGHT

To my Lord and Savior, my amazing family, my beautiful love Cristina, and my special Lady Bird

— ADAM JORGENSEN

To my wife Karlyn, who encourages and motivates me to attain any goal.

— PATRICK LEBLANC

To my wife Jessy; without her strength I would not have accomplished so much.

— MIKE DAVIS

ABOUT THE AUTHORS

 BRIAN KNIGHT, SQL Server MVP, MCITP, MCSE, MCDBA, is the owner and founder of Pragmatic Works. He is also the co-founder of BIDN.com, SQLServerCentral.com, and SQLShare.com. He runs the local SQL Server users group in Jacksonville, Florida (JSSUG). Brian is a contributing columnist at several technical magazines and does regular webcasts at Jumpstart TV. He is the author of a dozen SQL Server books. Brian has spoken at conferences like PASS, SQL Connections, and TechEd, SQL Saturdays, Code Camps, and many pyramid scheme motivational sessions. His blog can be found at `http://www.bidn.com`. Brian lives in Jacksonville, Florida, where he has been baking at 350 degrees for the past 34 years.

 DEVIN KNIGHT, MCP, MCITP, is a Senior BI consultant at Pragmatic Works Consulting. Previously, he has tech edited the book *Professional Microsoft SQL Server 2008 Integration Services* and was a co-author for the book *Knight's 24-Hour Trainer: Microsoft SQL Server 2008 Integration Services*. Devin has spoken at past conferences like PASS and at several SQL Saturday events. He is a contributing member to the Business Intelligence Special Interest Group (SIG) for PASS as a leader in the SSIS Focus Group. Making his home in Jacksonville, Florida, Devin is the Vice President of the local users' group (JSSUG).

 ADAM JORGENSEN, MBA, MCITP: BI, is the President of Pragmatic Works Consulting, a global Business Intelligence software and solutions firm based in Jacksonville, Florida. He has been delivering innovative SQL Server and Business Intelligence solutions for over a decade. These systems deliver critical operations and intelligence functions for firms such as Toyota Motor Company, Fidelity, Depositors' Trust, NASDAQ, Goldman Sachs, Clipper Windpower, and Microsoft. His passion is finding new and innovative avenues for clients and the community to embrace Business Intelligence and lower barriers to implementation. Adam's focus is on mentoring executive and technical teams in realizing the value in their data, while accelerating their learning curve. He engages with firms to strategize how proper technological leverage will decrease cost, improve agility, and deliver continually increasing margins. Adam is a co-founder of Business Intelligence Developer Network (BIDN.com). He is the co-host of SQLLunch.com, a weekly live virtual event combining new and experienced presenters to provide a free global knowledge outlet. Adam is a regular contributor to the SQLPASS virtual user groups, and he speaks often at industry group events, major conferences, Code Camps, and SQL Saturday events on strategic and technical topics.

PATRICK LEBLANC, SQL Server MVP, MCTS, is currently a Business Intelligence Architect, trainer, and consultant for Pragmatic Works. He has worked with SQL Server for more than a decade. His experience includes working in the educational, advertising, mortgage, medical, and financial industries. He is also the founder of TSQLScripts.com, SQLLunch.com, and the President of the Baton Rouge Area SQL Server User Group. Patrick is a regular speaker at various SQL Server community events, including SQL Saturdays, User Groups, and the SQL Lunch.

 MIKE DAVIS, MCTS, MCITP, is a Senior Business Intelligence Consultant for Brian Knight at Pragmatic Works in Jacksonville, Florida. He was a co-author for *Knight's 24-Hour Trainer: Microsoft SQL Server 2008 Integration Services.* Mike is an experienced speaker and has presented at many events such as several SQL Server User Groups across the United States, Code Camps, SQL Server Launches, and SQL Saturday events. He is an active member at his local user group (JSSUG) in Jacksonville. In his spare time he likes to play guitar and darts.

ABOUT THE TECHNICAL EDITOR

SHAWN HARRISON is an experienced BI trainer and BI Developer for Pragmatic Works. He has expertise in Integration Services, Reporting Services, and computer networking. He's helped hundreds of customers with SSIS, architecting, and developing solutions. Shawn contributes to the local SQL Server Users' group and has spoken at SQL Saturday events.

CREDITS

ACKNOWLEDGMENTS

THANKS TO EVERYONE WHO MADE THIS BOOK POSSIBLE. As always, I owe a huge debt to my wife, Jenn, for putting up with my late nights, and my children, Colton, Liam, Camille, and my newest son, John, for being so patient with their tired dad who was always overextended. Thanks also to the makers of Guinness and other hard liquors for sustaining my ability to keep on writing technical books. Thanks for all the user group leaders out there who work so hard to help others become proficient in technology. You make a huge difference! Finally, thanks to my vocal coach, Jorge Segarra, for getting me ready for my American Idol tryout this upcoming season.

— BRIAN KNIGHT

I MUST GIVE THANKS TO GOD, who without in my life I would not have such blessings. Thanks to my wife Erin who has had amazing patience during the late nights of writing, editing, and video recording. To our wonderful son, Collin (a.k.a. Boy King) who will finally get his daddy back at night. Thanks to the group of writers Brian, Mike, Adam, and Patrick, who all worked very hard to meet our aggressive schedule and missed time with their families also. Special thanks to my brother Brian Knight. If it weren't for him, an opportunity like this would have never entered my life. He's truly an inspiration in his work and personal life and I hope I can become as good a husband and dad as he is. Lastly, I would like to thank my Big League Wiffle Ball coach Greg Maddux for giving me the encouragement that led to striking out a league record number of batters this year. Don't worry, Coach Maddux, next year we will win the state finals.

— DEVIN KNIGHT

THANK YOU TO MY FAMILY, Cristina for your love, support, encouragement, and for being a daily reminder of God's blessings. Your lifetime of support, love and "subtle" correction has made me the man I am and reminds me of the man I should be. A special thanks to my puppy Lady Bird for always reminding me where I stand in that relationship. Thank you to Brian and my other co-authors, Devin, Mike, and Patrick, without whom we would not have pulled this off. A huge thank you to the team at Pragmatic Works for putting up with "I'm sorry I need to write tonight, can we do it in the morning?" You are all an immense source of pride and encouragement. Lastly, thank you to John Wiley and Sons for letting us do this book and to you readers who have been asking for it.

— ADAM JORGENSEN

FIRST, I WOULD LIKE TO THANK MY WIFE, the love of my life, for supporting me. Even though there were some late nights, she never let me lose focus. I would also like to thank my two children, Patrick Jr. and Kalyn. I had to miss some of our normal bike rides and Wii days, but they understood. Thanks, family, for supporting me and understanding when I needed just a little quiet time to meet some of the deadlines. I would also like to thank Brian Knight for including me on this project: what a great experience. Thanks to my other co-authors, Devin, Mike, and Adam, for giving me some great tips on writing and recording the videos. A special thanks to my therapist for helping me acknowledge and accept the second person living inside of me, my EGO! Finally, I would like to thank GOD for giving me everything that I have.

— Patrick LeBlanc

THANKS TO ALL OF THE GUYS AT PRAGMATIC WORKS for their help and support in this book. Thanks to the other authors and technical editors who made this book possible. Thanks to Wiley publishing, especially Kevin Kent, for putting up with all of my late writings. Thank you to my mother, who made me the man I am today. And finally, thank you to the Flying Spaghetti Monster for showing us all the truth.

— Mike Davis

CONTENTS

INTRODUCTION

DURING THE ECONOMIC DOWNTURN that started in 2009, not many industries thrived in technology. However, Business Intelligence did thrive, seeing double-digit growth at Microsoft as companies strived to be more efficient with fewer resources. At Pragmatic Works, the Business Intelligence company where this author team works, we started in 2009 with a small staff of four full-time consultants and went into 2010 with nearly 30. You've picked the right technology to explore!

The best thing about Business Intelligence is it has a huge business impact on your users' daily lives. The reports and data that you bring to your users help those users make better decisions faster and shine a light on how to save their company's money. Business Intelligence can also use data mining to upsell customers or find how much profit a user will make on a given date.

WHO THIS BOOK IS FOR

This is a beginner book and assumes that you only know SQL Server 2005 or 2008 to run queries against the database engine. This book is structured with tutorials for a beginner; it focuses on only the essential components and teaches you what need to complete your project at work or school. As such, this is not a reference book filled with a description of every property in a given task.

WHAT THIS BOOK COVERS

This book covers how to create Business Intelligence using SQL Server 2008 R2 and assumes no previous knowledge of the Microsoft Business Intelligence set of products from SQL Server 2005 or 2008. Even though this is a SQL Server 2008 R2 book, much of the book can be used for past versions of SQL Server. The book also covers Microsoft SharePoint 2010, which is a major leap forward as a Business Intelligence platform.

By the time you've completed this book, you'll be able to design and load a data warehouse. You'll also be able to create an interactive drag and drop report by storing your data in Analysis Services. Finally, you'll see how to report against your data using Reporting Services and SharePoint 2010.

HOW THIS BOOK IS STRUCTURED

We took a much different approach to how we structured this book. Our main tenet was to only teach you what we thought you would need to perform your job task. Because of that, it's not a tutorial book. Instead it's a blended approach of a small amount of descriptions, a large tutorial, and videos to enhance your experience. Each lesson walks you through how to use components of the technology and contains a tutorial. In this tutorial, called "Try It," you can choose to read the requirements and hints and begin coding, or you can read the step-by-step instructions if you learn better that way. Either way, if you get stuck or want to see how one of us do the solution, watch the video on the DVD to receive further instruction.

This book contains 40 lessons, which are broken into sections. The lessons are usually only a dozen pages long and focus on the smallest unit of work in Business Intelligence that we could work on. Each section has a large theme around a given section in Business Intelligence:

> **Section I: Data Warehousing and Business Intelligence:** In the first section, you'll learn how to model your data warehouse fact and dimension tables as well as how all the Business Intelligence components interconnect.

> **Section II: SQL Server Integration Services:** Seventy-five percent of your time in a Business Intelligence project is with loading the warehouse. You'll learn here how to load your data with SSIS and apply complex rules to your load.

> **Section III: SQL Server Analysis Services:** To make your solution scale and offer drag and drop queries for your ad-hoc users, you'll likely want Analysis Services. In this section, you'll see how to create a cube and do data mining.

> **Section IV: SQL Server Reporting Services:** In this section, you'll see how to write amazing dashboards and reports to properly convey your data to your users.

> **Section V: Containers:** The most popular Business Intelligence client is Excel. In this section, you'll learn how to use Excel for Business Intelligence.

> **Section VI: SharePoint:** In this section, you'll learn how to present your data effectively in SharePoint through PerformancePoint, Reporting Services, and PowerPivot.

WHAT YOU NEED TO USE THIS BOOK

To do the examples in this book, you'll need to have SQL Server 2008 R2 installed with the Business Intelligence features enabled (Analysis Services, Reporting Services, and Integration Services). You'll also need access to a Microsoft SharePoint 2010 Enterprise Edition site that has PerformancePoint and PowerPivot enabled. If you want to do PowerPivot and the Excel examples, you'll want to ensure that Office 2010 installed.

INSTRUCTIONAL VIDEOS ON DVD

Because the author team believes strongly in the value of video training, this book has an accompanying DVD containing hours of instructional video. At the end of each lesson in the book, you will find a reference to an instructional video on the DVD that accompanies that lesson. In that video, one of us will walk you through the content and examples contained in that lesson. You'll also find whiteboard sessions with the author team, which explain why you would use a certain technology or architecture. So, if seeing something done and hearing it explained helps you understand a subject better than just reading about it, this book and DVD combination is just the thing for you to get started.

CONVENTIONS

To help you get the most from the text and keep track of what's happening, we've used a number of conventions throughout the book.

 Boxes like this one hold important, not-to-be forgotten information that is directly relevant to the surrounding text.

 Notes, tips, hints, tricks, and asides to the current discussion are offset and placed in italics like this.

 References like this one point you to the DVD to watch the instructional video that accompanies a given lesson.

As for styles in the text:

➤ We highlight new terms and important words when we introduce them.

➤ We show keyboard strokes like this: Ctrl+A.

➤ We show file names, URLs, and code within the text like so: `persistence.properties`.

➤ We present code in two different ways:

```
We use a monofont type with no highlighting for most code examples.
We use bold to emphasize code that's particularly important in the present
context.
```

SUPPORTING PACKAGES AND CODE

As you work through the lessons in this book, you may choose either to type in any code and create all the packages manually or to use the supporting packages and code files that accompany the book. All the packages, code, and other support files used in this book are available for download at www.wrox.com. Once at the site, simply locate the book's title (either by using the Search box or by using one of the title lists) and click the Download Code link on the book's detail page to obtain all the files that accompany this book.

Because many books have similar titles, you may find it easiest to search by ISBN; this book's ISBN is 978-0-470-88963-3.

Once you download the compressed file, just decompress it with your favorite compression tool. Alternately, you can go to the main Wrox code download page at www.wrox.com/dynamic/books/download.aspx to see the code available for this book and all other Wrox books.

ERRATA

We make every effort to ensure that there are no errors in the text or in the code. However, no one is perfect, and mistakes do occur. If you find an error in one of our books, like a spelling mistake or faulty piece of code, we would be very grateful for your feedback. By sending in errata you may save another reader hours of frustration and at the same time you will be helping us provide even higher quality information.

To find the errata page for this book, go to www.wrox.com and locate the title using the Search box or one of the title lists. Then, on the book details page, click the Book Errata link. On this page you can view all errata that has been submitted for this book and posted by Wrox editors. A complete book list including links to each book's errata is also available at www.wrox.com/misc-pages/booklist.shtml.

If you don't spot "your" error on the Book Errata page, go to www.wrox.com/contact/techsupport.shtml and complete the form there to send us the error you have found. We'll check the information and, if appropriate, post a message to the book's errata page and fix the problem in subsequent editions of the book.

P2P.WROX.COM

For author and peer discussion, join the P2P forums at p2p.wrox.com. The forums are a Web-based system for you to post messages relating to Wrox books and related technologies and interact with other readers and technology users. The forums offer a subscription feature to e-mail you topics of interest of your choosing when new posts are made to the forums. Wrox authors, editors, other industry experts, and your fellow readers are present on these forums.

At http://p2p.wrox.com you will find a number of different forums that will help you not only as you read this book, but also as you develop your own applications. To join the forums, just follow these steps:

1. Go to p2p.wrox.com and click the Register link.
2. Read the terms of use and click Agree.

3. Complete the required information to join as well as any optional information you wish to provide and click Submit.

4. You will receive an e-mail with information describing how to verify your account and complete the joining process.

 You can read messages in the forums without joining P2P but in order to post your own messages, you must join.

Once you join, you can post new messages and respond to messages other users post. You can read messages at any time on the Web. If you would like to have new messages from a particular forum e-mailed to you, click the Subscribe to this Forum icon by the forum name in the forum listing.

For more information about how to use the Wrox P2P, be sure to read the P2P FAQs for answers to questions about how the forum software works as well as many common questions specific to P2P and Wrox books. To read the FAQs, click the FAQ link on any P2P page.

Knight's Microsoft® Business Intelligence 24-Hour Trainer

SECTION I
Data Warehousing and Business Intelligence

1

Why Business Intelligence?

Congratulations on your choice to explore how Business Intelligence can improve your organization's view into its operations and uncover hidden areas of profitability and analysis. The largest challenges most organizations face around their data are probably mirrored in yours. Challenges include:

➤ **Data is stored in a number of different systems on different platforms,** such as inventory and logistics in SAP, financials in Oracle, web analytics in SQL Server, and manufacturing on the mainframe. This can make data difficult to get to, require multiple accounts for access, and keep teams and departments at arm's length from each other.

➤ **Pockets of knowledge about the data are spread throughout teams that don't regularly interact.** This spread causes data to be analyzed in different ways and metrics to be calculated inconsistently, which, in turn, leads to unpredictable analysis and inappropriate actions being taken based on the data.

➤ **Documentation is limited or nonexistent.** Many times documentation is not created for reports or the metadata underneath them, and this lack of documentation is a critical problem. If you don't know where the data is coming from for the report, or how certain metrics are being calculated, then you can't truly understand or communicate the value of the data and calculations.

➤ **Consolidated reporting is very time-consuming, when it is possible at all.** With reports coming from so many different places, you run into the same problems mentioned in the previous point. These challenges require more people to know different reporting systems, lead to more administrative headaches, and so on.

➤ **Reporting teams spend significant time finding and aligning data instead of analyzing and mining it for actionable information.** If reporting teams need to go out and gather data from across the company constantly, this doesn't leave much time for analyzing and interpreting the data. These challenges cause many reporting teams to rework large portions of their reports several times as opposed to spending that time understanding what the users are asking for and delivering more actionable information.

HOW INTELLIGENT IS YOUR ORGANIZATION?

Business Intelligence (BI) is a term that encompasses the process of getting your data out of the disparate systems and into a unified model, so you can use the tools in the Microsoft BI stack to analyze, report, and mine the data. Once you organize your company's data properly, you can begin to find information that will help you make actionable reports and decisions based on how the data from across your organization lines up. For instance, you can answer questions like, "How do delays in my manufacturing or distribution affect my sales and customer confidence?" Answers like this come from aligning logistics data with sales and marketing data, which, without a Business Intelligence solution, would require you to spend time exporting data from several systems and combining it into some form that you could consume with Excel, or another reporting tool.

Business Intelligence systems take this repetitive activity out of your life. BI automates the extracting, transforming, and loading (ETL) process and puts the data in a dimensional model (you'll create one in the next two lessons) that sets you up to be able to use cutting-edge techniques and everyday tools like Microsoft Excel to analyze, report on, and deliver results from your data.

Getting Intelligence from Data

How do you get information from data? First, you need to understand the difference. As you learned earlier, data can come from many different places, but information requires context and provides the basis for action and decision-making. Identifying your data, transforming it, and using the tools and techniques you learn from this book will enable you to provide actionable information out of the mass of data your organization stores. There are several ways to transform your data into actionable information and each has its pros and cons.

Typical solutions for reporting include a few different architectures:

➤ **Departmental reporting:** Many organizations have their own departmental reporting environments. This situation leads to a significant increase in licensing costs, since using different vendors for each department and reporting environment increases spending on hardware and software licensing, end-user training, and ramp-up time.

➤ **Individual data access:** Some organizations find it easier to grant lots of individual users access to the data. This is not only dangerous from a security perspective, but likely to lead to performance problems, because users are not the most adept at creating their own queries in code. Also, with all the industry and federal compliance and regulation governing data access, widespread access can quickly lead to a security audit failure, especially in a publicly held company.

➤ **BI add-on from each vendor:** When teams seek out and apply different strategies, it exacerbates the original problem of data being all over the organization. The data will still be segmented, and additionally the analysis on it will be inconsistent and applied based on each team's individual understanding of how its data fits into the enterprise, instead of the correct view based on the organizational goals.

➤ **Automated reports from different systems:** It may be nice to get the automated reports and they likely serve a purpose, but they usually cannot be counted on to run an enterprise. Strategic reporting, dashboard drill-through, and detailed analysis require a BI implementation to support them and provide the "at your fingertips" data and analysis that your end users, managers, and executives are craving.

You have likely seen some form of all of these problems in your organization. These are the opposite of what you want to accomplish with a great BI infrastructure.

BI to the Rescue

A well-thought-out BI strategy will mitigate the problems inherent to each of the previously listed approaches. A good BI approach should provide the targeted departmental reporting that is required by those end users while adjusting the data so it can be consumed by executives through a consolidated set of reports, ad hoc analysis using Excel, or a SharePoint dashboard. Business Intelligence provides a combination of automated reporting, dashboard capabilities, and ad hoc capabilities that will propel your organization forward.

BI provides a single source of truth that can make meetings and discussions immediately more productive. How many times have you gotten a spreadsheet via e-mail before a meeting and shown up to find that everyone had his or her own version of the spreadsheet with different numbers? Business Intelligence standardizes organizational calculations, while still giving you the flexibility to add your own and enhance the company standard. These capabilities allow everyone to speak the same language when it comes to company metrics and to the way the data should be measured across the enterprise or department.

Integrating Business Intelligence with your organization's current reporting strategy will improve the quality of the data as well as the accuracy of the analysis and the speed at which you can perform it. Using a combination of a data warehouse and BI analytics from Analysis Services and Excel, you can also perform in-depth data mining against your data. This enables you to utilize forecasting, data-cluster analysis, fraud detection, and other great approaches to analyze and forecast actions. Data mining is incredibly useful for things like analyzing sales trends, detecting credit fraud, and filling in empty values based on historical analysis. This powerful capability is delivered right through Excel, using Analysis Services for the back-end modeling and mining engine.

BI = Business Investment

A focused Business Intelligence plan can streamline the costs of reporting and business analytics. The Microsoft BI stack does a great job of providing you with the entire tool set for success within SQL Server Enterprise Edition. We provide more details on that shortly, but the most important bit of information you should take away right now is that the cost of managing multiple products and versions of reporting solutions to meet departmental needs is always higher than the cost of a cohesive strategy that employs one effective licensing policy from a single vendor. When organizations cannot agree or get together on their data strategy, you need to bring them together for the good of the organization. In the authors' experience, this single, cohesive approach to reporting is often a gateway to a successful BI implementation. Realizing the 360-degree value of that approach and seeing the value it can have in your organization are the two most important first steps.

Microsoft's Business Intelligence Stack

Microsoft's Business Intelligence stack comes with SQL Server and is greatly enhanced with the addition of SharePoint Server.

SQL Server Enterprise includes industry-leading software components to build, implement, and maintain your BI infrastructure. The major components of the Microsoft BI stack that are included with SQL Server are the following:

➤ SQL Server Database Engine

➤ SQL Server Integration Services (SSIS)

➤ SQL Server Analysis Services (SSAS)

➤ SQL Server Reporting Services (SSRS)

These programs work together in a tightly integrated fashion to deliver solutions like those you'll build in this book. See Figure 1-1 for more details.

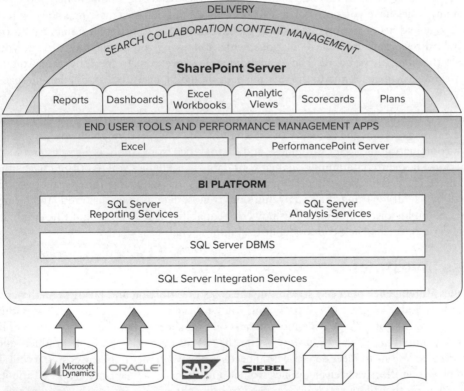

FIGURE 1-1

In Figure 1-1 you see the layers of Microsoft's Business Intelligence stack. SharePoint is at the top as the most end user–facing program for reporting, dashboard, and analytic capabilities. On the next level down you see the more common end user tools, and continuing down you can see the development tools, the core components, and some of the multitude of potential data sources you can consume with the products we discuss in this book.

BI Users and Technology

Different levels of users will have different sorts of questions around which they will use these BI technologies we are discussing. To see this at a glance, review Table 1-1. In that table you can see a breakdown that helps answer which users will rely on which tool for their reporting and data analysis and makes clear that Microsoft's Business Intelligence stack does address the needs of users at every level.

TABLE 1-1

END USERS	POWER USERS	EXECUTIVES/CLIENTS
1. Excel	1. Excel	1. Excel
2. Reporting Services	2. Report Builder	2. SharePoint Dashboards
3. SharePoint Dashboards	3. Reporting Services	
	4. SharePoint Dashboards	

TRY IT

Your Try It for this lesson is a bit different than most others in the book. Throughout the book you will be challenged with hands-on tasks to enhance your understanding. For this lesson, your Try It is to make sure the things you learned in this lesson are in your mind as you learn the technologies to apply them. For instance, ask yourself these questions as you go through the rest of the book.

➤ What systems in my organization could I tie together using SSIS?

➤ What types of analysis could be made easier with the tools in Analysis Services?

➤ What users would benefit from the types of reporting I can do in Reporting Services and Excel?

➤ What types of data in my organization would be useful for dashboard- and portal-based analytics in SharePoint and PerformancePoint?

If you can keep these things in mind as you're learning and developing, you will succeed in harnessing the goals of a Business Intelligence implementation as you move through the data in your organization.

 As this chapter is just an introductory overview, it does not have an accompanying video.

2

Dimensional Modeling

Dimensional modeling is the process you use to convert your existing OLTP data model to a model that is more business-centric and easier for Business Intelligence tools to work with. Tools like SSIS, Analysis Services, and the others you'll learn about in this book are geared specifically toward variations of this type of model. In this lesson you will learn what makes a dimensional model different and then have the opportunity to convert a simple model yourself.

As seen in Figure 2-1, the OLTP model is highly normalized. This is to enhance the quick insertion and retrieval of data. The goal in designing a data warehouse or star schema is to denormalize the model in order to simplify it and to provide wider, more straightforward tables for joining and data-retrieval speed. This denormalization allows you to "model" the database in a business-focused way that users can understand, and dramatically increases performance of the types of analytical queries that we're performing.

Why do you need to do this denormalization in order to report on your data, you may ask? The largest reason is that you need to consolidate some of the redundancy between tables. Consolidating redundancy will put the database into a *star schema* layout, which has a central fact table surrounded by a layer of dimension tables, as shown in Figure 2-2.

As you can see in Figure 2-2, we have abstracted out tables such as DimProduct, DimCustomer, DimPromotion, and DimDate and put the additive and aggregative data, like sales amounts, costs, and so on into a single fact table, FactInternetSales (more on fact tables in Lesson 3; for now focus on the dimensions). This abstraction allows you to implement a number of important elements that will provide great design patterns for dealing with the challenges discussed later in this chapter.

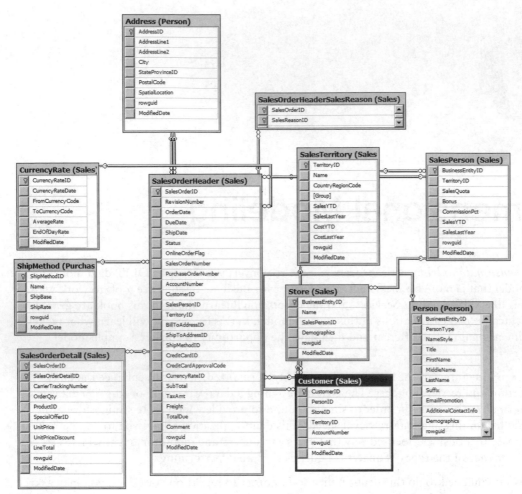

FIGURE 2-1

Moving from the OLTP model to a dimensional model is important for a number of reasons, not the least of which is performance, but within the dimensional model we can handle many situations with the data that are very difficult, if not impossible, to handle in a more typical OLTP third-normal-form model. Some of these situations are:

➤ **Slowly changing dimensions:** How do you handle historical changes and reporting, for instance, if someone's last name changes and you need to show the old last name on the historical reporting, and the current on the new reporting? How can you efficiently handle that situation in a highly normalized fashion? This would involve multiple tables and require some complicated updates. We will go over this later in the lesson.

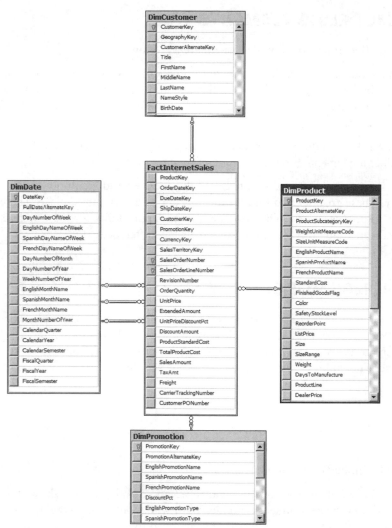

FIGURE 2-2

➤ **Role-playing dimensions:** How are you going to handle multiple calendars with multiple relationships to different tables if the calendars change? For instance, your fiscal calendar or accounting periods may change from year to year, but will need to maintain relationships to the previous methods for historical and trend analysis. More on this later.

➤ **Integrating primary key structures from multiple systems:** Some systems will have alphanumeric keys, and others will have integer or composite keys. Integrating different key types is a real challenge that often leads to hybrid, system-crossing keys kept in sync with some complicated ETL. Hybrid keys are not necessary in the dimensional model because you abstract all of that.

KEY DIMENSIONAL MODELING ELEMENTS

The key elements that make up the dimensional model system are as follows:

➤ The dimensions in the model provide a single complete and historically accurate source for the data. For instance, in the example we discuss in this lesson the customer dimension has a record of all the customers and their historically accurate information based on the dates for which the record was accurate.

➤ The solution you will see later in this lesson supports changes with the StartDate and EndDate columns in DimProduct implemented to track the effective dates of the rows in the table.

➤ You'll notice a new key on the dimension table called ProductKey and a column called ProductAlternateKey. These are added to support the new key structure put in place. There will be more on how to do this shortly. This structure provides portability for the warehouse and the ability to integrate numerous systems despite their key differences.

HOW DOES DIMENSIONAL MODELING WORK?

Before you try some dimensional modeling for yourself, we want to show you an example. For our example, we use the AdventureWorks2008R2 sample databases from Microsoft available at www.codeplex.com. We create a simple start schema from the reseller sales information in the OLTP version of the database. The tables we use from OLTP will be as follows:

➤ Customer

➤ Person

➤ Address

The table we will create will be called DimCustomer.

First, take notice of the differences and key elements in Figures 2-3 and 2-4. Figure 2-3 shows the OLTP tables, and Figure 2-4 shows the new dimension table. We'll walk you through the numbered items in Figure 2-4 to show you what key design elements we employed to make this a successful transition from normalized dimension data to a set of dimension tables.

1. **New CustomerKey column to provide SurrogateKey.** We are using a new column we created to provide the primary key for this new dimension table. Best practice is to add a suffix of "SK" to the name of this column, so it would read CustomerSK or CustomerKeySK.

2. **We have modified the primary key column that is coming over from the source OLTP system to act as the alternate key.** All this means is that if we need to bring in data from several systems whose primary keys have overlapped or are in different formats, we can do it with a combination of our alternate (or business) key and our surrogate key CustomerKey.

3. **Much of the demographic data and store sales data was also tapped to get columns** like DateFirstPurchase and CommuteDistance so you can find out more about your customers. Some of these columns could be calculated in the ETL portion of your processing by comparing information like a work and home address, for example.

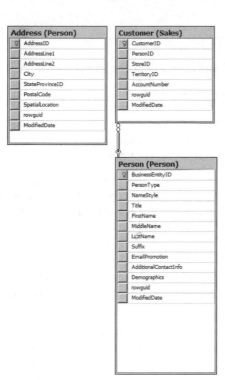

FIGURE 2-3

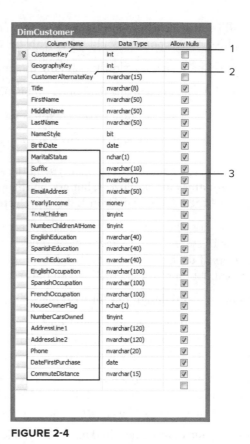

FIGURE 2-4

Once the dimension tables are in place, you can easily see why this is a better model for working with large analytical queries and analysis. For instance, now if you refer to multiple customers in a single order, you need only one customer dimension with a fact table row that has multiple key relationships to the customer table. This is much better than having a bill-to customer table and a ship-to customer table to handle subsidiaries or other issues.

Multiple dates are also very common in most fact tables; for instance, an inventory fact table may have a product's arrival date, ship date, expiration date, and return date. This requires multiple links to a product table for multiple columns; instead we can link directly to DimDate for these values with our numeric surrogate keys. Remember, these keys keep all the tables in the warehouse linked as your new key system.

You can see the StartDate and EndDate columns and how they control the historical loading. (The mechanics of historical loading are discussed in the SSIS lessons in Section II of this book.) These columns allow you to expire a row when a historical change is required. For instance, when a product line gets a new account manager, you would expire the current product line row and insert into the dimension table a new row with an EndDate of null that links to the new product manager.

This way, all your historical reporting is accurate, and your current reporting is accurate as well. Otherwise, historical reporting could mistakenly tie sales to the wrong manager.

There are three main types of slowly changing dimensions:

➤ **Type I:** Updates changing data only, no historical tracking

➤ **Type II:** Tracks historical records, expires the row, and puts a new one into the table

➤ **Type III:** Same as Type II, but only tracks a certain number of revisions

It is common to have columns from each type in the same table; for instance, if you need to track history on last names for employees, but not on their addresses, you may have a Type II LastName column and a Type I Address column. This is perfectly acceptable and common.

This design has also been proven to improve performance significantly since the main goal of a data warehouse or BI system is to extract data as quickly as possible. The more denormalized type of this model lends itself to the quick retrieval of data from the tables to serve to populate a cube, run a report, or load data into Excel. You'll do all of these things in later lessons!

Here are some general design tips for working with your dimension tables:

➤ **Try to avoid unnecessary normalizing.** In a star schema, this practice is called *snowflaking* and while sometimes it is warranted, it usually isn't, unless your dimension table is so large it needs to be physically separated on the storage array.

➤ *CamelCasing,* **the capitalization of each word with no spaces or underscores, will help you down the road.** You're not working with Analysis Services yet, but you will be very soon, and CamelCasing will help streamline your work in SSAS. For now, you have to trust us.

➤ **Begin your table name with Dim** (Dim<Tablename>). This allows for better sorting of dimension and fact tables.

➤ **Don't over index.** Until you know what queries you'll be running against the tables, don't assume you need lots of indexes on all your tables.

TRY IT

In this Try It you're going to take what you've just read about and apply it to create your own product dimension table with columns from a typical source OLTP system.

Lesson Requirements

The columns you put in your table are up to you, but your dimension will need to track history. Also, the dimension table will be getting data from other sources, so it will need to be able to handle that. You will create your table in SQL Server Management Studio.

Hints

➤ Make sure to remember to use the right types of key columns for your new dimension table.

➤ Remember the concepts this lesson discussed that are required for handling data coming from multiple systems.

Step-by-Step

1. The first thing you should do is identify some columns you might want in your table. Table 2-1 has a number of standard product dimension columns that you can pick from.

   TABLE 2-1

ProductName	Model	Line	Category
SubCategory	Price	Cost	Color
Weight	ManufactureCountry	Market	AgeRange

2. Now, in order to make these into a proper dimension table, you need to review your requirements. Your first requirement was to make sure you can track history, so you need to make sure you have a StartDate and EndDate column so you can expire rows as they become updated.

3. Your next requirement was to make sure the dimension table could handle data from multiple systems either now or in the future, which means you need to apply the best practice you learned about surrogate keys. This will add a ProductKeySK and a ProductAlternateKey column to the table as well.

   The finished product should look something like Figure 2-5.

FIGURE 2-5

This table will work with multiple systems with its surrogate key structure and will perform well if the rest of the warehouse follows similar best practices for design.

Congratulations, you have just designed your first dimension table. Don't forget to remember these concepts and refer to them as they become relevant in the lessons in the rest of the book. Great job!

 Please select Lesson 2 on the DVD to view the video that accompanies this lesson.

3

Fact Table Modeling

A fact table is modeled to be the center of the star schema in a data warehouse. It consists of two primary types of data:

- ➤ **Key columns,** which point to the associated dimension tables
- ➤ **Data columns,** which normally contain additive or numeric data representing a transaction or snapshot of a situation at a point in time. Numeric data is more common in financial or inventory situations.

You need fact tables because they allow you to link the denormalized versions of the dimension tables and provide a largely, if not completely, numeric table for Analysis Services to consume and aggregate. In other words, the fact table is the part of the model that holds the dollars or count type of data that you would want to see rolled up by year, grouped by category, or so forth. The fact table holds "just the facts" and the keys to relate the needed dimension tables. Since many OLAP tools, like Analysis Services, look for a star schema model and are optimized to work with it, the fact table is a critical piece of the puzzle.

The process of designing your fact table will take several steps:

1. **Decide on the data you want to analyze.**

   Will this be sales data, inventory data, or financial data? Each type comes with its own design specifics. For instance, you may have to load different amounts of data based on the type of analysis you're doing.

2. **Once you've identified your data type, pick the level of granularity that you're seeking.**

   When you consider the question of granularity, or the "grain" of each row, in the fact table, you want each row to represent a certain level of granularity. This means that you need to decide on the lowest level of analysis you want to perform. For example, each row may represent a line item on a receipt, a total amount for a receipt, or the status of a particular product in inventory for a particular day.

3. **Decide how you will load the fact table** (more on this in Lesson 9).

Transactions are loaded at intervals to show what is in the OLTP system. An inventory or *snapshot* fact table will load all the rows of inventory or snapshot-style data for the day, always allowing the user to see the current status and information based on the date the information was loaded.

Fact tables are often designed to be *index light*, meaning that indexes should be placed only to support reporting and cube processing that is happening directly on that table. It is a good idea to remember that your fact tables will often be much larger in row count and data volume than your dimensions. This means you can apply several strategies to manage the tables and improve your performance and scalability.

➤ **Implementing table partitioning:** Table partitioning can significantly help your management of this type of larger fact table. Implementing a sliding-window partitioning scheme, where you roll off old partitions and roll on new ones periodically, can drive IO and query times down and access speeds up since you will be accessing only the specific areas of data on the disk that are needed for your query. Processing speeds for data loading and cube processing will also be faster since the new versions of SQL Server 2008 and 2008R2 allow for increased parallelization of queries across partitions.

➤ **Configuring and implementing data compression in SQL Server 2008 and 2008R2:** There are two types of compression in SQL Server 2008 and 2008R2. The details of these are out of the scope of this lesson, but you should investigate using these in your data warehouse, because of the significant performance and disk space improvements you will see. Compression will deliver a decreased amount of IO for queries and a lower total amount of IO will be needed to satisfy them, resulting in faster, more nimble tables, even though some fact tables will have millions of rows.

➤ **Using physical foreign key constraints to enforce relationships:** There is some debate over this one, with hardcore performance purists focused on the minimal amount of overhead that the key constraints can employ during a load process or heavy-duty reporting. For this minimal overhead, however, Analysis Services will optimize its processing based on the fact that it can assume these keys are keeping the data valid and disable some of the internal checks built into the processing algorithm. This will allow Analysis Services to consume the data from your fact and dimension tables much faster than if it did not have those keys.

Now that you have some insight into the fact table design process, it's time to try building one yourself.

TRY IT

In this Try It you will build a fact table based on the dimensions from Lesson 2.

Lesson Requirements

This lesson requires you to create a fact table to use in your sample model for this section. Make sure to use SQL Server Management Studio or TSQL to create your tables, whichever you're more comfortable with. We are going to use SQL Server Management Studio. To complete the lesson you need to build the table, and include any valuable cost, sales, and count fact columns, along with the key columns for the important dimensions. Next are a couple of hints to get you started.

Hints

➤ Make sure you include references to the SK columns in your dimension tables.

➤ Think about granularity and make sure your row layout implements the level of granularity that you're looking for.

Step-by-Step

1. Make sure you identify the dimensions that are important to your analysis and then include references to those surrogate key columns in your fact table.

2. Add columns for each numeric or additive value that you're concerned about rolling up or aggregating.

3. Check out the example in Figure 3-1. Yours should look similar.

FactResellerSales
ProductKey
OrderDateKey
DueDateKey
ShipDateKey
ResellerKey
EmployeeKey
PromotionKey
CurrencyKey
SalesTerritoryKey
SalesOrderNumber
SalesOrderLineNumber
RevisionNumber
OrderQuantity
UnitPrice
ExtendedAmount
UnitPriceDiscountPct
DiscountAmount
ProductStandardCost
TotalProductCost
SalesAmount
TaxAmt
Freight
CarrierTrackingNumber
CustomerPONumber

FIGURE 3-1

 Please select Lesson 3 on the DVD to view the video that accompanies this lesson.

SECTION II
SQL Server Integration Services

Understanding SSIS

If you're new to SQL Server Integration Services (SSIS), it can be a very intimidating and overwhelming tool. It consists of a myriad of diverse components, each of which can perform a multitude of operations. SSIS is a tool that can be used to construct high-performance workflow processes, which include, but are not limited to, the extraction, transformation, and loading of a data warehouse (ETL). It encompasses most of the tools required to migrate data from various data sources, including flat files, Excel workbooks, databases (SQL, Oracle, MySQL, DB2), and many other sources. Coupling SSIS with the SQL Server Agent you have the ability to construct an entire ETL framework that can fully or incrementally load your warehouse on a time-based interval that meets your organization's needs. In this section we demystify some of the key components of SSIS. We focus primarily on those that are essential in the development of most SSIS packages.

BUSINESS INTELLIGENCE DEVELOPMENT STUDIO (BIDS)

BIDS is the Graphical User Interface (GUI) that you will use to develop, debug, and maybe deploy SSIS packages, which are the building blocks of SSIS. This tool allows you to develop packages that can:

➤ Execute SQL Tasks

➤ Extract data from various sources

➤ Load data into various sources

➤ Perform data cleansing

➤ Lookup, Merge, and Aggregate data

Note that this is not an exhaustive list; it does, however, include those tasks that are essential to building an ETL solution for a data warehouse. If you want to use BIDS you must select it during the SQL Server installation process.

To start BIDS, click Start ➪ All Programs ➪ Microsoft SQL Server 2008 R2 ➪ SQL Server Business Intelligence Development Studio. BIDS is a shell of Microsoft Visual Studio. If you have Visual Studio installed, it will open and you will select a BIDS project when starting your SSIS development. If you want to improve the way the application starts you can add a startup parameter to the application shortcut. To do this, right-click the BIDS shortcut and the screen in Figure 4-1 will appear.

Ensuring that the Shortcut tab is active, append -NOSPLASH to the end of the target URL. Close and reopen BIDS. You should notice that the splash screen that appeared when you initially opened BIDS no longer appears.

Now that you have BIDS open, create your first SSIS project. On the BIDS menu screen, click File ➪ New ➪ Project, and the New Project screen will appear. Select Integration Services Project from the Template pane. On the New Project screen you will need to specify the solution name, file location, and project name. Before proceeding

FIGURE 4-1

we should provide a brief explanation of solutions and projects. A *solution* is a container of projects. One solution can include several Integration Services projects, but a solution can also contain other types of projects. For example, you can also include a Reporting Services project in the same solution as the Integration Services project. An Integration Services *project*, on the other hand, is a container of packages. The project will typically contain several data sources and SSIS packages. As a result, you can create a project within a solution that is specific to the task that you are trying to accomplish or complete. In addition to creating solutions and projects and designing packages, BIDS will allow you to save copies of the packages to an instance of SQL Server or the file system, create a deployment utility that can install multiple packages and any dependencies to an instance of SQL Server or the file system at once, and also provide multiple tools that can assist in monitoring and troubleshooting your packages.

SOLUTION EXPLORER

Once you have opened BIDS and created your Integration Services project, you can now begin designing your SSIS packages. By default, when you create an Integration Services project in BIDS a package named Package.dtsx is included and opened in the project. You can view the package inside the Solution Explorer. The Solution Explorer will also show the projects and solution. If the solution does not appear, select Tools ➪ Options from the menu bar. Then select Project and Solutions in the navigation pane of the Option screen that appears. Select the checkbox labeled "Always show solution" and click OK. Return to the Solution Explorer and you will see items similar to the ones in Figure 4-2.

The Solution Explorer allows you to easily navigate between projects and the items that are contained within a project. In this case it is Data Sources, Data Source Views, and SSIS Packages. In the later sections of this book we will explain how to create data sources and packages. However, note that any data sources created in the Solution Explorer can be used by any packages created within the same project.

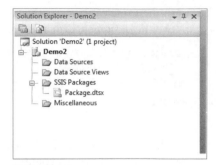

FIGURE 4-2

SSIS DESIGNER

The SSIS Designer contains four tabs. The first is the Control Flow tab, which orchestrates the entire flow of the SSIS package. The next tab is Data Flow, which is where the actual movement and cleansing of data will take place. Then there is the Event Handlers tab, which can be used to perform actions like those that can be performed on the Data Flow and Control Flow tabs. Event handlers can be constructed for the entire package or for a specific task in the package on a specific tab. Each of the three aforementioned tabs is accompanied by a corresponding toolbox. Figure 4-3 shows a sample data flow in the SSIS Designer.

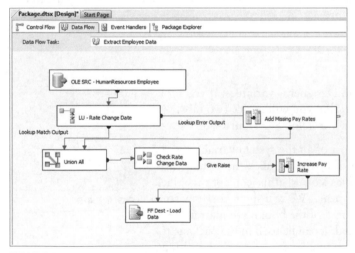

FIGURE 4-3

Finally, there is the Package Explorer tab. This tab provides a tree view that groups and lists each item. Since a package can contain many tasks, Connection Managers and other items, this summarized view makes it easier to navigate, locate, and configure items within a specific package.

In addition to the four tabs, the designer also includes the Toolbox and Connection Manager sections. Each tab has a corresponding toolbox, except the Package Explorer tab. The selected tab will determine the contents of the toolbox. Regardless of the active tab, each task can be dragged onto the design surface and configured as needed. When the Control Flow tab is active, the toolbox will contain two types of tasks: container and workflow. If the Data Flow tab is active it will contain source, transformation, and destination tasks. The Error Handler tab has a corresponding toolbox with the same contents as the Control Flow tab's toolbox. The major difference is that directly above the design surface are two drop-down lists, as shown in Figure 4-4.

FIGURE 4-4

The Executable drop-down list contains a collection of all the tasks defined on the data flow. The "Event handler" drop-down list contains a collection of all the possible handlers that can be associated with a particular executable. You can design workflows on the Event Handlers design surface just as you would on the Control Flow and Data Flow tabs using the toolbox that corresponds to the Event Handlers tab.

The final section, the Connection Manager, allows you to create connections to various types of data sources. The difference between connections created in the Connection Manager and those created in the Solution Explorer under the Data Sources folder is that the connections created in the Connection Manager section are exclusive to a specific package. In other words, the connections created in the Connection Manager can be used only within the containing package. Therefore, if you realize you are creating the same connection over and over again within different packages you may want to create it under the Data Sources folder in the Solution Explorer. That way it can be reused by every package within your project.

VARIABLES

Another element available in the SSIS Designer is variables. If you look toward the bottom of the Toolbox section you will notice two tabs. One is labeled Toolbox and the other Variables. See Figure 4-5.

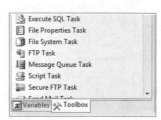

FIGURE 4-5

When you click the Variables tab, a list of all the system variables and user-defined variables will appear. If they do not, click the system variables icon ⊠ and the show all variables icon ⊠ (this icon appears blue). This will cause all the variables to appear. (We will show you how to create user-defined variables in Lesson 5 of the book.) No matter the type of variable, system or user-defined, it can be used in the package to hold data, assist in control flow, and audit changes, among other things.

Remember, this is not an exhaustive list of all the elements available in SSIS. We have covered only a few key elements that are critical to the development of SSIS packages that will perform ETL operations. In later lessons of this book, we will introduce additional elements that will assist in the development of these packages.

SSIS ARCHITECTURE

As mentioned in the previous section, the SSIS Designer contains four distinct tabs. Of the four, two are typically used in most SSIS packages, Control Flow and Data Flow. As mentioned earlier, Control Flow orchestrates the entire workflow of the package. It contains three elements: Containers, Tasks that provide functionality to the package, and Precedence Constraints. The containers add structure and order to the package workflow. These tasks primarily consist of loop and sequence containers. The additional tasks provide functionality, such as executing ActiveX and SQL scripts, bulk insert operations, and e-mail operations, to mention a few. The precedence constraints connect and control the flow of tasks from one to the other.

The Data Flow tab provides a different type of functionality from the Control Flow tab. It becomes active only once a Data Flow task is added to the design surface of the Control Flow tab. The Data Flow tab contains three types of tasks, which are labeled as follows: Data Flow Sources, Data Flow Transformations, and Data Flow Destinations. The data flow sources provide you with the ability to extract data from various data sources, which include OLE DB, flat files, XML, ADO.NET, and others. In addition, using the OLE DB source you can connect to many types of databases, including SQL Server, Oracle, and DB2. The data flow transformations are tasks that can assist you in transforming, massaging, or cleansing the data so that it meets your business requirements. For example, you may need to add a column to a result set that contains the first and last name, as opposed to having them in two separate fields. In this case, you could use a Derived Column task that will take advantage of the expression language built into SSIS. The final type of task, data flow destinations, contains tasks that allow you to load data into various data sources. Much like data flow sources, the destinations consist of ADO.NET, Excel, flat files, and OLE DB, but also include DataReader, SQL Server, and Recordset destinations.

Once you have implemented all the necessary containers, tasks, and precedent constraints, on both the control and data flows, you can debug your package by executing it in BIDS. You can execute a package several different ways in BIDS.

One way to run a package is to press F5 on your keyboard another is to click the green icon ▶ on the toolbar. Finally, you can right-click the package in the Solution Explorer and select Execute Package. Any way will run the package. Once a package is executed, a new tab appears in the SSIS Designer labeled Execution Results. See Figure 4-6 for an example.

FIGURE 4-6

The Execution Results tab will provide a detailed listing of every step of the package including validation and the execution of each task contained within the package. If a warning occurs it will be designated with the following icon ⚠. If an error occurs there will be at a minimum two statements indicating the failure. The first will provide the details of the error, and the second usually just states that the task has failed. The results will be similar to what is shown in Figure 4-7.

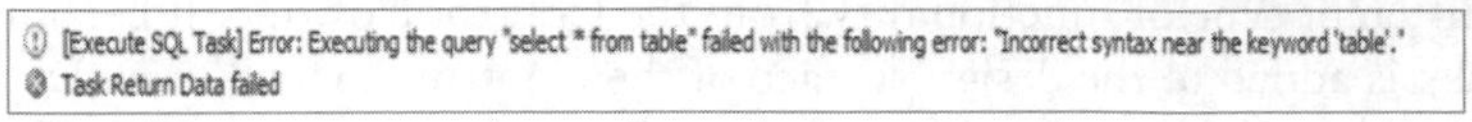

① [Execute SQL Task] Error: Executing the query "select * from table" failed with the following error: "Incorrect syntax near the keyword 'table'."
⊘ Task Return Data failed

FIGURE 4-7

Note that the first line provides the details of the error and the second states which task failed.

TRY IT

In this Try It you will first create a solution and a project. Once these are complete, you will create an extract file that contains a list of the name of every person from the Person.Person table in the AdventureWorks2008 database.

Lesson Requirements

In this lesson you will create an Integration Services project. Then you will create an SSIS package that will read the contents of the Person.Person table. You will add a new column to the result set that will contain the person's first and last names as one field.

 The download for this lesson available at www.wrox.com *includes the solution for this Try It.*

Hints

Developing Integration Services projects requires a development environment. BIDS provides a comprehensive tool set for developing, testing, debugging, and deploying SSIS packages. Using BIDS, create an Integration Services project that is contained within a solution. Open BIDS and select File ⇨ New ⇨ Project from the menu. Ensure that you select Business Intelligence Projects from the "Project types" section and that Integration Services Project is selected in the Templates section.

To extract data from a database you need to:

➤ Create a connection to the database

➤ Add a Data Flow task to the control flow

➤ Add a data flow source, derived column, and data flow destination to the Data Flow tab

Step-by-Step

1. To open BIDS, click Start ➪ All Programs ➪ Microsoft SQL Server 2008 R2 ➪ SQL Server Business Intelligence Development Studio.

2. From the menu select File ➪ New ➪ Project, and the screen shown in Figure 4-8 will appear.

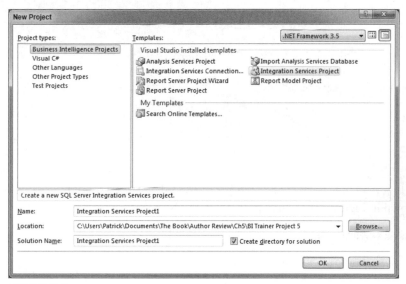

FIGURE 4-8

3. Ensure that Business Intelligence Projects is selected in the "Project types" section and that Integration Services Project is selected in the Templates section.

4. In the text box labeled Name, type **BI Trainer Project 4**.

5. Accept the default for the text box labeled Location.

6. Accept the default for the drop-down list labeled Solution.

7. Ensure that the checkbox labeled "Create directory for solution" is checked.

8. In the text box labeled Solution Name, type **BI Trainer Project 4**. Click OK.

9. If Package.dtsx is not open, double-click it in the Solution Explorer.

10. Ensuring that the Control Flow tab is active, drag a Data Flow tab onto the design surface.

11. Right-click the table and select Rename from the context menu.

12. Type **Extract Person Data**. Your screen should resemble the one in Figure 4-9.

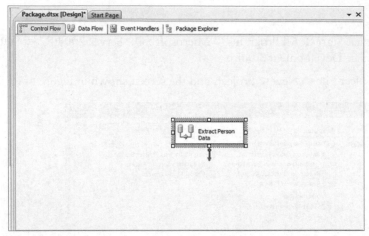

FIGURE 4-9

13. Right-click in the Connection Manager section and select New OLE DB Connection. The screen shown in Figure 4-10 will appear. Click the New button.

FIGURE 4-10

14. In the Connection Manager screen, type **localhost** in the drop-down list labeled "Server name" and type or select AdventureWorks2008 in the drop-down list labeled "Select or enter database name." Click OK twice.

15. Double-click the Data Flow item and now the Data Flow tab is active.

16. Drag an OLE DB source onto the design surface.

17. Rename the task **OLE DB – Person Source**.

18. Double-click the task and the screen shown in Figure 4-11 will appear.

FIGURE 4-11

19. In the drop-down list labeled "Data access mode" select SQL Command.

20. In the text box labeled "SQL command text," type the following:

```
SELECT FirstName, LastName FROM Person.Person
```

Click OK.

21. Drag a Derived Column task onto the design surface.

22. Drag the green arrow from the OLE DB source onto the derived column.

23. Rename the derived column **Add Full Name**.

24. Double-click the Derived Column task and the screen shown in Figure 4-12 will appear.

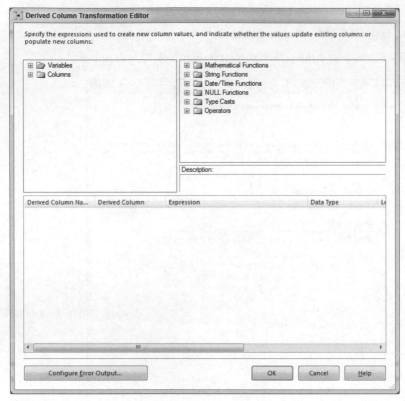

FIGURE 4-12

25. In the lower section of the screen, select <add as new column> from the column Derived Column. Enter the value **FullName** in the column Derived Column Name. Finally, in the column Expression enter **[FirstName]+" "+[LastName]**.

Click OK.

26. Drag a Flat File Destination task onto the design surface.

27. Rename the task **FF - Person Full Name Dest**.

28. Drag the green arrow from the derived column onto the Flat File Destination task.

29. Double-click the Flat File Destination task and the screen shown in Figure 4-13 will appear.

FIGURE 4-13

30. Click New next to the drop-down list labeled "Flat File connection manager."

31. Select Delimited from the Flat File Format screen that appears. Click OK.

32. Then the Flat File Connection Manager will appear.

33. Click Browse and select a directory on your computer where the flat file will reside. Name the file **FullName.txt**.

34. Accept all the defaults and click OK.

35. Back on the Flat File Destination Editor click Mappings, located at the top left of the screen.

36. Ensure that each column is mapped accordingly, for example, FirstName to FirstName. Click OK.

37. Right-click the package in the Solution Explorer and select Execute Package.

38. When the package is complete it will resemble the screen shown in Figure 4-14.

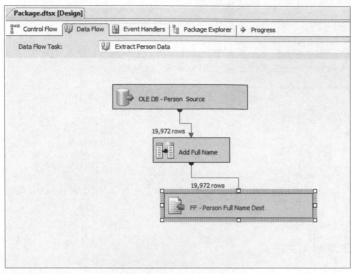

FIGURE 4-14

39. If you click the Progress tab you can view each individual step that was executed during the package run.

40. Click the square blue button on the menu bar to stop the package.

41. Browse to the location on your computer that you specified in Step 33.

42. Open the FullName.txt file. The text file should contain three columns, FirstName, LastName, and FullName, which were derived in the package.

 Please select Lesson 4 on the DVD to view the video that accompanies this lesson.

5

Using the Control Flow

The control flow organizes and orchestrates the execution of the entire package. When you're designing your SSIS packages, the Control Flow tab is the starting point. As mentioned in Lesson 4, each tab has a toolbox that contains items specific to that tab. You have three types of items available to you in the control flow. First, there are two types of items available in the Control Flow tab toolbox: control flow items and maintenance plan items.

➤ The control flow items are divided into two types: container and execution tasks.

➤ The maintenance items include tasks such as Backup, Index Rebuild, and Update Statistics tasks.

One final item available to you in the control flow, one not contained in the toolbox, is the precedence constraint.

These items available to you in the control flow can be configured with a graphical user interface, with the exception of the Data Flow task.

CONTROL FLOW CONTAINERS

The control flow includes three types of containers whose purpose is to add structure to the entire package. These containers are as follows:

➤ The **Sequence Container** organizes tasks and potentially other containers into smaller sets of tasks to assist in structuring the workflow of the package.

➤ The **For Loop Container** will create a workflow that repeats until some condition is evaluated as false.

➤ The **Foreach Loop Container** creates a repetitive control flow that uses a data set or enumeration to execute looping.

You can drag multiple containers onto the design surface of the control flow. In addition, you can drag multiple items within a container, including other containers. For example, Figure 5-1 shows a sample control flow that includes a Sequence Container that contains an Execute SQL task.

If there are multiple containers on the control flow design surface, all the items contained within the task must complete before any subsequent tasks will finish. This is, of course, if they are linked together by precedence constraints. If they are not linked, they may execute in parallel.

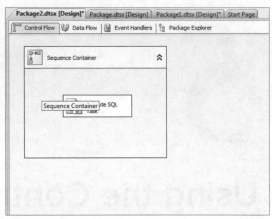

FIGURE 5-1

CONTROL FLOW TASKS

The control flow also contains executable tasks. These include, but are not limited to, File System, FTP, Execute SQL, and various other tasks. Each task has a graphical user interface (GUI) that can be used to configure the properties required to run each task. You can access each GUI by double-clicking the task. For example, Figure 5-2 shows a control flow that contains a Foreach Loop Container that contains a Bulk Insert task. The container may loop over a list of files and insert the contents of the files into a database.

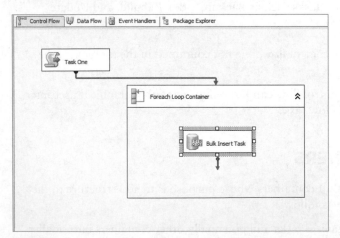

FIGURE 5-2

You do not have to drag the task into a container. As you can see in Figure 5-2, the designer contains a Script task that will execute prior to the Foreach Loop Container.

PRECEDENCE CONSTRAINTS

Once all the containers and tasks have been added to the Control Flow designer, you will need to connect them using *precedence constraints*. A precedence constraint will connect a minimum of two items, a task to a task, a task to a container, a container to a container or a container to a task. The precedence constraint will determine if the next task or container will be executed based on the state (success, complete, fail) of the constraint. Each item that is added to the design surface automatically includes a connector or precedence constraint. These constraints relate and connect the items to each other. One thing to note is that the constraint defaults to a successful completion. In other words, in Figure 5-2, the Foreach Loop will not execute until the preceding Script task successfully completes.

Therefore, if you wanted to change the default behavior, you would double-click the connector and the box shown in Figure 5-3 should appear.

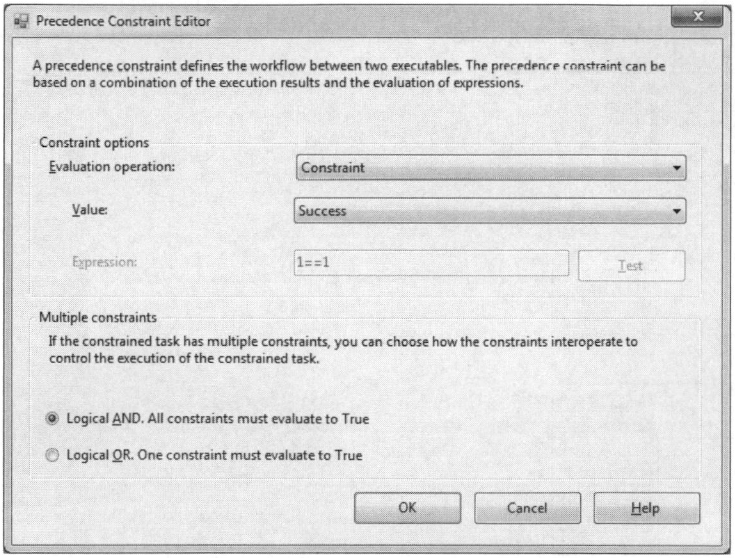

FIGURE 5-3

Using this screen, you can specify how you want the workflow between the two executables to occur. For example, if you want the Foreach Loop to execute if the Script task completed and success is not a factor, you should select Completion from the Value drop-down list.

CONNECTION MANAGER

Since many of the tasks and at least one of the containers may require a connection to a data source, you must create a connection manager to a source that is required by any of the tasks included in the control flow. Any connections created with the connection manager are exclusive to the package in which it was created. However, you can create a connection to a data source in the Solution Explorer. The connection can be used by all packages contained within the same project.

CONTROL FLOW DESIGNER

You will use the Control Flow design surface to create your package workflow. If you suspect that your control flow will contain several small sets of actions or any repeating actions, then the first step is to add a container to the design surface. This is an optional step in the control flow design because some control flows contain only one task. As a result, adding a container does not serve much of a purpose. The next step is to add a task either on the design surface or to a container that already exists on the design surface. Once you have added and configured all your containers and tasks, the final step is to connect them using precedence constraints. Figure 5-4 shows a sample package that includes various containers, tasks, and precedence constraints.

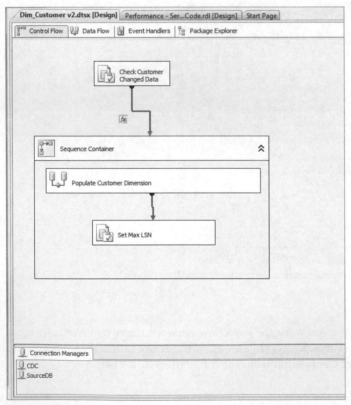

FIGURE 5-4

As you can see, in Figure 5-4 I have an Execute SQL task, followed by a precedence constraint that is configured to use a constraint and an expression. Figure 5-5 shows the implementation.

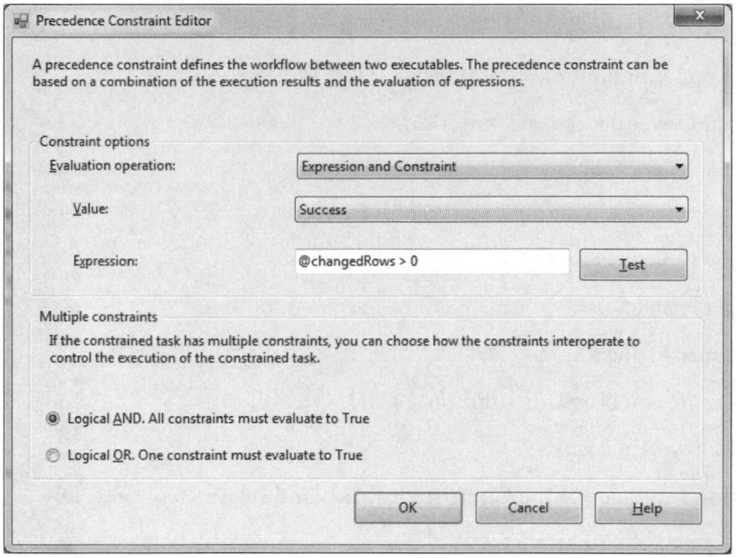

FIGURE 5-5

In Figure 5-5 the connector has been configured to control the execution of the next task based on its completion of the first task, and an expression has been included that will further restrict the flow of the operation. If the variable that is specified in the expression is not greater than zero, the next step in the workflow will not execute.

TRY IT

In this Try It you will learn to configure a Foreach Loop Container on the Control Flow designer. Inside the loop you will also learn to configure an Execute SQL task to modify data in the HumanResources.EmployeePayHistory table.

Lesson Requirements

For this lesson you will need the AdventureWorks2008 database, which can be downloaded from www.codeplex.com. You will also need to know the name of your SQL Server. To complete this lesson you will create an SSIS package. The package will loop through the contents of a table in the AdventureWorks2008 database. As it is looping, the package will update a column in each row.

> *The download for this lesson, available at* www.wrox.com, *includes the solution for this Try It.*

Hints

➤ You will use a Foreach Loop Container and an Execute SQL task.

➤ The Execute SQL task requires a database connection.

Step-by-Step

1. In BIDS select File ➪ New ➪ Project.

2. Select Integration Services Project.

3. Name the project **BI Trainer Project 5**.

4. Place a check next to "Create directory for solution." Click OK.

5. Ensure that the Control Flow tab is active.

6. Right-click the Connection Manager of the Control Flow tab and select New OLE DB Connection.

7. In the Connection Manager screen, type **localhost** in the drop-down list labeled "Server name" and type or select AdventureWorks2008 in the drop-down list labeled "Select or enter database name." Click OK twice.

8. Right-click the connection in the Connection Manager and select Rename. Change the name of the connection to **AdventureWorks2008**.

9. Ensuring that you click the white space in the Control Flow designer space, right-click and select Variables.

10. Click the item in the Variable menu labeled New Variable.

11. Type **results** for the variable name and change the data type to Object.

12. Select New Variable from the Variable menu again.

13. Type **businessEntityID** for the variable name and accept Int32 as the data type.

14. When you are done, your variables should look like what is shown in Figure 5-6.

15. Click the toolbox tab, then drag an Execute SQL task onto the design surface.

16. Double-click that task and the Execute SQL task Editor will appear. See Figure 5-7.

17. Ensure that OLE DB is selected in the ConnectionType text box. Then click in the text box labeled Connection. This will activate the drop-down list. Select AdventureWorks2008 from the drop-down list.

FIGURE 5-6

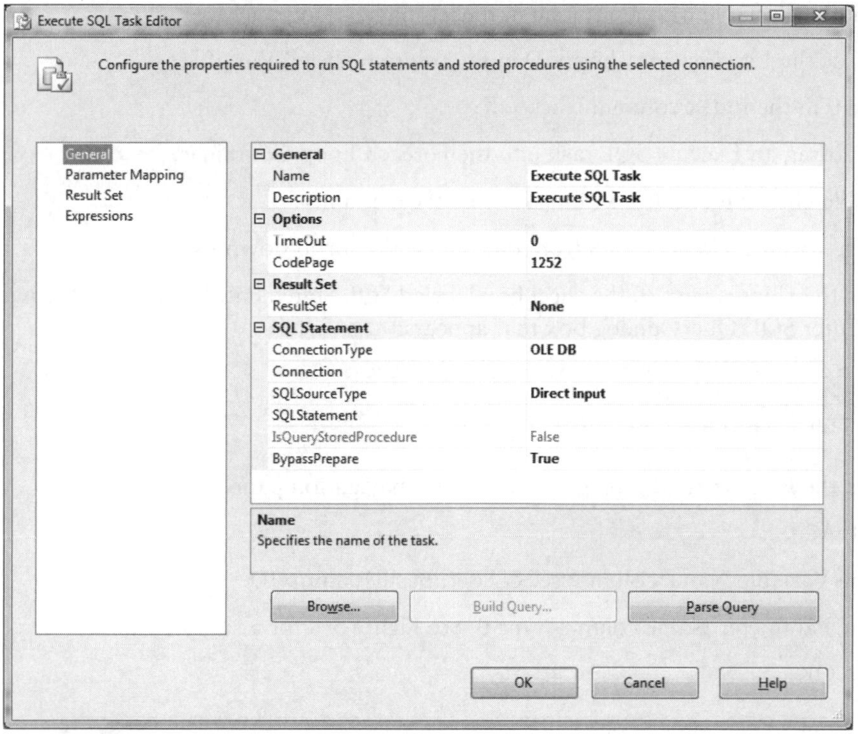

FIGURE 5-7

18. Click in the text box labeled SQLStatement and ellipses will appear. Click the ellipses. Paste the following query into the Enter SQL Query dialog box that appears:

```
select BusinessEntityID
from HumanResources.EmployeePayHistory
```

19. Choose "Full result set" from the drop-down list labeled Resultset.

20. Click the Result Set Item in the left navigation pane.

21. Click Add.

22. Type 0 in the Result Name column.

23. In the Variable Name column, select User::results from the drop-down list. Click OK.

24. Drag the Foreach Loop container onto the Control Flow design surface. Double-click the Foreach Loop Container.

25. Click the Collection item in the left navigation pane.

26. Choose Foreach ADO Enumerator from the drop-down list labeled Enumerator under the Foreach Loop Editor group.

27. Choose User::results from the drop-down list labeled "ADO object source variable."

28. Select Rows in the first table radio button.

29. Click the Variable Mappings item in the left navigation pane.

30. Choose the User::businessEntityID in the column labeled Variable.

31. Type 0 in the Index column. Click OK.

32. Next, drag an Execute SQL task into the Foreach Loop Container.

33. Double-click the Execute SQL task inside the container.

34. Select AdventureWorks2008 from the Connection drop-down list.

35. Click the ellipses next to the checkbox labeled SQL Statement. Paste the following query into the Enter SQL Query dialog box that appears:

```
update HumanResources.EmployeePayHistory
set rate = rate*1.10
where businessentityID = ?
```

36. Click the Parameter Mapping item in the left navigation pane.

37. Click Add.

38. In the Variable Name column, select User::businessEntityID.

39. In the Parameter Name column, type 0. See Figure 5-8 for a sample view.

Click OK.

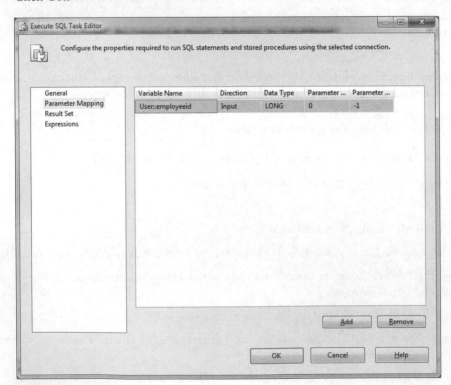

FIGURE 5-8

40. Drag the connector from the Execute SQL task that is not inside the container onto the Foreach Loop Container. See Figure 5-9 for an example.

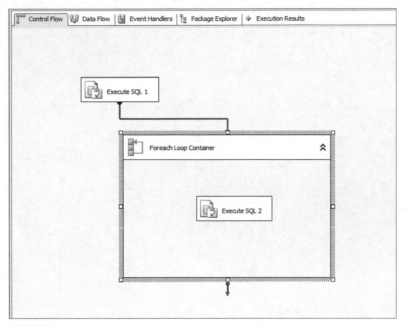

FIGURE 5-9

41. Right-click your package in the Solution Explorer and select Execute. The Execute SQL task outside of the container will immediately turn green, and the one on the inside will blink from yellow to green, eventually turning green. Once this occurs, the package has successfully completed.

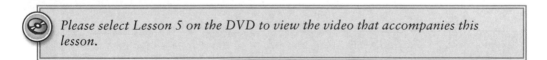

Please select Lesson 5 on the DVD to view the video that accompanies this lesson.

Using the Data Flow

Now that you understand how to organize the workflow of your package, it is time to learn how to use the data flow. In this lesson you will focus on designing and implementing processes that extract data from various sources, then transform or cleanse the data, and finally load the data into a destination source. The data flow toolbox exposes several data sources, transformation tasks, and destination sources that may play a role in the architecture of your data warehouse ETL process. Each of the aforementioned items can be connected to each other by various paths. These paths connect the inputs and outputs of the components on the data flow design surface.

Initially, the Data Flow tab resembles Figure 6-1.

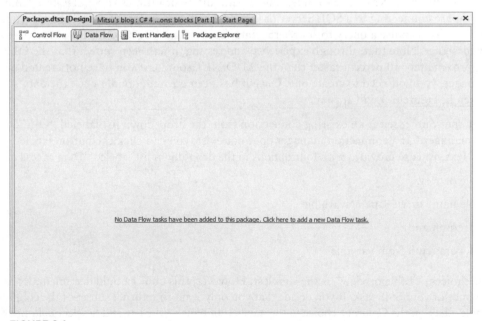

FIGURE 6-1

There are two methods that will activate this tab. You can click the hyperlink on the Data Flow tab or you can activate the Control Flow tab and drag a Data Flow task onto the control flow design surface. No matter which approach you choose, a Data Flow task will be added to the design surface of the control flow. Unlike with the other tasks added to the design surface of the control flow, double-clicking the Data Flow task will activate the corresponding Data Flow tab.

Multiple Data Flow tasks can be placed on the control flow design surface. If you do this you can switch back and forth between the data flows by selecting the data flow of choice from the drop-down list labeled Data Flow Task, which is located above the data flow design surface. See Figure 6-2.

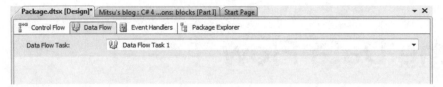

FIGURE 6-2

Finally, as with the control flow, if one of the components on the data flow designer requires a data source, a connection manager must be added to the package. If the connection manager was created earlier, when you were designing the control, it can be reused on the design flow.

DATA FLOW SOURCES (EXTRACTING DATA)

SSIS provides various sources for extracting data. With an SSIS package you can extract data from Microsoft Excel, flat files, XML data sources, and several different OLE DB and ADO.NET data sources. If you are connecting to a SQL Server or Oracle database, you can extract directly from a table or view or you can use a query to source the data. To do this, drag an OLE DB source onto the design flow designer. Note that, through experience and testing, it has been shown that the OLE DB source is approximately 30 percent faster than the ADO.NET source. If you have not created a connection manager, you will need to create one. Once it has been created, double-click the data source and the screen in Figure 6-3 will appear.

To configure the source, select an existing connection from the drop-down list labeled "OLE DB connection manager." If a connection manager does not exist, you can click the button labeled New to add one. Next, you are provided with four options in the drop-down list labeled "Data access mode":

➤ Table or view

➤ Table name or view name variable

➤ SQL command

➤ SQL command from variable

Of the four choices, "Table or view" is the simplest. However, this choice could detrimentally affect the performance of your SSIS task. If you decide that you only want to return a subset of the columns from the table, click on the Columns choice in the navigation pane to the left and deselect columns from the list of Available External Columns (Figure 6-4).

FIGURE 6-3

FIGURE 6-4

You might have assumed that a server-side filter would occur; unfortunately, that is not the behavior. All the data from the selected table will be returned and a client-side filter will be performed. Therefore, instead of selecting "Table or view," you should select option "SQL command." With this choice you can ensure that only the required data is being transferred over the network to the client.

As with most of the configurable properties of an SSIS task, you can use a variable in place of hard-coded text. For example, if you want to source the query or table dynamically based on some condition in the work flow, you can assign the variable a value. Then you can use that variable as the value for your table or query. See Figure 6-5 for an example:

FIGURE 6-5

No matter your choice, variable or hard-coded, you should always select a method that is based on a query instead of a table or view. One thing to note is that if your expression syntax is incorrect, the expression will turn red. If you hover over the expression or click OK, you will be provided with detailed information about the error. Once the error is corrected, if any existed in the first place, click OK.

DATA FLOW TRANSFORMATIONS

Once you have created a data source, it is time to perform any transformations that may be needed on the data. SSIS provides several tasks to assist in cleansing the data before it is loaded into its final destination. The data flow includes tasks that can aggregate data, join data, count data, sort data, and do many other things to it. Other tasks can split the data based on a condition or look data up based on matching keys between two data sources.

A task that is commonly used during ETL for a data warehouse is the Derived Column task. The purpose of this task is either to create a new column in the existing data set or to replace an existing column. To configure this task, you must first drag a connection from a data source onto the task. Once the connection is made, double-click the Derived Column task and the window shown in Figure 6-6 will appear.

FIGURE 6-6

Expand the folder labeled Columns in the top left pane. Notice that the columns listed here are based on the query that was provided in the OLE DB source. I can add a new column to this result set by selecting "Add as new column" from the drop-down list labeled Derived Column in the lower pane. For example, assume that FirstName and LastName are two columns available in the tree. If you wanted to add a FullName column whose value was a concatenation of the two columns, with FirstName first and LastName last and a space between the two, you would type the following expression in the column labeled Expression in the lower pane.

```
FirstName+" "+LastName
```

Then you could change the column name from Derived Column 1 by replacing the value in the column labeled Derived Column Name with FullName.

If additional transformations are needed on the data set before it is loaded into the destination, simply drag over any component and connect it to the derived column. For example, if you wanted to load only rows that meet a certain condition, you could use a Conditional Split task. Or if you wanted to load the data into multiple destinations you could use a Multicast task.

DATA FLOW PATHS

You can connect the items that have been added to the Data Flow designer by using the data flow paths that protrude from each element. At a minimum each item will have a success path (green arrow) and an error path (red arrow). To use these paths, simply drag one from an item onto the next item you want to execute. At that point, the items will execute in the sequence that you have specified.

In some cases, you can customize the output of a data flow path. For example, with the Lookup task you can specify what if anything is output from the error flow path. In Figure 6-7 you can see the four configurable options.

➤ If you choose the first option, **"Ignore failure,"** from the drop-down list labeled "Specify how to handle rows with no matching entries," the Lookup task will behave much like an OUTER JOIN in T-SQL.

➤ Choosing **"Redirect rows to error output"** will send any rows that do not match down the error flow path. Two additional columns are added to the output columns.

➤ The **"Fail component"** option will do just that. If any rows do not match, the component execution will fail.

➤ Finally, if you choose **"Redirect rows to no match output,"** a new green arrow will be added to the task. Any rows that do not match will be sent down this path.

DATA FLOW DESIGNER

The data flow provides you with the tools needed to build an effective and efficient data cleansing or ETL process. The typical steps involved in designing the data flow are as follows:

1. Add a data flow source to the design surface. Do not forget to add a connection manager.

2. Add as many transformation tasks as are required to meet your business needs.

3. Connect the data flow source to the transformation tasks and perform any additional connections using the data flow paths exposed by each source and transformation.

4. Add data flow destination(s).

5. Connect the final transformations to the destinations using the data flow paths.

The five preceding steps are typical of most data flows for building a data warehouse ETL process. Figure 6-8 shows a data flow that extracts the data from a database, performs a few transformations to massage the data, and finally loads the cleansed data into a database using a data flow destination.

FIGURE 6-7

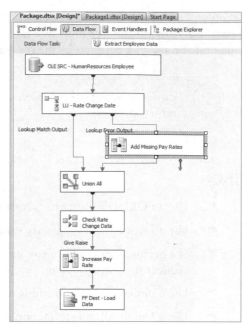

FIGURE 6-8

Note that the preceding steps list the minimum elements that may be used in designing a typical ETL process. Additional sources, transformations, and destinations may be included as you determine your needs.

TRY IT

In this Try It, you will learn to design a data flow that will extract employee pay data from a SQL Server database. Then you will learn to use a Lookup task to determine the last time each employee received a pay increase. If the person does not have any pay data, you will add a Derived Column task to the data flow. The task will add two columns to the output set.

➤ The first column will be Rate, and it will have a value of 10.

➤ The second column will be RateChangeDate, and it will have a value equal to today's date.

On the other hand, if the person does have pay data and has been working for more than 10 years, you will increase the pay rate by 10 percent. Finally, you will export the data to a flat file data source.

Lesson Requirements

To complete this lesson you will need the AdventureWorks2008 database, which can be downloaded from www.codeplex.com. You will also need to know the name of your SQL Server.

You will create an SSIS package. The SSIS package will extract data from the AdventureWorks2008 database HumanResource.Employee table. In addition, the package will either increase the employee's pay rate or assign a base rate as the rows are extracted from the table.

 The download for this lesson, available at www.wrox.com, *includes the solution for this Try It.*

Hints

- ➤ Use an OLE DB source to extract the data.
- ➤ Use a Lookup task to identify each person's last change date.
- ➤ If a person does not have any pay change data, ensure that you configure the Lookup task to redirect to an error output.
- ➤ Use a derived column to add Rates and RateChangeDates for the unmatched rows.
- ➤ Use a Union All transformation to combine the two result sets.
- ➤ Use a Conditional Split transformation to determine if a person has been employed for more than 10 years.
- ➤ Add another derived column that will add a new column to increase the pay rate.
- ➤ Finally, output the data to a flat file destination.

Step-by-Step

1. In BIDS, click File ➪ New ➪ Project.
2. Select Integration Services Project.
3. Name the project **BI Trainer Packages 6**.
4. Place a check next to "Create directory for Solution." Click OK.
5. Ensure that the Control Flow tab is active.
6. Right-click in the connection manager of the Control Flow tab and select New OLE DB Connection.
7. In the connection manager screen, type **localhost** in the drop-down list labeled "Server name" and type or select **AdventureWorks2008** in the drop-down list labeled "Select or enter database name." Click OK twice.
8. Right-click the connection in the connection manager and select Rename. Change the name of the connection to **AdventureWorks2008**.
9. Drag a Data Flow task onto the control flow design surface.
10. Double-click the Data Flow task or click the Data Flow tab.

11. Drag an OLE DB data source onto the design surface.

12. Double-click the OLE DB source.

13. Select AdventureWorks2008 from the drop down-list labeled OLE DB Connection Manager.

14. Select SQL Command from the drop-down list labeled "Data access mode."

15. Paste the following query into the text box labeled "SQL command text."

```
SELECT
      BusinessEntityID,
      NationalIDNumber,
      JobTitle,
      BirthDate,
      MaritalStatus,
      HireDate,
      Gender,
      SalariedFlag,
      VacationHours,
      SickLeaveHours
FROM HumanResources.Employee
```

16. Your screen should resemble the one in Figure 6-9.

Click OK.

FIGURE 6-9

17. Drag a Lookup task onto the design surface.

18. Drag the green data flow path from the OLE DB connection onto the Lookup task.

19. Double-click the Lookup task.

20. Select "Redirect rows to error output" from the drop-down list labeled "Specify how to handle rows with no matching entries."

21. Click Connection in the left window pane.

22. Select AdventureWorks2008 from the drop-down list labeled OLE DB connection manager.

23. Select the radio button labeled "Use result of a query."

24. Paste the following query into the text box below that radio button:

```
SELECT
    BusinessEntityID, RateChangeDate,Rate
FROM HumanResources.EmployeePayHistory
```

25. Click Columns in the left window pane.

26. Click the BusinessEntityID column in the list of columns labeled Available Input Columns.

27. Drag the BusinessEntityID column from the Available Input Columns onto the BusinessEntityID column in the list of columns labeled Available Lookup Columns.

28. In the list of columns labeled Available Lookup columns, ensure that only the RateChangeDate and Rate columns are checked. See Figure 6-10.

Click OK.

29. Drag a Derived Column task onto the design surface.

30. Drag the red Lookup Error Output data flow path onto the Derived Column task.

31. Double-click the Derived Column task. In the lower pane, in the column labeled Derived Column Name, type **Rate**.

32. In the column labeled Derived Column, select <add as new column>.

33. In the column labeled Expression, type (DT_CY)10.00.

34. Under that row, type **RateChangeDate** in the column labeled Derived Column Name.

35. In the column labeled Derived Column, select <add as new column>.

36. In the column labeled Expression, type **GETDATE**(). Click OK.

37. Drag a Union All transformation onto the design surface.

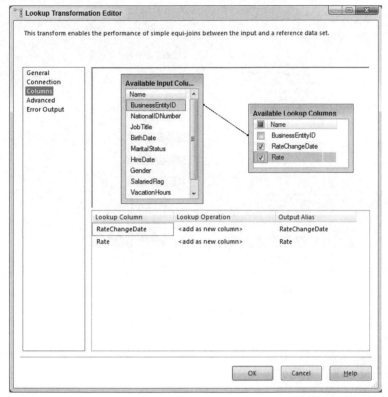

FIGURE 6-10

38. Drag the Lookup Match Output Data Path onto that task.

39. Drag the green arrow from the Derived Column task onto the Union All task.

40. Add a Conditional Split task onto the design surface.

41. Drag the green arrow from the Union All task onto the Conditional Split.

42. Double-click the Conditional Split task.

43. In the lower pane of the Conditional Split Transformation Editor, type **Give Raise** in the column labeled Output Name.

44. Then type the following expression in the column labeled Condition:

```
DATEDIFF("yy",RateChangeDate,GETDATE()) > 10
```

45. Finally, type **No Raise** in the column labeled "Default output name." See Figure 6-11. Click OK.

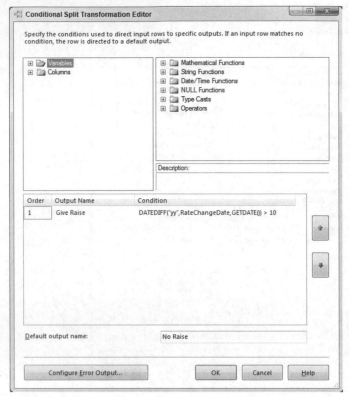

FIGURE 6-11

46. Drag a Derived Column task onto the design surface.

47. Drag the green arrow from the Conditional Split task onto the newly added Derived Column task. A dialog box like the one in Figure 6-12 will appear.

48. Select Give Raise from the drop-down list labeled Output and click OK.

49. Double-click the derived column.

FIGURE 6-12

50. In the lower pane, in the column labeled Derived Column Name, type **NewRate**.

51. In the column labeled Derived Column, select <add as new column>.

52. In the column labeled Expression type **Rate*1.10** and type **NewPayRate** in the column labeled Derived Column Name. Click OK.

53. Drag a flat file destination onto the design surface.

54. Drag the green data flow path onto the flat file destination.

55. Double-click the flat file destination.

56. Click New.

57. Select the radio button labeled Delimited on the Flat File Format screen. Click OK.

58. In the Flat File Connection Manager Editor, type **c:\Raises.txt** in the text box labeled "File name." Click OK.

59. Click Mapping in the left pane. Click OK.

60. Right-click the package in the Solution Explorer and select Execute Package.

61. Browse to the C: drive, locate the Raises.txt text file, and open it.

 Please select Lesson 6 on the DVD to view the video that accompanies this lesson.

7

Solving Common SSIS Scenarios

As you work with SSIS, you may realize that certain tasks become commonplace. You may find yourself implementing the same solution over and over again, for example, moving data from one database to another. You would typically do this by using the data flow, as in Figure 7-1.

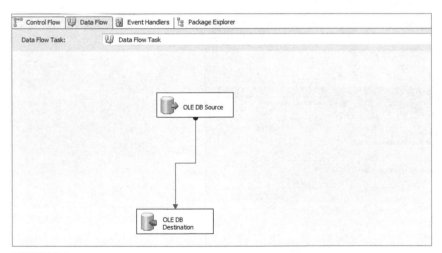

FIGURE 7-1

In Figure 7-1 you see a data flow source that will extract data from some source. The data flow source is connected to a data flow destination, which is where the data will be exported. You may place some data flow transformations between the source and destination, but ultimately the goal is the same, moving data from one data source to another.

You may also encounter a situation in which you need to import data from multiple text files into one single destination. You would typically do this by using a Foreach Loop container on the control flow, as in Figure 7-2.

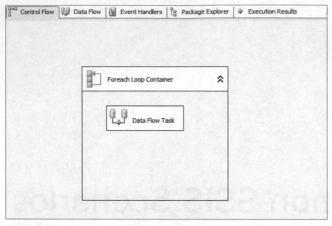

FIGURE 7-2

As you can see in Figure 7-2, the Foreach Loop container contains a Data Flow task that will handle the movement of the data from the text file to the destination. Double-click the Foreach Loop container to open the Foreach Loop Editor, shown in Figure 7-3.

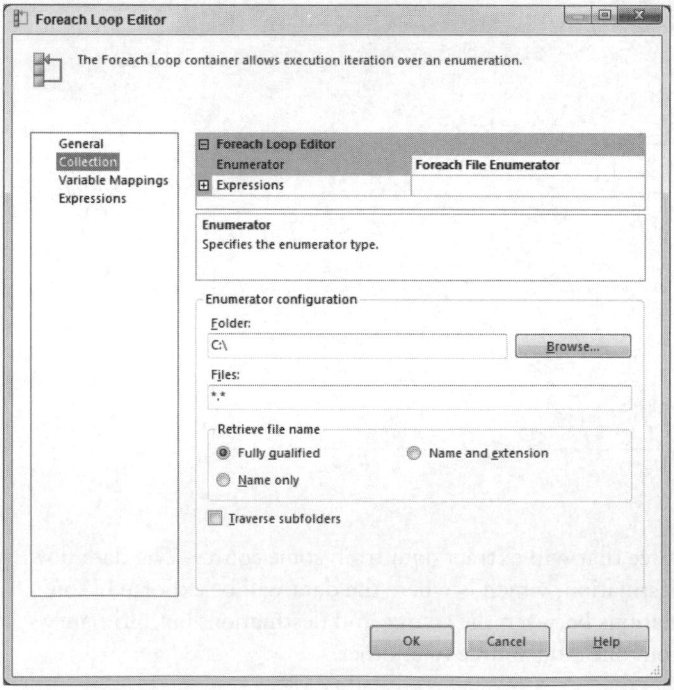

FIGURE 7-3

To configure the Foreach Loop to enumerate a list of files, click Collection in the left navigation pane. Select Foreach File Enumerator in the drop-down list labeled Enumerator. Then specify a file path in the text box labeled Folder. Next, click Variable Mappings in the left navigation pane. When configuring a Foreach Loop container that will move through a list of files, you typically declare a variable that will hold each file name as the container loops through the list. Select that variable from the column labeled Variable and accept the value of 0 for the column labeled Index. Click OK and the container is configured.

Finally, you may be asked to move and rename the file(s) after the data has been imported. This is often a method that is used to ensure that the data is not imported more than once. Figure 7-4, which is similar to Figure 7-2, includes a File System task.

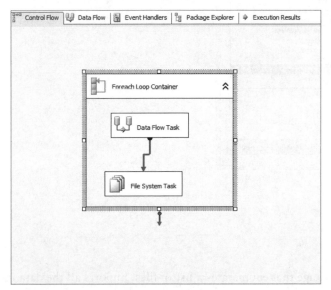

FIGURE 7-4

This task, if configured properly, can rename and move the file in one step. By double-clicking the File System task, you can configure source and destination locations. You can also specify whether you want to move, copy, or rename the file. To use the task, you should begin by deciding on the operation you want to perform. Do this by selecting the choice from the drop-down list labeled Operation. As you can see in Figure 7-5, there are several options from which to choose.

If you are trying to move and rename a file in one step, choose the Rename file option. Then you will decide on the destination and source locations.

FIGURE 7-5

TRY IT

In this Try It, you will create an SSIS package that enumerates a list of files, imports all the data in each file, and, finally, renames and moves each file to a new location.

Lesson Requirements

To complete this lesson, you will create an SSIS package that uses a Foreach Loop container to loop over a list of files. As the package loops over each file, it uses a data flow to import the data into a database and finally moves the file to a new location.

Before building your SSIS package you will need to run Lesson7Create.sql. Then you should create a folder on your C: drive named **Lesson7**. In that folder create two folders, one named **DataFiles** and the other **Archive**. Finally, copy the text files included in this lesson's download into the DataFiles folder.

The download for this lesson, available at www.wrox.com, *includes the Lesson7Create.sql, the text files you need for this Try It, and the final solution.*

Hints

➤ You will use a Foreach Loop container, Data Flow task, and File System task.

➤ The package will require three data sources, two files, and one database.

➤ You will make the connection string based on an expression.

Step-by-Step

1. Open and execute Lesson7Create.sql.

2. In BIDS, click File ➪ New ➪ Project.

3. Select Integration Services Project.

4. Name the project **BI Trainer Packages 7**.

5. Place a check next to "Create directory for Solution." Click OK.

6. Ensure that the Control Flow tab is active.

7. Right-click in the Connection Manager of the Control Flow tab and select New OLE DB Connection.

8. In the Connection Manager screen, type **localhost** in the drop-down list labeled "Server name" and type or select **AdventureWorks2008** in the drop-down list labeled "Select or enter database name." Click OK twice.

9. Right-click the connection in the Connection Manager and select Rename. Change the name of the connection to **AdventureWorks2008**.

10. Right-click the control flow designer and select variables from the context menu.

11. Click the "Add new variable" icon in the Variables menu.

12. Add a new string variable named **DestinationFileLocation**. Set the value to `C:\Lesson7\Archive`.

13. Add a new string variable named **SourceFileLocation**. Set the value to `C:\Lesson7\DataFiles`.

14. Add a new string variable named **SourceFileName**.

15. Drag a Foreach Loop container onto the control flow design surface. Double-click the container.

16. Select Collection from the left navigation pane.

17. Ensure that Foreach File Enumerator is selected in the drop-down list labeled Enumerator.

18. In the text box labeled Folder type or paste **C:\Lesson7\DataFiles**.

19. Select the radio button labeled "Name only" from the "Retrieve file name" group. The Foreach Loop Editor should resemble what is shown in Figure 7-6.

20. Click Variable Mappings in the left navigation pane.

21. Select User:SourceFileName from the column labeled Variable.

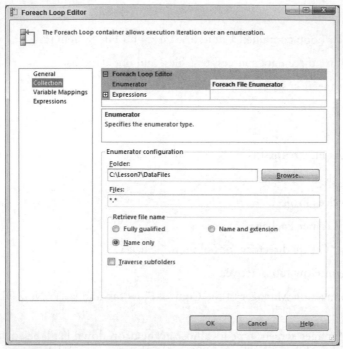

FIGURE 7-6

22. Accept the default of 0 from the column labeled Index. Click OK.

23. Right-click in the Connections Manager section of the control flow.

24. Select New File Connection. The File Connection Manager Editor will appear.

25. Select Create File from the drop-down list labeled "Usage type."

26. Paste or type the following in the text box labeled File: **C:\Lesson7\Archive\FileOne.txt**.

27. Rename the file connection to **Archive**.

28. Right-click the file connection and select Properties.

29. Locate Expression in the Properties window. Click the ellipsis.

30. In the Property column, select ConnectionString.

31. Click the ellipsis in the column labeled Expression.

32. Type or paste the following value in the text box labeled Expression:

```
@[User::DestinationFileLocation]+"\\"+ @[User::SourceFileName]+"_
"+  (DT_WSTR, 4) DATEPART("yyyy", GETDATE())+(DT_WSTR, 2) DATEPART
("mm", GETDATE())+(DT_WSTR, 2) DATEPART("dd", GETDATE())+".txt"
```

Click OK twice.

33. Drag a Data Flow task into the Foreach Loop container.

34. Activate the Data Flow tab.

35. Drag a flat file source onto the data flow designer. Double-click the file source and the Flat File Source Editor will appear, as in Figure 7-7.

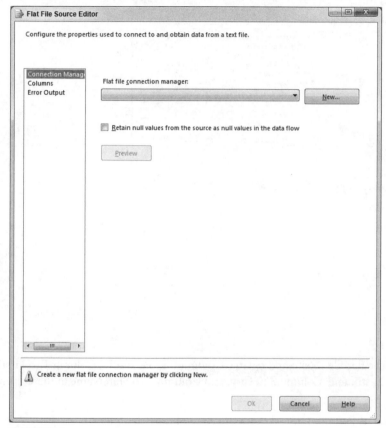

FIGURE 7-7

36. Click New next to the drop-down list labeled "Flat File connection manager."

37. Type **Source** in the text box labeled Connection Manager Name on the Flat File Connection Manager Editor.

38. Type or paste **C:\Lesson7\DataFiles\FileOne.txt** into the text box labeled "File name."

39. Click Columns in the left navigation pane. Click OK twice.

40. Right-click the file connection and select Properties.

41. Locate Expression in the Properties window. Click the ellipsis.

42. In the Property column, select ConnectionString.

43. Click the ellipsis in the column labeled Expression.

44. Type or paste the following value into the text box labeled Expression (Figure 7-8):

```
@[User::SourceFileLocation]+"\\"+  @[User::SourceFileName]+".txt"
```

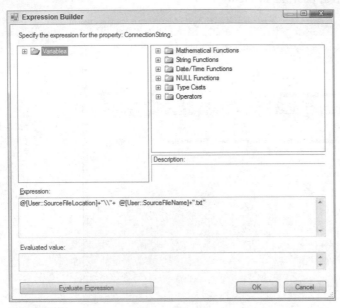

FIGURE 7-8

Click OK twice.

45. Double-click the flat file source and rename Column 0 to **PersonID,** Column 1 to **FirstName,** Column 2 to **LastName,** Column 3 to **City,** and Column 4 to **StateName** in the Output columns. Click OK.

46. Drag an OLE DB Destination task onto the control flow designer.

47. Drag the data flow connector from the flat file source onto the newly created OLE DB destination.

48. Double-click the destination and select dbo.Lesson7Imports from the drop-down list labeled "Name of the table or the view."

49. Click Mappings in the left navigation pane.

50. The OLE DB Destination Editor that appears should resemble Figure 7-9. Click OK.

51. Activate the Control Flow data tab.

52. Drag a File System task into the Foreach Loop container.

53. Drag the precedence constraint from the Data Flow task onto the File System task.

54. Double-click the File System task.

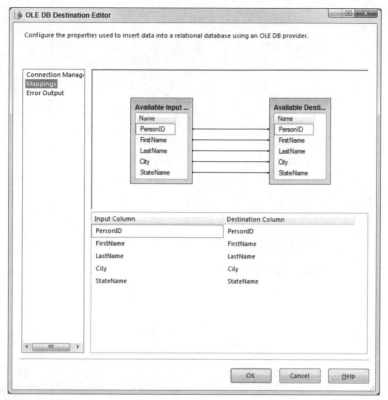

FIGURE 7-9

55. Select "Rename file" from the drop-down list labeled Operation.

56. Select Archive from the drop-down list labeled DestinationConnection.

57. Select Source from the drop-down list labeled SourceConnection. Click OK.

58. After executing the package, open C:\Lesson7\Archives. You will notice that three files have been renamed to this location.

 Please select Lesson 7 on the DVD to view the video that accompanies this lesson.

8

Loading Dimensions

An integral part of a data warehouse is the dimension tables. If you have a data warehouse you've probably been anticipating a section that will assist you in designing an SSIS package that will load your dimension tables. Before SSIS, building the logic to load a dimension would require thousands of lines of code. However, because SSIS includes a Slowly Changing Dimension Wizard in the data flow, many of the challenges have been removed from designing and creating the extraction, transformation, and loading of your dimension table.

If you don't have an existing warehouse and are about to get started building, we would like to provide you with a bit of terminology for slowly changing dimensions (SCDs). The SCD task on the data flow of an SSIS package can handle Type 0, 1, and 2 dimensions. One specific advantage of the task is that these types can be set on a column-by-column basis. A Type 0 dimension, which is specified as a *fixed attribute*, does not make any changes to the column. For example, you may want to ensure that all TaxIDs for a customer or vendor remain the same; therefore, you would set the column as a fixed attribute. A Type 1 dimension (*changing attribute*) will update the value of a column, but does not track the history of the change. Finally, a Type 2 dimension (*historical dimension*) will track column data changes. For example, if the discount percentage for a promotion changes, and it was specified as a Type 2 column, the original row expires, and a new row with the updated data is inserted into the dimension table.

Two terms that you will see in the wizard are *inferred members* or *late arriving facts*. Inferred members exist when you are loading a fact table and the corresponding dimension data does not exist. For example, you may have a salesfact that contains sales data and one of the dimensions contains promotion data. If a row is inserted into the salesfact and the data in the promotion dimension is not up to date, a temporary, or stub, row will be inserted into the dimension table. The row that was inserted into the fact will be associated to that row. Once the dimension record does come from the source, the SCD transformation will update the row as if it were a Type 1 dimension, even if it is set to a Type 2.

USING THE SLOWLY CHANGING DIMENSION TASK

Before you start using the SCD task, you must first add a Data Flow task to your Control Flow designer; then you will need to create and configure a source on the Data Flow designer. Once you have done this, drag an SCD task onto the Data Flow design surface and drag the Data Flow connector from your source onto the SCD task. Your design surface should resemble Figure 8-1.

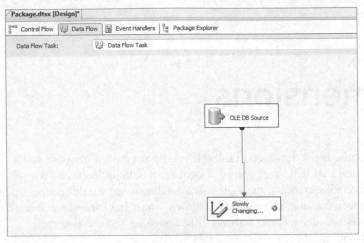

FIGURE 8-1

Ignore the red X on the SCD task: once you configure the task it will disappear. Next, double-click the SCD task to open the Slowly Changing Dimension Wizard. The first screen is the startup screen; simply click Next. On the next screen (Figure 8-2) you will need to select the Destination Connection Manager and the table. This connection is typically a connection to your data warehouse and the table is the dimension that will hold the data from the source. After your have made those selections, map the source input columns to the target destination columns. Finally, choose one key to be your business key: in most cases this is the primary key from the source system or operational data store. This key is often called the *alternate key*.

On the next screen (Figure 8-3) you will specify a dimension type (0, 1, or 2) for each column. As mentioned earlier, Type 0 is a fixed attribute, Type 1 is a changing attribute, and Type 2 is a historical attribute.

FIGURE 8-2

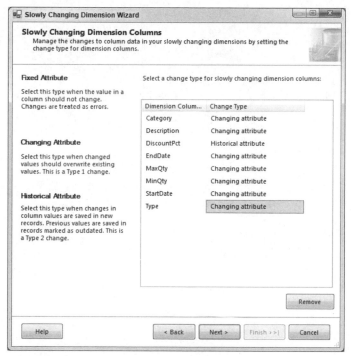

FIGURE 8-3

The next screen (Figure 8-4) contains two sections. Each section's availability depends on the types of the attributes that were selected in the previous screen. Since I did not denote any columns as Type 0 (fixed) attributes, the checkbox labeled "Fail the transformation if changes are detected in a fixed attribute" is disabled. However, if any attributes had been specified as Type 0, you could have used this option to fail the entire task if any columns that you expected to remain the same changed. For example, if the Special Offer name were a Type 0 attribute and it changed in the source system, then the task would have failed. The next option, Changing Attributes, will allow you to change expired or outdated rows if the source data has changed. For example, assume that a special offer has two rows, the effective row and an expired row. If a new row is inserted with an updated value for Offer Description, then the Offer Description in every row will be updated to the new value.

If during the configuration of the screen in Figure 8-3 you selected "Historical attribute" for any of the available columns, you will be asked how to set a row as expired and how to create a new row (Figure 8-5).

There are two sections on the screen. The top section allows you to choose one column in which you can set the value as Current or Active for the current row and set the expired row as Expired or False for outdated rows. The bottom section provides more robust capabilities. You have the ability to set start and end date columns to a date or user variable. Regardless of what you choose, all of this can be customized later. The final screen is the Inferred Dimension Members screen, which I discussed earlier in this lesson.

Now that you have completed the wizard you will notice new template code (Figure 8-6) has been created and your dimension is ready to load.

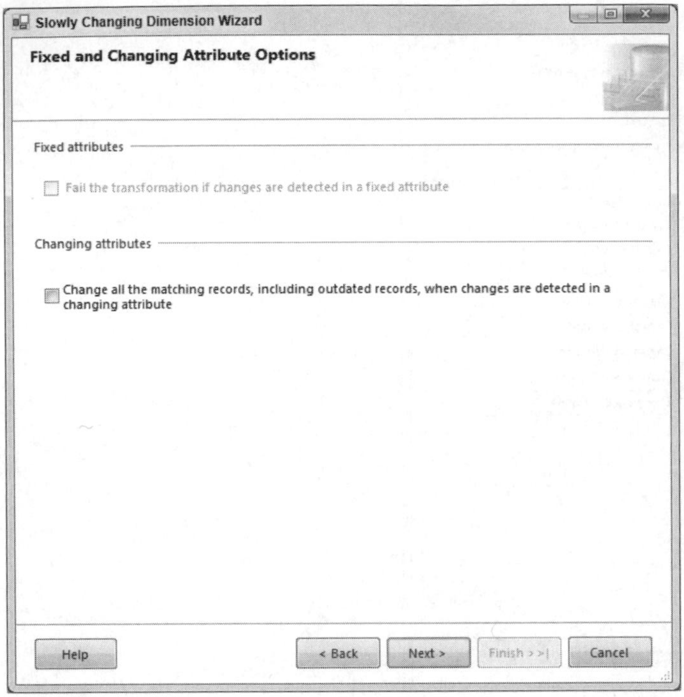

FIGURE 8-4

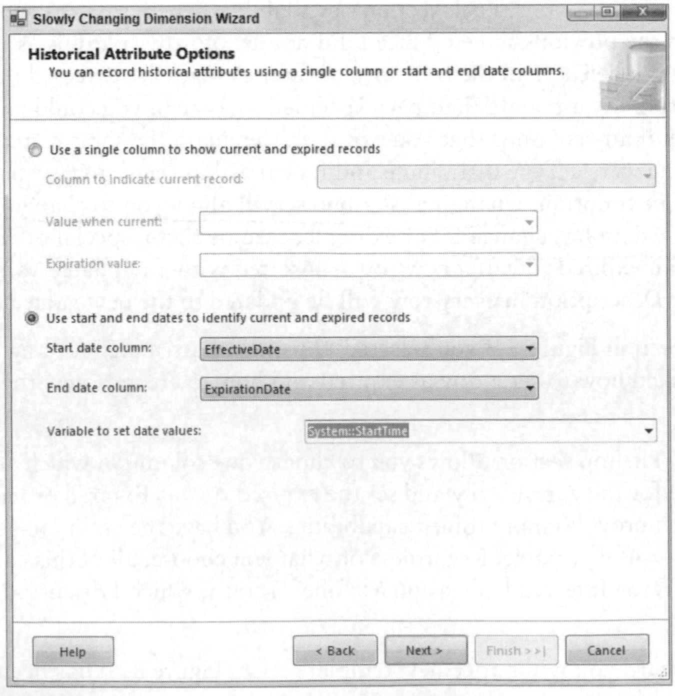

FIGURE 8-5

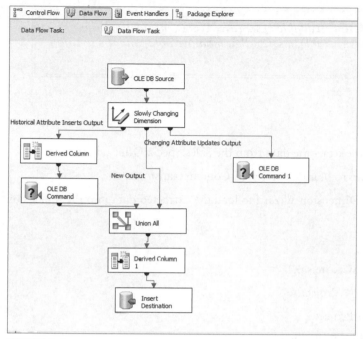

FIGURE 8-6

Review the tasks and data flows that have been added to the package. Notice that three paths lead from the SCD task. When the data flow is executed each row is checked to see whether it is a new row, a duplicate row, or a Type 1 or 2 update. You can change any task that has been added by the SCD wizard; however, if you rerun the wizard any custom changes will have to be recreated.

TRY IT

In this Try It, you will learn how to use the Slowly Changing Dimension task and its accompanying wizard to load a new special offer dimension. Then some changes will be made to the source data, and you will see how they are applied to the dimension table by means of the task.

Lesson Requirements

Before building your SSIS package, you will need to run Lesson8Create.sql. You will use the Slowly Changing Dimension Wizard to extract the data from the source database into the warehouse. Your source data is in the AdventureWorks2008 database in a table called Sales.SpecialOffer. You should set the DiscountPct column as a Type 2 dimension column. Also, you will also be required to replace NULL data in the MaxQty column with a value of 0. After you run the package once, execute Lesson8Changes.sql to modify data in the source table. You will then rerun the package and watch the changes flow through the Slowly Changing Dimension task and get applied to the destination dimension table.

The download for this lesson, available at www.wrox.com, *includes a script file that will create the dimension table, a script that modifies data, and the solution to the Try It section.*

Hints

➤ Use the OLE DB source to extract the data from the Sales.SpecialOffer table.

➤ To set the MaxQty column to 0, use the Derived Column transform.

➤ Use the Slowly Changing Dimension Wizard to load the extracted data into the dimension.

Step-by-Step

1. Open and execute Lesson8Create.sql.

2. In BIDS select File ➪ New ➪ Project.

3. Select Integration Services Project.

4. Name the project **BI Trainer Packages 8**.

5. Place a check next to Create Directory for Solution.

6. Click OK.

7. Ensure that the Control Flow tab is active.

8. Right-click in the Connection Manager of the Control Flow tab and select New OLE DB Connection.

9. In the Connection Manager screen, type **localhost** in the drop-down list labeled "Server name" and type or select **AdventureWorks2008** in the drop-down list labeled "Select or enter database name."

10. Click OK twice.

11. Right-click the connection in the Connection Manager and select Rename. Change the name of the connection to **Source**.

12. Repeat Steps 8 through 11, but instead of selecting AdventureWorks2008 as the database, select AdventureWorksDW2008 and rename it **Destination**.

13. Drag a Data Flow task onto the Control Flow design surface.

14. Click the Data Flow tab.

15. Drag an OLE DB data source onto the Data Flow design surface.

16. Double-click the data source and select Source from the drop-down list labeled OLE DB Connection Manager.

17. Select Sales.SpecialOffer from the drop-down list labeled "Name of the table or the view."

18. Click OK.

19. Drag a Derived Column task onto the Data Flow designer.

20. Drag the green data flow connector from the source onto the Derived Column task.

21. Double-click the derived column.

22. In the column labeled Derived Column select Replace "MaxQty."

23. In the column labeled Expression paste the following expression:

```
ISNULL(MaxQty) ? 0 : MaxQty
```

24. Click OK.

25. Drag a Slowly Changing Dimension task onto the Data Flow design surface.

26. Drag the green data flow connector from the Derived Column task onto the Slowly Changing Dimension task.

27. Double-click the Slowly Changing Dimension task.

28. Click Next.

29. Select Destination from the drop-down list labeled Connection Manager.

30. Select DimSpecialOffer from the drop-down list labeled "Table or view."

31. Select SpecialOfferID from the column labeled "Input Columns," next to the value labeled SpecialOfferAlternateKey.

32. In the same row, select "Business key" in the column labeled "Key Type."

33. Select Category from the column labeled "Input Columns," next to the column labeled SpecialOfferCategory.

34. Select Description from the column labeled "Input Columns," next to the column labeled SpecialOfferDescription.

35. Select Type from the column labeled "Input Columns," next to the column labeled SpecialOfferType. At this point, your screen should resemble Figure 8-7.

36. Click Next.

37. On the Slowly Changing Dimension Columns screen (Figure 8-8) set all columns to "Changing attribute" except DiscountPct. Set DiscountPct to "Historical attribute."

38. Click Next twice.

39. On the Historical Attribute Options (Figure 8-9) screen select the radio button labeled "Use start and end dates to identify current and expired records."

40. In the drop-down list labeled "Start date column" select EffectiveDate.

41. In the drop-down list labeled "End date column" select ExpirationDate.

42. In the drop-down list labeled "Variable to set date values" select System::StartTime.

FIGURE 8-7

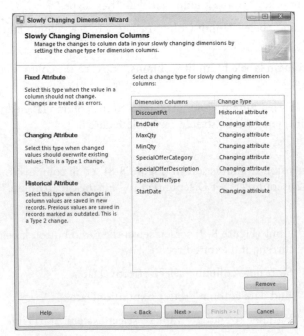

FIGURE 8-8

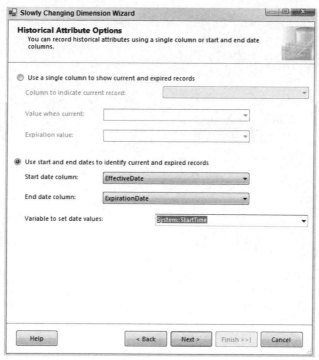

FIGURE 8-9

43. Click Next.

44. On the Inferred Dimension Members screen uncheck the box labeled "Enable inferred member support."

45. Click Next.

46. Click Finish.

47. Right-click the package in the Solution Explorer and select Execute Package. The results will look like Figure 8-10.

48. Run Lesson8Changes.sql to make changes to the source data. This script will make two Type 2 changes and one Type 1 change.

49. Rerun the package. You will notice that one row is sent down the changing attributes path and two rows are sent down the historical attributes path (Figure 8-11).

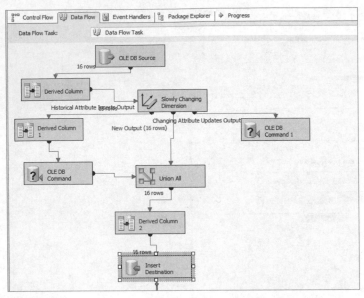

FIGURE 8-10

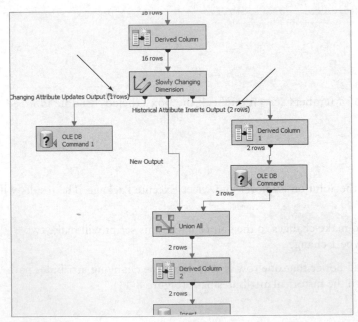

FIGURE 8-11

 Please select Lesson 8 on the DVD to view the video that accompanies this lesson.

Loading a Fact Table

In most cases, fact tables are much easier to load than dimension tables. Typically, you are inserting only rows into the fact table and very few updates, if any. The components used to construct the load are much simpler than those for the Slowly Changing Dimension transform that you used in Lesson 8.

When loading a fact table, the first thing you will do is look up the primary key or surrogate from the dimension table using the *natural key* that is contained within the fact table source data. The natural key, which is also known as the *business* or *alternate key*, is also stored as a column in each dimension. During the fact load process a lookup transform is used to identify the surrogate key or the dimensions table's primary key. This value is stored in the fact table.

You may also be required to include some additional calculations or formulas before you load the fact table. For example, you may be loading line item data and your source data may contain only a Quantity value and an Item Cost value, although your requirements are to store a LineCost column. This value is the result of multiplying the quantity and the cost. As a result, you use a derived column task to apply the formula and create a LineCost column.

You may also encounter a situation in which you need to aggregate data because the data is at a more granular level than required. Assume that your source data contains Vendor, Item, Date, and SalesAmount columns and your fact table includes only Item, Date, and SalesAmount. You could use an aggregate transform to roll the data up. When configuring the transform, you should set the Item as the Group By value, then set the operation on SalesAmount to Sum and set the operation to Max on Date.

TRY IT

Now that you are aware of all the components required to load a fact table, it's time to try actually loading one. In this Try It you will load a fact table called FactSales.

Lesson Requirements

Before beginning the lab, run Lesson9CreateTable.sql in the AdventureWorksDW2008 database. The data that you will use is in Lesson9Data.csv.

 The download for this lesson, available at www.wrox.com, *includes a script that will create the fact table, a* .csv *file that will be the source data for the fact table, and the solution to the Try It section of this lesson.*

Hints

➤ The fact build is a series of Lookup transforms.

➤ In this process you will have four lookups.

➤ You will use a Derived Column transform to add an ExtendedTotal column to the result set.

➤ In the lookups, you will look up the alternate key and return the surrogate key.

➤ You will use the DimCustomer, DimSaleTerritory, DimDate, and DimCurrency dimensions.

Step-by-Step

1. Run Lesson9CreateTable.sql to create the fact table.

2. In BIDS, click File ➪ New ➪ Project.

3. Select Integration Services Project.

4. Name the project **BI Trainer Packages 9**.

5. Place a check next to "Create directory for Solution."

6. Click OK.

7. Ensure that the Control Flow tab is active.

8. Right-click in the Connection Manager of the Control Flow tab and select New OLE DB Connection.

9. In the Connection Manager screen, type **localhost** in the drop-down list labeled "Server name and type" or select or enter **AdventureWorksDW2008** in the drop-down list labeled "Select or enter database name."

10. Click OK twice.

11. Right-click the connection in the Connection Manager and select Rename. Change the name of the connection to **AdventureWorksDW2008**.

12. Click OK.

13. Drag a Data Flow task onto the Control Flow design surface.

14. Activate the Data Flow tab.

15. Drag a flat file data source onto the Data Flow design surface.

16. Double-click the source.

17. Click the button labeled New on the Flat File Editor.

18. Type **FactSource** in the text box labeled "Connection manager name."

19. Click Browse and locate the Lesson9Data.csv file (Figure 9-1).

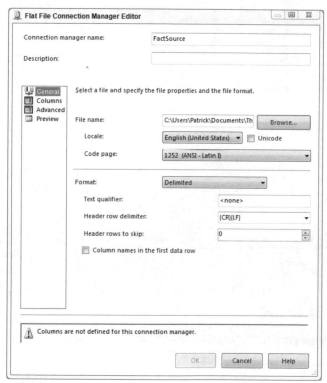

FIGURE 9-1

20. Check the box labeled "Column names in the first data row."

21. Click Advanced in the left navigation pane (Figure 9-2).

22. Change the data type for CurrencyAlternateKey to Unicode string [DT_WSTR] and set OutputColumnWidth to 3 (Figure 9-3).

FIGURE 9-2

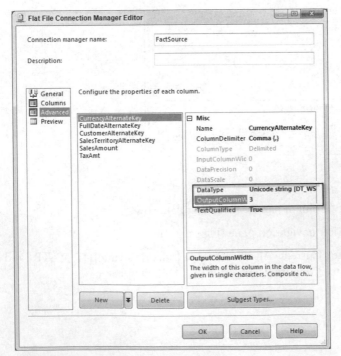

FIGURE 9-3

23. Change the data type for the FullDateAlternateKey to database date [DT_DBDATE].

24. Change the data type for CustomerAlternateKey to Unicode string [DT_WSTR] and set the OutputColumnWidth to 15.

25. Change the SalesAmount and TaxAmt columns' data types to decimal and change the SalesTerritoryAlternateKey to four-byte signed integer [DT_I4].

26. Click OK twice.

27. Drag a Lookup transform onto the Data Flow design surface.

28. Drag the data flow path (green arrow) from the flat file source onto the Lookup transform. Rename the transform to **Customer Lookup**.

29. Double-click the Lookup transform.

30. Select "Ignore failure" from the drop-down list labeled "Specify how to handle rows with no matching entries."

31. Click Connection in the left navigation pane.

32. Ensure that the AdventureWorksDW2008 connection is selected.

33. Select DimCustomer from the drop-down list labeled "Use a table or a view."

34. Click Columns in the left navigation pane.

35. Select CustomerAlternateKey from the AvailableInputColumns list and drag it onto the CustomerAlternateKey in the Available Lookup Columns list (Figure 9-4).

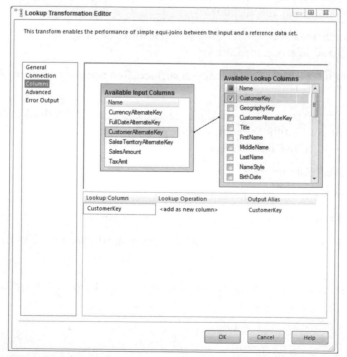

FIGURE 9-4

36. Select the checkbox next to the CustomerKey column in the Available Lookup Columns list.

37. Click OK.

38. Drag a Lookup transform onto the Data Flow design surface. Rename the transform to **Currency Lookup.**

39. Drag the data flow path (green arrow) from the Customer Lookup onto the Currency Lookup. When the Input Output Selection screen appears, choose Lookup Match Output from the Output drop-down list and click OK.

40. Repeat Steps 30 through 39, selecting the DimCurrency table and matching the CurrencyAlternateKey and selecting the CurrencyKey.

41. Drag a Lookup transform onto the Data Flow design surface. Rename the transform **SalesTerritory.**

42. Drag the data flow path (green arrow) from the Currency Lookup onto the SalesTerritory Lookup. When the Input Output Selection screen appears, choose Lookup Match Output from the Output drop-down list and click OK.

43. Repeat Steps 30 through 39, selecting the DimSalesTerritory table and matching the SalesTerritoryAlternateKey and selecting the SalesTerritoryKey. Click OK.

44. Drag a Lookup transform onto the Data Flow design surface. Rename the transform **Date Lookup.**

45. Drag the data flow path (green arrow) from the SalesTerritory Lookup onto the Date Lookup. When the Input Output Selection screen appears choose Lookup Match Output from the Output drop-down list and click OK.

46. Repeat Steps 30 through 39, selecting the DimDate table and matching the FullDateAlternateKey and selecting the DateKey.

47. Drag a Derived Column transform onto the design surface. Rename the transform **Add Extended Total.**

48. Drag the data flow path (green arrow) from the Date Lookup onto the Derived Column transform. When the Input Output Selection screen appears, choose Lookup Match Output from the Output drop-down list and click OK.

49. Double-click the Derived Column transform.

50. In the column labeled Derived Column Name, type **ExtendedTotal.**

51. In the column labeled Derived Column, select <add as new column>.

52. In the column labeled Expression, type **[TaxAmt]+[SalesAmount].** (See Figure 9-5.)

53. Click OK.

54. Drag an OLE DB destination onto the Data Flow design surface. Rename it **FactSales Destination.**

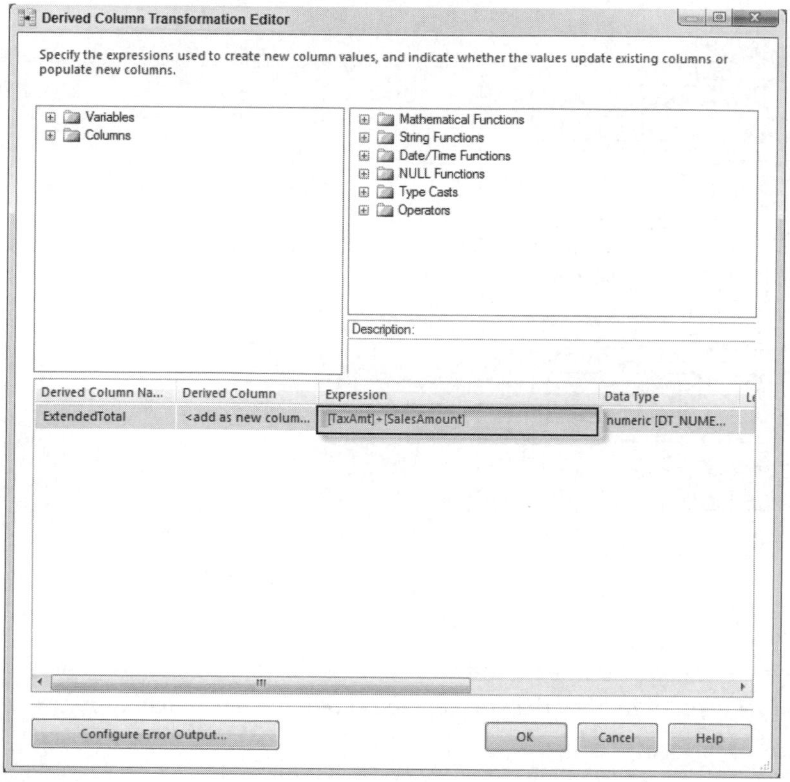

FIGURE 9-5

55. Drag the data flow path (green arrow) from Add Extended Total onto the destination.

56. Double-click the destination source.

57. Ensure that AdventureWorksDW2008 is selected in the drop-down menu labeled OLE DB connection manager.

58. Select dbo.FactSales from the drop-down menu labeled "Name of the table or view."

59. Click Mappings in the left navigation pane.

60. Select DateKey in the Input Column list next to the OrderDateKey in the Destination Column List.

61. Select TaxAmt in the Input Column list next to the TaxAmount in the Destination Column List.

62. Click OK.

63. Run the package and the final result should look like Figure 9-6.

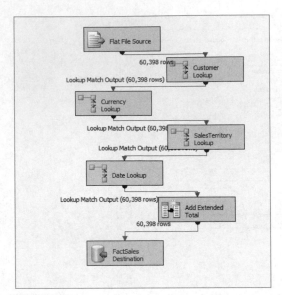

FIGURE 9-6

 Please select Lesson 9 on the DVD to view the video that accompanies this lesson.

10

Deploying SSIS Packages

Now that all of your packages have been created, you will need to deploy them to either an instance of SQL Server or a file system location using one of the many approaches that are available. Each approach ultimately accomplishes the same goal; however, the method of choice will probably depend on the number of packages you plan to deploy. As with most Microsoft tools, you have numerous ways to accomplish the same task. Both Business Intelligence Development Studio (BIDS) and SQL Server Management Studio (SSMS) include tools and wizards that simplify the deployment of SSIS packages. There are three main deployment choices available to you:

> Deploy a single package using SSMS.

> Deploy a single package to a SQL Server instance or file location using BIDS.

> Create a deployment utility using BIDS.

The first two methods allow you to deploy only a single package at a time. The third approach, on the other hand, allows you to configure and deploy multiple packages simultaneously.

DEPLOYING A SINGLE PACKAGE USING SSMS

If you are deploying only a single SSIS package this maybe a viable approach. Using SSMS, connect to the SSIS instance to which you will be deploying the package. As stated earlier, you can deploy a package to an instance of SQL Server or to a file location. When you are connected to an SSIS instance, expand the Stored Packages folder in the Object Explorer (Figure 10-1).

Right-click the folder labeled MSDB and the Import Package screen will appear (Figure 10-2). On this screen you will select the package location, which in this case will be File System. Now you must enter the SQL Server name and the username and password if you are using SQL Authentication. If you are going to connect with your Windows account, choose Windows Authentication. This authentication method will use your Windows domain credentials to deploy the package. Next you will use the ellipsis button next to the "Package path" text box to locate the package that you plan to upload. Then you are required to provide a package name (the field is pre-populated with the current package name). You can accept the default or you can change the name of the package. Finally, you must specify your package protection level. Once you are finished, click OK and your package will be deployed.

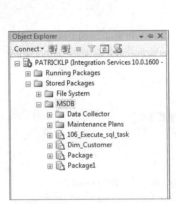

FIGURE 10-1

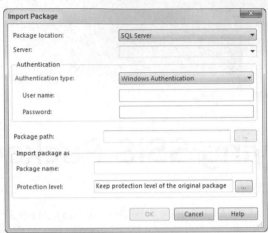

FIGURE 10-2

This approach is limited in two ways. First, you can update only a single package at a time. If you have several packages to deploy, this could be a very cumbersome approach. Second, if your packages rely on any configuration files, you will be required to change the values manually either before or after deployment. As a result, this method may not be optimal for a multi-package deployment that includes configuration files.

DEPLOYING A SINGLE PACKAGE USING BIDS

You can also deploy a single SSIS package using BIDS. First, open the SSIS project that contains the package you want to deploy. Once the project is open, you will need to open the package that will be deployed. Then, select File ⇨ Save Copy of Package As, and the Import Package screen (Figure 10-2) will again appear. You will follow the same steps outlined in the previous section to deploy your package. As when deploying a package using SSMS, you are limited to deploying one package at a time and cannot modify your package configurations at the time of deployment. Keep this in mind when deciding on your package deployment strategy.

CREATING A DEPLOYMENT UTILITY USING BIDS

If you are planning to deploy more than one package and require a more flexible SSIS deployment strategy, I suggest that you use this approach. There are three steps required to build the deployment utility, and one optional step:

1. Create a package configuration file (this is the optional step).

2. Create an SSIS project, set the CreateDeploymentUtility property of the project to `true`, and build the project.

3. Copy the deployment folder and its content to the target server.

4. Run the .SSISDeploymentManifest executable, which is the Package Deployment Wizard, on the target server.

To create an SSIS deployment utility, first right-click the project in the Solution Explorer and the Integration Services Project Properties screen will open. When the screen is opened, ensure that either Configuration Properties or Deployment Utility is selected on the menu. No matter the choice, you can set three project properties. The first is AllowConfigurationChanges. If you set this property to `true` and your package contains configuration files, you will have the ability to change your configurations when you run the wizard. The second property is CreateDeploymentUtility. You must set the value for this property to `true` so that the deployment wizard is created when you build the project. Finally, using the DeploymentOutputPath you can specify where to save the wizard when the project is built.

Once you have built the project, navigate to the file location that you specified as the output path. Copy the deployment folder to the target server. Then you will need to run the .SSISDeploymentManifest file. Once the wizard starts you will see the Microsoft wizard welcome screen. Click Next to begin selecting where you want to deploy the packages — to an instance of SQL Server or to a file location. You can also decide if you want the deployment wizard to validate your packages when deployment is complete. After selecting your deployment destination, indicate the installation folder if you chose a file deployment, and the target SQL Server if you chose a server deployment.

If you chose SQL Server deployment, enter a server name, and the username and password you want to use for SQL Authentication. If you want to use Windows Authentication instead, select Using Windows Authentication and your Windows credentials will be used during the deployment process. On the same screen click the ellipsis button next to the text box labeled "Package path." The SSIS Package Explorer screen will appear. Select your deployment path and click OK. Once you have selected your authentication method or file location for a file deployment, you must choose the installation folder.

On the Select Installation Folder screen you can use the Browse button next to the text box labeled Folder to select the folder to which you want to deploy the SSIS packages and any associated dependencies. After you have selected the installation folder the installer will confirm that the wizard has enough information to install the packages from your project. At this point the wizard will gather all the information required to deploy the packages. Now that the wizard has all the information it needs, you are given an opportunity to modify any configurations that you have set in the packages' configuration files. The Configure Packages screen allows you to edit the configurations that you specified during the design of the SSIS packages.

The deployment wizard then validates the packages and finally provides a summary of the deployment. The summary includes information such as the packages that will be deployed, the deployment location, the configuration file information, a list of dependencies, and a log file name. At this point you click Finish and the packages are deployed.

TRY IT

In this Try It, you learn how to create a SSIS deployment wizard using BIDS. The deployment wizard is the most flexible and scalable approach for deploying SSIS packages using the tools that are native to SQL Server.

Lesson Requirements

Deploy the Dimension and Fact SSIS packages created in earlier lessons. You will be using BIDS to create the deployment wizard and deploy the packages to a local SQL Server.

Hints

➤ The fastest and most flexible way to configure and deploy multiple SSIS packages is to use a Package Deployment Wizard, which is created when you build an SSIS project. Right-click the SSIS project in the Solution Explorer and select Properties. You will set the c property to `true` so that it creates the deployment wizard when you build the project.

Step-by-Step

1. Open the SSIS project that contains the packages you want to deploy. You could use the project from the Lesson 9 Try It section.

2. Right-click the project in the Solution Explorer and select Properties or click Project in the toolbar and then select Properties.

3. Click Deployment Utility from the Configuration Properties. Set the AllowConfigurationChanges and CreateDeploymentUtility property values to `true`. Then set the DeploymentOutputPath to the file location where you want to create the deployment wizard.

4. Specify the location where you want to create the deployment utility in the DeploymentOutputPath. Your screen will resemble Figure 10-3.

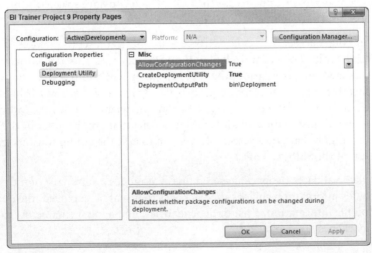

FIGURE 10-3

5. Click Build in the tool bar and select Build Solution.

6. Copy the Deployment folder to the target server.

7. Run the Package Deployment Wizard.

8. Click Next on the Welcome screen.

9. Choose "SQL Server deployment" as the deployment method and select "Validate packages after installation." This will install the packages on a SQL Server (Figure 10-4).

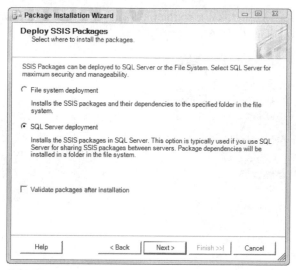

FIGURE 10-4

10. Click Next.

11. The Specify Target SQL Server screen appears (Figure 10-5). Enter a SQL Server name.

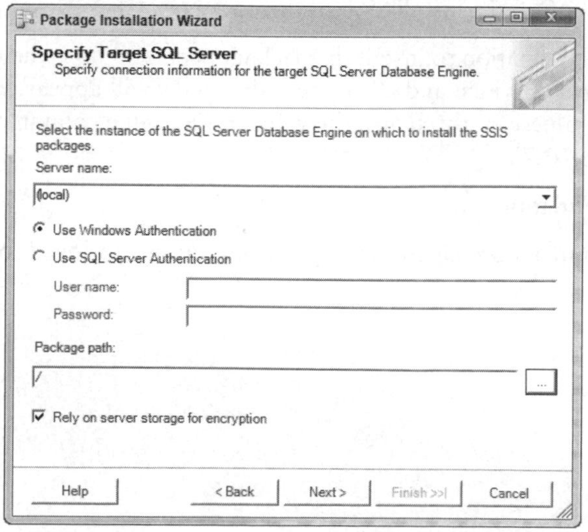

FIGURE 10-5

12. Choose Windows Authentication.

13. Click the ellipsis button next to the "Package path" text box and specify a deployment path.

14. Check the "Rely on server storage for encryption" checkbox.

15. Click Next.

16. On the Select Installation Folder screen, browse to the file location to which you want to install the package dependencies (Figure 10-6).

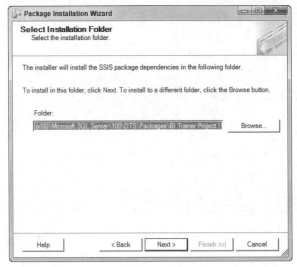

FIGURE 10-6

17. At this point the wizard will confirm the installation of the packages. Click Next.

18. Once the wizard has enough information to install the package, you will have the Configure Packages screen expand the Property item and all configurable items will appear. If you want to modify any of the existing values simply change the value in the Value column of the Configurations section (Figure 10-7).

19. Click Next on the Package Validation screen.

20. Finally, click Finish on the Summary screen and your packages will be deployed to the SQL Server specified in Step 11.

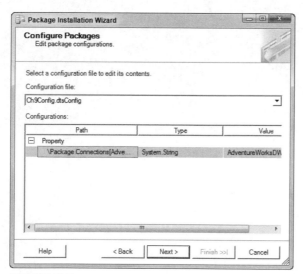

FIGURE 10-7

 Please select Lesson 10 on the DVD to view the video that accompanies this lesson.

SECTION III
SQL Server Analysis Services

11

Understanding SSAS

Now that you've loaded your data warehouse, you may find that with all that great data, your report backlog is starting to grow. Most organizations that we ask have a report backlog of 50 or more reports and a report writer who is constantly battling to catch up. SQL Server Analysis Services (SSAS) to the rescue! SSAS allows your users to create complex ad hoc reports without having to involve IT.

SSAS is another service that you've already licensed if you've purchased SQL Server, one that can pre-aggregate data and make it easier for your users to query data via familiar interfaces like Excel or Reporting Services. SSAS has two major functions: a high-performance cubing technology and a data-mining technology. We focus on the cubing technology until Lesson 19, when you'll get your hands dirty in data mining.

As you may remember, a data warehouse is made up of fact and dimension tables. The fact tables hold measures, which are the numeric columns that you want to put on the report. The dimensions hold the columns in which you'd like to filter your data. SSAS adopts many of the same items but has changed their names. For example, *measure groups* in SSAS are collections of measures within a single fact table. The columns in dimensions (Product Name, Gender, City, or State, for example) are called *attributes*.

To develop an SSAS database you need to create an SSAS project similar to what you did in SSIS. The first step, once the project is created, is to create a data source. The data source is a connection to your data warehouse. Second, create a data source view to act as a layer between your data source and your data warehouse and to protect you from changes. Third, run the Cube Wizard to create the first cube and dimensions. Finally, modify the cube and dimensions to scale better and be properly formatted.

SSAS ARCHITECTURE

The architecture of SSAS (shown in Figure 11-1) is quite a bit different from what you're used to in SQL Server. The Analysis Services server listens on a TCP/IP port for requests to come in from clients. Those users can be slicing and dicing data from one of many clients like Excel, SharePoint, a third-party application, or a custom application. Those same users can read data out of the cube by using Reporting Services for more standard reporting. If you want to write a custom application, you can use ADOMD or ADOMD.NET. From a management perspective, the Analysis Management Object (AMO) is used to manage SSAS from a .NET language. AMO is out of the scope of this book and you will likely never use it during your everyday management of SSAS.

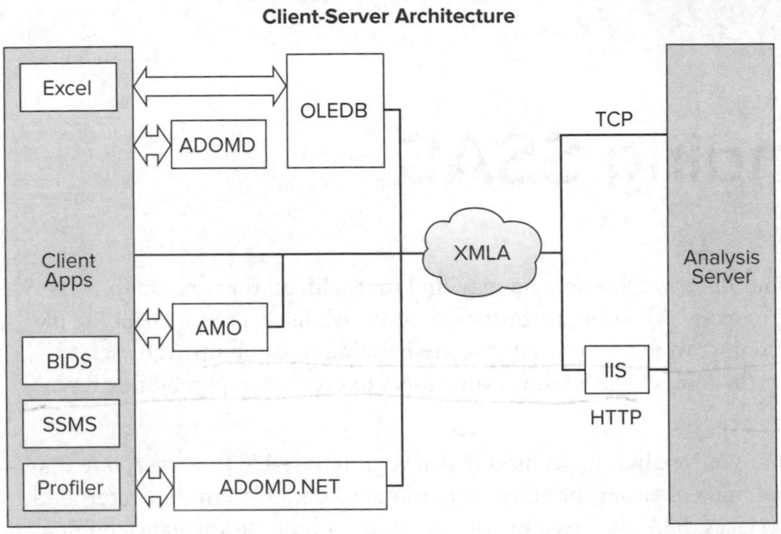

Client-Server Architecture

FIGURE 11-1

CUBES

At the highest level, to start with SSAS, you must create an SSAS database. The SSAS database is a container of one or more cubes and can be created only by an admin of the SSAS instance. Once the database is created, you can create any number of cubes, which are containers for one or more measure groups or dimensions, inside the database. The data in the cube is refreshed periodically from the data warehouse through a processing step. During the processing step a series of queries run against the data warehouse to retrieve all the distinct values of each column in the dimensions and load the measure groups.

Measure Groups

The measure group equates in SSAS to a fact table. It is a collection of measures, which are numeric items you can place in the data area of a report. As you're configuring the measures in the BIDS environment in the Cube Editor, the first thing you will do is define how you want the measure to roll up. In other words, if someone were to drag over the Sales Amount measure onto the report, should the number be summed, averaged, or something else, like merely counted? Each number like this will have its own logic for its aggregation and can also be formatted differently.

Dimensions

Dimensions define how you wish to slice your measures. Each column in a dimension, like First Name, Last Name, and Product Name, is called an *attribute*. When you process a dimension, queries against the underlying dimension table in the data warehouse are run to retrieve all the distinct values on an attribute-by-attribute basis. These distinct values are called *members*. For example, the Gender attribute might have members like Male and Female.

As you can see in the example report in Figure 11-2, a user has brought the Category Name and Subcategory Name into the rows area of the report and the Color attribute into the columns area of the report. The user is evaluating the Sales Amount by these various attributes. If you feel your users are consistently going to view data a given way in a dimension, you can create a user hierarchy. These hierarchies give the user the means to find the data quickly. For example, most date dimensions have a hierarchy for Year → Quarter → Month → Date. In our example in Figure 11-2, there's a hierarchy for Category → SubCategory → Product. While a user could still drag over Year, Quarter, and Month individually, creating this hierarchy allows the user to drag over a single element that contains all those attributes.

Category Name ▼	Subcategory Name	Black Sales Amount	Blue Sales Amount	Multi Sales Amount	NA Sales Amount
⊟ Accessories	⊞ Bike Racks				$39,360.00
	⊞ Bike Stands				$39,591.00
	⊞ Bottles and Cages				$56,798.19
	⊞ Cleaners				$7,218.60
	⊞ Fenders				$46,619.58
	⊞ Helmets	$72,954.15	$74,353.75		
	⊞ Hydration Packs				
	⊞ Tires and Tubes				$245,529.32
	Total	$72,954.15	$74,353.75		$435,116.69
⊟ Bikes	⊞ Mountain Bikes	$4,879,678.15			
	⊞ Road Bikes	$3,779,439.14			
	⊞ Touring Bikes		$2,169,055.53		
	Total	$8,659,117.30	$2,169,055.53		
⊟ Clothing	⊞ Caps			$19,688.10	
	⊞ Gloves	$35,020.70			
	⊞ Jerseys			$86,782.64	
	⊞ Shorts	$71,319.81			
	⊞ Socks				
	⊞ Vests		$35,687.00		
	Total	$106,340.51	$35,687.00	$106,470.74	
Grand Total		$8,838,411.96	$2,279,096.28	$106,470.74	$435,116.69

FIGURE 11-2

Attribute Relationships

Attribute relationships tie multiple attributes in a single SSAS dimension together, much as foreign keys tie various tables together in SQL Server. This ultimately helps with the cube's performance in query time and processing time. It also helps with security and the user experience. It will be one of the most important changes you'll make to each dimension in Lesson 14. This, and every other dimension property, is set in the Dimension Editor.

MDX

Multi-Dimension eXpression Language or MDX is the query language that will be used to retrieve data from a cube and is discussed in much more detail in Lesson 17. It's similar to T-SQL in SQL Server but is by nature multidimensional. In MDX, you refer to intersection points between two coordinates called *tuples*.

You must also place each tuple and attribute on an axis. The first two axes are columns and rows. In Figure 11-2, you saw Subcategory on the rows and Color on the columns. In the following code you can see the query that can be used to produce what you saw in Figure 11-2.

```
SELECT ([Product].[Color].Children,
        [Measures].[Sales Amount]) ON COLUMNS,
       ([Product].[Category Name].Children,
        [Product].[Subcategory Name].Children ) on ROWS
FROM [CubeName]
```

Don't worry if the query is still a bit confusing. We'll be spending an entire lesson on the MDX query language. Lesson 17 will be detailed enough to make you functional in MDX but not an expert. You'll use that functionality to create calculations and KPIs, which will be covered in Lesson 18.

BIDS FOR SSAS

As with the rest of the BI suite, you'll use the Business Intelligence Development Studio (BIDS) to develop an SSAS solution. To create an SSAS project, simply select Analysis Services Project when creating a new project while Business Intelligence Projects is selected as a template (as shown in Figure 11-3). You can also select Import Analysis Services Project to reverse-engineer a project from an Analysis Services database already in production.

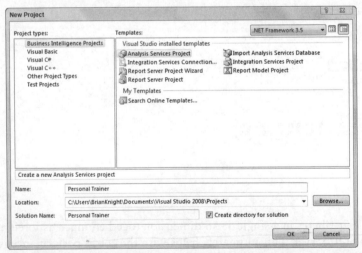

FIGURE 11-3

Once you click OK after naming the project, an empty project will be created, in which you can create the SSAS objects. After you're ready to deploy your project to the server, simply select Build ⇨ Deploy <*Project Name*> from the menu. Deploying this to the SSAS instance will send the schema to the server and then automatically process the data by default.

You can adjust to where the cube is deployed once the project is created by going to Solution Explorer, right-clicking the project, and selecting Properties. This opens the Project Properties dialog box. In the Deployment tab (shown in Figure 11-4) you can adjust the name of the database and server to which the project will be deployed.

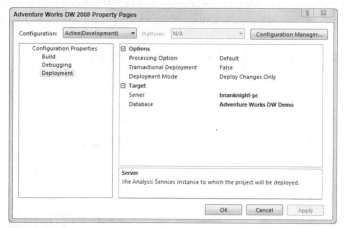

FIGURE 11-4

After the cube is created you can double-click a .cube file in Solution Explorer to open the Cube Editor (shown in Figure 11-5). The Cube Editor is where you can modify the measure groups and how those measure groups relate to the dimensions. You can also add server-side KPIs and calculations, and control the partitions from the Cube Editor.

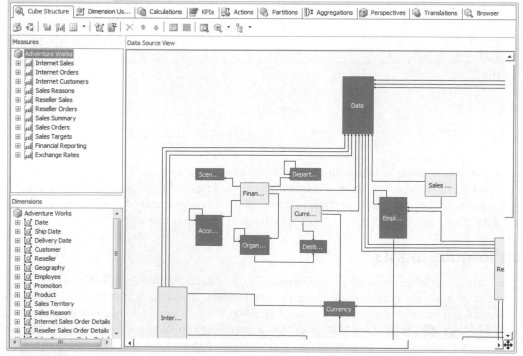

FIGURE 11-5

When you double-click the .dim file in Solution Explorer, you open the Dimension Editor. Here you edit the dimension (shown in Figure 11-6), attribute relationship, and properties. The fantastic thing is that if a dimension is used in different ways as a role-playing dimension (we'll get deeper into that term when we create a cube), you'll need to manage the dimension only one time and your changes will be shown across each of the role-playing dimensions.

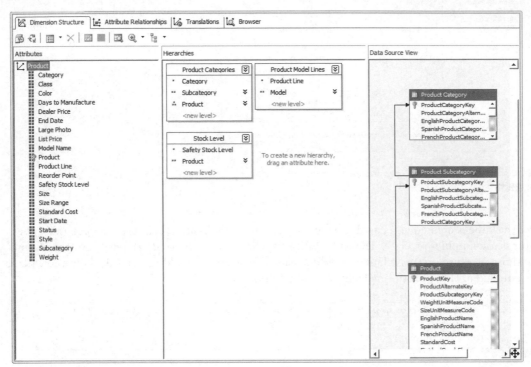

FIGURE 11-6

TRY IT

In this Try It, you're going to deploy the AdventureWorks sample cube, which you are going to use later in this SSAS section of the book. This database is not installed by default, but by the deployment of a project. That project is available to you only once you've installed the AdventureWorks sample databases from CodePlex.com (`http://msftdbprodsamples.codeplex.com/`).

Lesson Requirements

After you install the AdventureWorks sample databases (the database that ends in DW or DW2008 is the important one), you're ready to open the project for deployment. If you don't have the AdventureWorks database, you can install it from `http://msftdbprodsamples.codeplex.com`. The project file will be located in the C:\Program Files\Microsoft SQL Server\100\Tools\Samples\AdventureWorks 2008 Analysis Services Project directory by default and you'll need to pick Standard or Enterprise, based on the edition of SQL Server you have installed. Your goal in this lesson is simply to deploy the AdventureWorks SSAS database and cubes.

Hints

➤ You can deploy the database in BIDS by selecting Build ⇨ Deploy <Project Name>. You may need to adjust the location to which you deploy this database by right-clicking your project in the Solution Explorer and selecting Properties.

Step-by-Step

1. Open Adventure Works DW 2008.dwproj in either the C:\Program Files\Microsoft SQL Server\100\Tools\Samples\AdventureWorks 2008 Analysis Services Project\enterprise or C:\Program Files\Microsoft SQL Server\100\Tools\Samples\AdventureWorks 2008 Analysis Services Project\standard directory, based on which version of SQL Server you have installed.

2. Right-click the project name and select Properties. Ensure that the correct SSAS instance is selected in the Deployment tab in that <Project Name> Properties page.

3. Select Build ⇨ Deploy <Project Name>.

4. The deployment process should take a few minutes the first time. If you're successful, the deployment tab will open and the project will deploy.

There are two reasons the project would not deploy. The first is that you may not have adequate access to the server to create a new SSAS database. To resolve that, have the sysadmin of that instance give you access by right-clicking the instance in Management Studio, selecting Properties, and adding your account to the Security tab. The other reason is the SSAS service may not have access to read the AdventureWorksDW2008 database. To fix that, ensure that the service account has access to read data out.

 Please select Lesson 11 on the DVD to view the video that accompanies this lesson.

12

Configuring a Data Source and Data Source View

One of the many great features of Analysis Services is that, despite its being a tool that is included when you purchase SQL Server, it does not limit you to using SQL Server relational databases as a source. Creating this connection to your source data will be the first step you take when designing any Analysis Services project.

CREATING A DATA SOURCE

You will make any connections required for your project by configuring a data source, which stores the connection string information of your source data. To create a data source, open the Solution Explorer (Ctrl+Alt+L) in any Analysis Services project, right-click the Data Sources folder, and select New Data Source. The Data Source Wizard will open, which walks you through the steps of configuring your source. Figure 12-1 shows the Connection Manager dialog box.

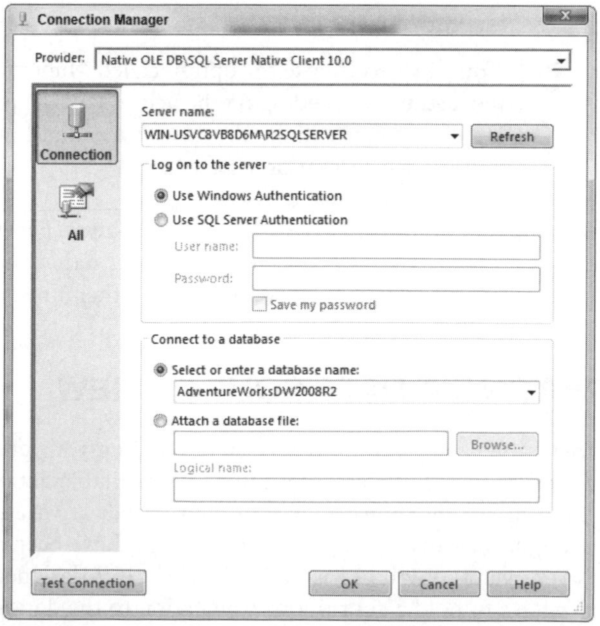

Here you will select the provider if it is different from the default Native OLE DB\SQL Server Native Client 10.0. This is the typical provider for connecting to a SQL Server relational

FIGURE 12-1

database. If you do choose the default data provider, you will identify the server on which your data source is stored, as well as the database name. Optionally, you can change the authentication used to connect to the source from Windows to SQL Server Authentication. Verify that your authentication can access the data source by clicking Test Connection.

On the next screen you see after configuring the connection, you will define the impersonation information. This is the information Analysis Services will use to connect to the data source throughout development, most noticeably during processing time. Your options here, shown in Figure 12-2, are "Use a specific Windows user name and password," "Use the service account," "Use the credentials of the current user," and "Inherit."

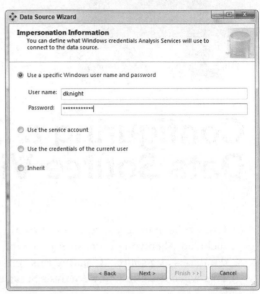

➤ If you select "Use a specific Windows user name and password," you will type in an account that can be used.

➤ When you select "Use the service account," Analysis Services will use one of the three built-in accounts that you may have selected during the installation: Network Service, Local System, or Local Service.

FIGURE 12-2

➤ The option to "Use the credentials of the current user" will take the rights of the user currently logged in.

➤ You can also choose the option called "Inherit," which tries to pick the account that will be most secure depending on the action you are performing. For example, when you are processing the cube, it will use the service account, but when you are doing a drill-through action it will use the current user's account.

You may find it easiest to explicitly give Analysis Services an account that has rights to all source data using the "Use a specific Windows user name and password" option. After deciding which option is best for you, click Next; you will then finish by naming the data source.

CREATING A DATA SOURCE VIEW

Inevitably, your second step when developing your project is to create a *data source view* (DSV). A DSV holds all the metadata from the available data sources in the project. It is a useful tool for filtering just the tables, views, or queries that are needed for your development. When tables are brought into a DSV, any relationships that have been established on the relational database will carry over and will be visible in the DSV. It is designed to cache the source metadata so that it does not have to hold a continuous connection to the data source.

To design a data source view open the Solution Explorer (Ctrl+Alt+L) in any Analysis Services project. Right-click the Data Source Views folder and select New Data Source View. You will be asked to select a data source. If you did not previously create a data source as we discussed earlier in this lesson, you can do it in the Select a Data Source dialog box.

Once you select the data source, click Next and you will be asked to define which tables or views you would like added to the DSV. The best practice when you have a data warehouse as a source is to select the fact table(s) you want added by highlighting them and then to add them to the "Included objects" pane by clicking the single right-facing arrow. As shown in Figure 12-3, once the fact table(s) is in the "Included objects" pane, you can click the Add Related Tables button to add all the dimension tables that have an already existing relationship. Click Next, and then give the data source view a name before clicking Finish.

When you complete the wizard, it opens a diagram view of the tables or views you selected with visible relationships already created, shown in Figure 12-4. You can design relationships manually in the DSV, if they do not already exist in the relational database, by simply clicking and dragging the foreign key column from the source table to the primary key column in the destination table.

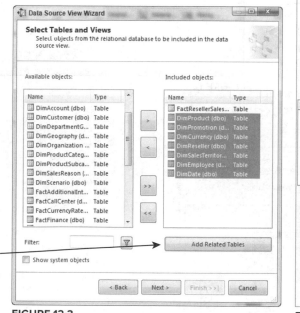

FIGURE 12-3

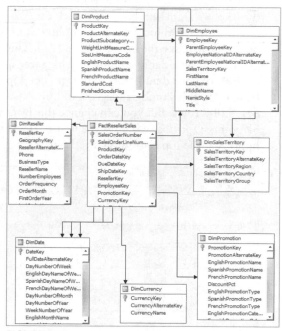

FIGURE 12-4

If you decide you want a query to be used in the DSV instead of a view or table, you can add it by right-clicking an existing table and selecting Replace Table ⇨ With New Named Query. This will open a Create Named Query editor where you can change the table or view into a query. This is commonly used for designing a testing or development cube to bring back a subset of the production data. You can also add a new named query if you right-click the diagram design surface and select New Named Query.

Adding Named Calculations

Another great feature of the data source view is the ability to create *named calculations*. Named calculations are small expressions written in the data source's coding language that are stored in the DSV and appear as a new column. This means that if your data source is SQL Server, then the expression is written in T-SQL. To add a named calculation, right-click the table name in the diagram and select New Named Calculation. Figure 12-5 shows an example of how you will give the new column a name and description and write an expression to define it.

Anytime you create a new column with a named calculation, you need to verify that the expression did what you anticipated. To double-check that the expression worked, right-click the table and select Explore Data. You will find the new column if you scroll all the way to the right.

Use this Explore Data feature not only to see a preview of your data but also to profile your data. With the Explore Data window open, click the Chart tab to view a graphical depiction of how your data breaks down, like the one in Figure 12-6. This is great to use as a data profiling tool for some quick analysis of your data before you begin developing. By default, this graphical depiction shows just the first 5,000 rows, but you can change this by clicking Sampling Options, which is the first of the three buttons at the top right of Figure 12-6.

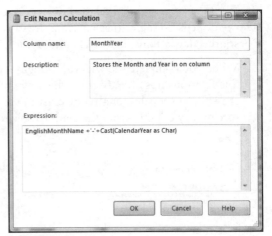

FIGURE 12-5

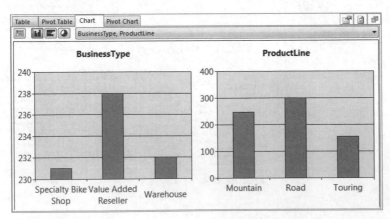

FIGURE 12-6

Giving Tables and Columns Friendly Names

When you are developing an Analysis Services project, it is important to understand that your end users will likely see table and column names exactly as they appear in the data source view. Keeping this in mind, it is always a best practice to give friendly names to both tables and columns so your users will better understand the data as they try to browse through it in a tool like Excel.

Generally speaking, end users have no idea what fact and dimension tables are in a data warehouse, so at the very least, rename your tables to remove any prefix you may have on the relational database (such as in the names *Dim*Customer or *Fact*Transaction). To give a table a friendly name, select the table name in the Tables window on the left side of the designer or in the diagram and open the Properties menu (F4). In the Properties menu, change the FriendlyName property to anything that will make the most sense to your end users.

Now that you have learned about the different features of the data source and data source view, try designing your own in the next section.

TRY IT

In this Try It, you will learn how to create connections to your source system using a data source. Also, once that connection is made you will create a data source view and make design changes to the resulting cube to make it friendlier to the end user.

Lesson Requirements

For this lesson you will need access to the AdventureWorksDW2008R2 or AdventureWorksDW2008 database, which can be downloaded from www.codeplex.com. You will first create a data source to connect to the previously mentioned database, and then design a data source view with FactInternetSales and all the tables it shares a relationship with. Ensure that table names are changed to help end users understand the data.

 The download for this lesson, available at www.wrox.com, *includes the completed Try It section with data source and data source view provided.*

Hints

- ➤ You will need to create a data source using your Windows account for the impersonation information.

- ➤ You will use FactInternetSales as your base table, but you will also add all related tables to the data source view.

- ➤ You will add a new named calculation to combine the customer's first and last names.

- ➤ You will need to create a second named calculation to easily find promotions that specify a minimum quantity that must be purchased before a discount is applied.

Step-by-Step

1. Open Business Intelligence Development Studio (BIDS) and navigate to File ➪ New ➪ Project. Create a new Analysis Services project called Knights24HourSSAS, and save it to the C:\Projects directory shown in Figure 12-7.

2. In the Solution Explorer, right-click the Data Sources folder and select New Data Source.

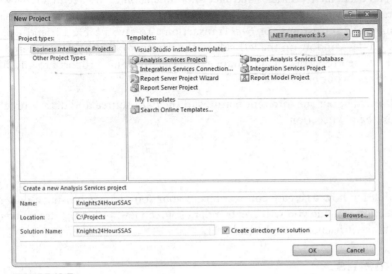

FIGURE 12-7

3. Click Next to bypass the welcome screen and then click New to define a new connection to the source data.

4. In the Connection Manager dialog (see Figure 12-8), type **localhost** for the "Server name" property (this is assuming you have only one instance of SQL Server installed on your machine), and then select AdventureWorksDW2008R2 from the "Select or enter a database name" property. Before you click OK, click Test Connection to make sure you have the permissions to the database with a Windows account.

5. You will return to the wizard, where you can click Next to continue.

6. Continue with the default "Use a specific Windows user name and password," and then type in the name of a Windows account that has permissions to the database. Click Next.

7. Complete the wizard by assigning the data source a name. Type **AdventureWorksDW2008R2** for the "Data source name" property and then click Finish.

8. Next, right-click the Data Source Views folder and select New Data Source View.

9. Click Next to bypass the welcome screen and then select AdventureWorksDW2008R2 as the relational data source before clicking Next again.

10. In the Select Tables and Views dialog of the wizard (see Figure 12-9) select FactInternetSales from the "Available objects" pane and click the single right-facing arrow to move it to the "Included objects" pane.

FIGURE 12-8

FIGURE 12-9

11. With the FactInternetSales table still selected, but now in the new pane, click Add Related Tables to add all tables that have an existing database relationship to FactIntenetSales. Click Next.

12. The last step in the wizard is to assign the data source view a name. Name it **AdventureWorksDW2008R2DSV** and click Finish.

13. Rename each table, removing the prefix Fact or Dim, by selecting each table either in the Diagram window or the Table pane and opening the Properties menu (F4). Use the FriendlyName property (see Figure 12-10) to remove any prefixes, making the names easier for your end users to understand.

14. Next, create a new named calculation on the table (now called just Customer) by right-clicking the table name and selecting New Named Calculation.

15. Give the named calculation a column name of **FullName** and make the expression use the following code before clicking OK (see Figure 12-11):

```
FirstName + ' ' +LastName
```

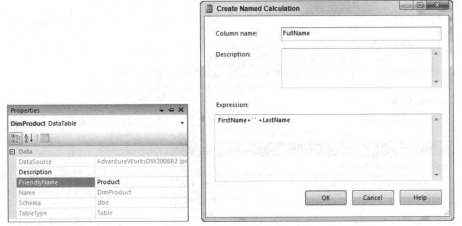

FIGURE 12-10   **FIGURE 12-11**

16. Ensure the named calculation is created correctly by right-clicking the table name Customer and selecting Explore Data. Scroll all the way to the right to see the new column values.

17. While exploring this table, select the Chart tab (Figure 12-12) to see some basic data profiling of the table. From the drop-down box uncheck everything except NumberCarsOwned, TotalChildren, and HouseOwnerFlag. Data profiling will help you understand your data a little better. Close the Explore Customer Table window when you are done.

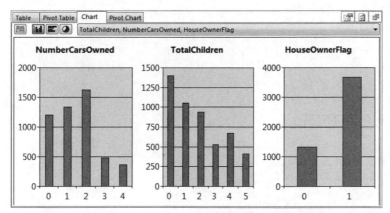

FIGURE 12-12

18. Create a second named calculation on the Promotion table with a column name of **MinimumRequired** (see Figure 12-13). Use the following expression to evaluate this column before clicking OK:

```
Case When
MinQty = 0 or MinQty is null Then 'NotRequired'
Else 'Required'
End
```

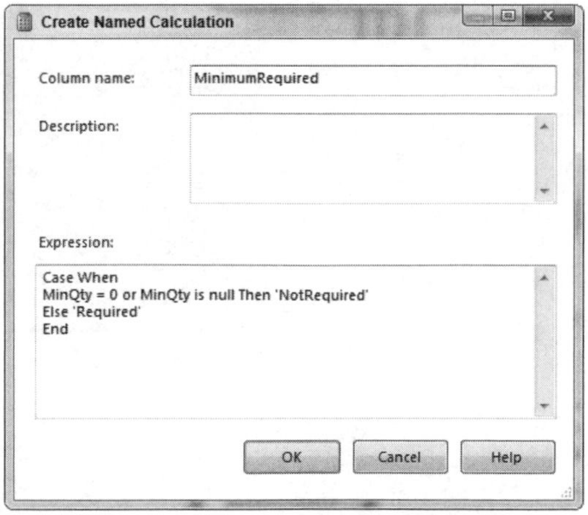

FIGURE 12-13

Congratulations! You are off to a great start. The next step is to use the data source and DSV that you have created in this lesson to develop a cube.

 Please select Lesson 12 on the DVD to view the video that accompanies this lesson.

13

Using the Cube Wizard

You have done a lot of work to get to this point, and all that work is about to be battle tested. You have likely designed a data warehouse and built database relationships, designed an ETL process in SSIS to load that database, and have just begun in SSAS with the data source and data source view. Now you are ready to create a cube, which is the subject of this lesson. A cube is a set of measures (facts) and dimensions that are related in a way that helps you analyze your data. Any small problems with the ETL and even bad relationships built in the database will be exposed while you design and process the cube. As you process the new cube you will soon discover any design flaws from previous steps in errors that appear during processing.

Creating the initial cube using the Cube Wizard is actually a very quick process. Designing the data source, data source view, and initial cube represent about five percent of the project. The other 95 percent is building out what the wizard creates so it can be more useful to your end users. Doing this includes, but is not limited to, correcting formatting, adding dimension hierarchies, and creating MDX calculations.

The Cube Wizard automates the process of creating the cube and can automatically create dimensions that are related for you as well. To get started you will open the Solution Explorer (Ctrl+Alt+L) with an Analysis Services project open, then right-click the Cubes folder and select New Cube. On the Select Creation Method screen you have three options: "Use existing tables," "Create an empty cube," and "Generate tables in the data source," as shown in Figure 13-1.

The "Use existing tables" option, which is the most commonly used, will examine the data source view and identify, based on the relationships, which tables are likely to be dimensions and which are likely to be measure groups. It will also determine which columns in a measure group are likely measures. This lesson walks you through using the "Use existing tables" option.

The second option, "Create an empty cube," creates a completely empty cube and requires you to create the dimensions. Selecting this option will have you select a data source view and then create the empty cube shell.

"Generate tables in the data source" is the last option. If you select this option, the wizard assumes you have not previously created a relational database on the backend and will walk you through designing it based on a template you can select from the Template drop-down box. You can find these templates in C:\Program Files\Microsoft SQL Server\100\Tools\Templates\olap\1033\Cube Templates, or, if you are working on a 64-bit machine, look in the same location but in the Program File (x86) folder.

Once you have selected the "Use existing tables" option, the next screen will ask you to select which tables in the data source view will be used as measure groups, as shown in Figure 13-2. You can either check off the tables yourself individually or click the Suggest button, in which case Analysis Services will try to determine which are measure groups based on the relationships. It does not always pick correctly, so, if you hit the Suggest button, make sure to verify that it chose correctly. You learned in Lesson 11 that, generally, fact tables are measure groups because they store all the measures, so, if you are designing based off a traditional data warehouse, you will select your fact tables here.

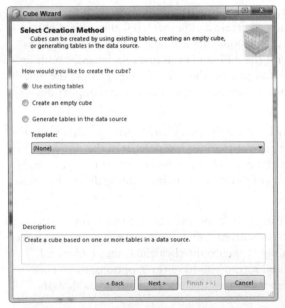

FIGURE 13-1

FIGURE 13-2

Now that you have selected a measure group, you must select which columns from the source table you wish to use as measures, as shown in Figure 13-3. You will find listed here only the columns that are not primary or foreign keys in the table. Analysis Services assumes correctly that none of those columns will serve as a measure. Here you can uncheck any columns that are not truly measures, as well as rename the measure group and measures before you click Next. Notice that the wizard has automatically added one measure on the bottom that does not exist in the physical table. This is a count of how many rows are found in the table, which is automatically added with every measure group.

On the Select New Dimensions screen you will select the tables from which you would like the wizard automatically to create dimension structures. If there are any tables listed from which you do not wish dimensions to be created, simply uncheck them. Notice in Figure 13-4 that the fact table is listed and a dimension would have been created if it had not been unchecked. However, often you may find the need to create a dimension from a fact table if you desire to slice your data by any column found in the fact table. A fact table that is used as a dimension is known as a *degenerate dimension*.

FIGURE 13-3

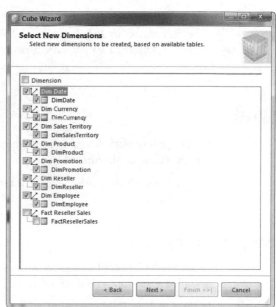

FIGURE 13-4

Once you have selected the tables from which you want to create dimensions, click Next and you will complete the wizard by naming the cube. Assign the cube a name and click Finish. This will automatically add the cube and any dimensions you assigned in the wizard to the Solution Explorer.

Now that you have learned what each step does in the Cube Wizard, try designing your own in the next section.

TRY IT

In this Try It, you will learn how to create a cube using the Cube Wizard. As you go through the wizard you will categorize which tables from the data source view are measure groups and which are dimensions. Also, once you select the Measure Group table you will identify which columns will be the measures that will be used throughout the cube.

Lesson Requirements

For this lesson you will need the completed Lesson 12, which can be downloaded from www.wrox.com. In that lesson, you created a data source and data source view that will be the basis for the cube you need to create. The new cube design will use measures from the InternetSales table, and the tables that are related will serve as dimensions.

 The download for this lesson, available at www.wrox.com, *includes this Try It section completed so you can compare your results to the finished product.*

Hints

➤ Select the InternetSales table as the measure group, and include all measures from that table, except Revision Number.

➤ You will use all the tables, except InternetSales, when selecting the tables that should be dimensions.

Step-by-Step

1. Open the Knights24HourSSAS Analysis Services project that was created in Lesson 12 or download the completed lesson from www.wrox.com.

2. In the Solution Explorer, right-click the Cubes folder and select New Cube.

3. Click Next to bypass the welcome screen and then select "Use existing tables" from the Select Creation Method screen. After that option is selected click Next.

4. Check InternetSales in the Select Measure Group Tables window, shown in Figure 13-5, and then click Next. This will be the main table used to track sales.

5. Leave all the measures checked by default except Revision Number; then click Next, as shown in Figure 13-6. All the remaining measures that are checked will be used to show users the tracking of individual and rolled-up sales.

6. Figure 13-7 shows the Select New Dimensions screen. Leave all tables checked except InternetSales, and then click Next. Each of the selected tables will have a dimension created for it.

FIGURE 13-5

FIGURE 13-6

FIGURE 13-7

7. The last step in the wizard is to name the cube. Change the Cube name property to **AWDW2008R2Cube** and click Finish.

8. Deploy the current cube by navigating to the Build menu and selecting Deploy Knights24HourSSAS.

9. Once the cube processing finishes successfully, move to the Browser tab. Expand the Promotion dimension and drag Promotion Key into the browser window to where it says Drop Row Data Here. Next expand the Measures and Internet Sales folders (see Figure 13-8), where you will find the measure called Sales Amount. Drag this measure into the browser window to where it says Drop Total or Detail Fields Here.

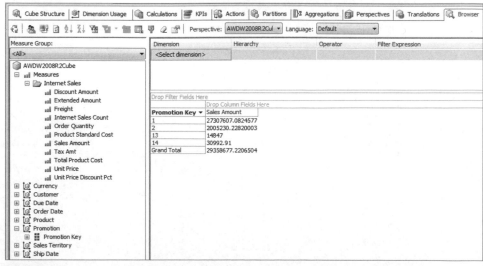

FIGURE 13-8

Notice that there are several problems with the data. The Internet Sales number is unformatted, and the promotion key does not tell you very much about what promotion was used. These will be fixed in the following lessons.

Congratulations! You have created your first cube. Remember that what you have completed in Lessons 12 and 13 represent about five percent of the actual cube development. In the next lessons you will learn how to correct formatting, add dimension hierarchies, create MDX calculations, and perform many other tasks that represent the other 95 percent of the project.

 Please select Lesson 13 on the DVD to view the video that accompanies this lesson.

14

Editing Your Dimension

Now that you have your cube deployed, the first thing to start working on is the dimensions. In SQL Server 2008, by default, only the dimension's primary key will be added as an attribute. All other attributes will need to be added manually. You'll also need to set the keys for each of the attributes and configure any attributes' relationships.

Nothing will find data integrity issues in your dimensions better than an SSAS project. As you deploy your project to the instance, SSAS runs a number of queries to determine the distinct records and the uniqueness of each key. Any problems with this process or with foreign key violations will cause the cube not to be able to process and require you to go back to SSIS to correct those issues.

 In this lesson, you'll add to the project from the last lesson. If you skipped that lesson, you can download Lesson13Complete.zip from this lesson's download on www.wrox.com *and deploy the project.*

DIMENSION EDITOR

You'll start editing any dimension in the Dimension Editor, which you can access by double-clicking the .dim file in the Solution Explorer window. For this example, I'm going to use the Date.dim dimension file that you created in the last lesson's Cube Wizard. Once in the editor you'll want to determine which attributes your users will want to use to slice and dice, and drag those over to the Attributes pane on the left from the Data Source View (DSV) pane on the right (both shown in Figure 14-1).

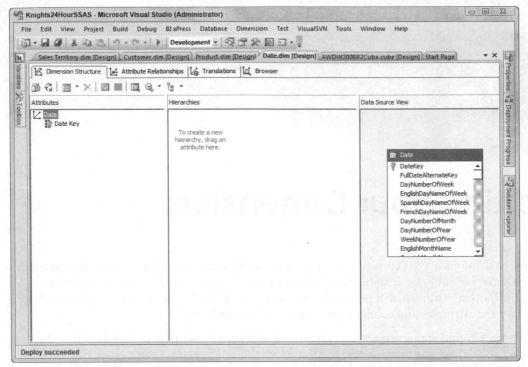

FIGURE 14-1

In the Date dimension, great attributes may be items like Calendar Year, Calendar Quarter, English Month Name, and Full Date Alternate Key. Figure 14-2 shows these attributes after they've been dragged over from the DSV pane. While these are all great attributes, they're terribly named for end-user friendliness. You can rename each attribute by simply right-clicking it and choosing Rename. Better names would be things like Year (Calendar Year), Quarter (Calendar Quarter), Month (English Month Name), and Day (Full Date Alternate Key).

FIGURE 14-2

User Hierarchies

With the attributes using better names, you're now ready to build your first user hierarchy. User hierarchies make it much easier to navigate through your hierarchies. Without them, users would have to drag over each Year → Quarter → Month → Day attribute one by one. Instead, you can create a simple user hierarchy called Calendar Drill-Down that contains all the attributes already preconfigured.

To create a hierarchy, simply drag the attributes from the left Attributes pane to the middle Hierarchies pane, as shown in Figure 14-3. In this figure you can see that in the Hierarchies pane there is one hierarchy that has four levels. You can create multiple hierarchies by dragging attributes over into the white space. You can also choose to rename a hierarchy by right-clicking it. For the time being, you can ignore the warning you're seeing above the hierarchy and dimension name.

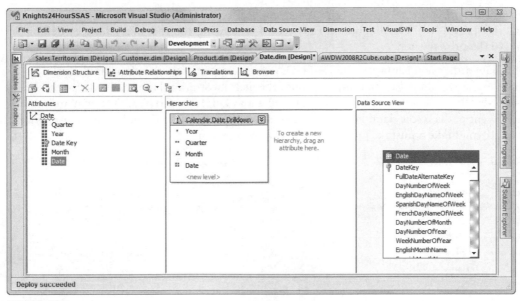

FIGURE 14-3

With the hierarchy created you may want to hide certain columns, like Date Key. To hide the column so users don't try to use it in the cube browser, select the attribute and change the AttributeHierarchyVisible property to `False` in the Properties window.

You can deploy your changes anytime by going to Build ➪ Deploy *<Project Name>*. The project should deploy successfully this time, but in a moment we'll break the deployment by adding attribute relationships.

ATTRIBUTE RELATIONSHIPS

Attribute relationships allow you to create relationships between your different dimension attributes, much like foreign key relationships in SQL Server. For example, even though your Customer dimension has Country, State, and City attributes, you may create attribute relationships among them by creating links between CustomerID (primary key) → City → State → Country. It's important to note that attribute relationships are not the same as hierarchies, although if they're not properly created, you may get warnings in your hierarchies.

Attribute relationships help in a number of areas outside of what you may expect. They help you in performance-tuning the processing of your cube and help your queries return results more efficiently. They also help in security. For example, imagine if a manager could see only the Europe customers. If attribute relationships did not exist, he could potentially see states in the United States or cities in those states even though he's not allowed to see countries outside of Europe. Creating attribute relationships implies a relationship between the United States attribute and any states and cities that attribute owns. The last thing they help with is member properties. If you have an attribute relationship off Customer's Name for Hair Color you will see the customer's Hair Color attribute when you are looking at that granularity and you choose to see that property.

To create an attribute relationship in the Dimension Editor, go to the Attribute Relationships tab (shown in Figure 14-4). The diagram in Figure 14-4 is showing you that everything by default is linking to the primary key.

For this date dimension (shown in Figure 14-5), to create an attribute relationship drag the Date attribute in the Attribute Relationships tab onto the next-most-granular attribute (Month). Then drag the Month attribute onto the Quarter attribute and Quarter onto Year. You may ultimately have different paths to the data. For example, you could get to a day through a week also, which is allowed. If you make a mistake, delete the arrow and try again.

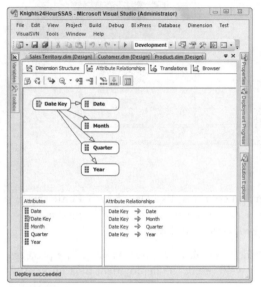 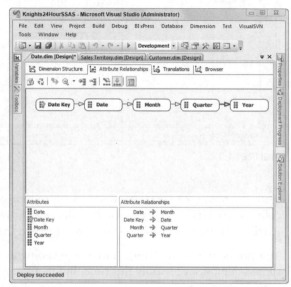

FIGURE 14-4   **FIGURE 14-5**

KEY COLUMNS

After you've created the attribute relationships, try to deploy the change to the server by going to Build ⇨ Deploy *<Project Name>*. You'll notice that the deployment process will return an error fairly quickly (as shown in Figure 14-6). In SSAS, the error messages are about as useful as a screen door on a submarine. Instead, you'll want to locate the warning message directly above the error to see the actual cause of the problem.

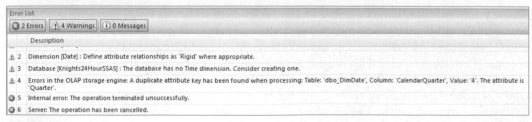

FIGURE 14-6

The cause of this error is a data duplication issue in the attribute relationship. As you can see from the message, SSAS thinks that the CalendarQuarter column has been duplicated in a given year. Keep in mind that SSAS processes a cube by running select distinct queries against each of the column keys. What makes a unique CalendarQuarter? A unique quarter should be the combination of a quarter and a year.

To create a key with multiple columns, go back to the Dimension Structure tab and select the Quarter attribute. While the attribute is selected, go to the Properties window (press F4 if it's closed) and click the ellipsis button next to the KeyColumns property. This opens the Key Columns dialog box (shown in Figure 14-7). Select the CalendarYear attribute and click the single right-facing arrow button to make a concatenated key. Typically, you'll want to order the columns to where the least granular column is on top.

After you click OK, you'll notice you have a new error on the Quarter attribute. SSAS doesn't know what column to show the users, since it will show the key by default, but now you have two columns that make up the key. To correct this, click the ellipsis button next to the NameColumn property, and select the column you'd like to show the users when they drag over the Quarter attribute (CalendarQuarter, as shown in Figure 14-8). Repeat these same steps for the Month attribute and then you'll be able to deploy the cube.

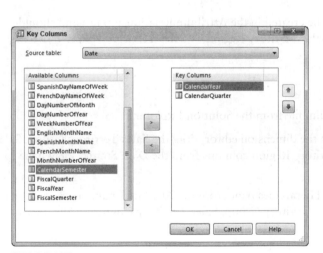

FIGURE 14-7

FIGURE 14-8

DIMENSION AND ATTRIBUTE TYPES

Dimensions and attributes can be classified to introduce new usability features to your users and to yourself. To classify a dimension, click the Date dimension and select Time from the Type drop-down box (in the Properties window). You can then do this for each attribute. For example, you can select the Date attribute and then change Type to Date (as shown in Figure 14-9). Change the Year attribute to Years, Quarter to QuarterOfYear, and Month to MonthOfQuarter.

TRY IT

You've learned in this lesson how to modify a dimension for performance and for usability. In this Try It, you're going to modify the Sales Territory dimension that was created in the last lesson to add a user hierarchy and add the necessary attribute relationships.

FIGURE 14-9

Lesson Requirements

To complete this lesson, first, modify the Sales Territory.dim file to add a new hierarchy with the following levels: Sales Territory Group → Sales Territory Country → Sales Territory Region. You will also want to create the attribute relationships to optimize the dimension. Last, hide the Sales Territory Key attribute to prevent users from dragging it over.

Hints

➤ The attribute relationship should be created in the Attribute Relationship tab and should look like Sales Territory Key → Sales Territory Region → Sales Territory Country → Sales Territory Group.

Step-by-Step

1. Double-click the Sales Territory.dim file from the Solution Explorer.

2. In the Dimension Structure tab of the dimension editor, drag the Sales Territory Group, Sales Territory Country, and Sales Territory Region columns from the Data Source View pane to the Attributes pane.

3. Drag the same attributes into the Hierarchies pane from the Attributes pane to create a hierarchy in the following order: Sales Territory Group, Sales Territory Country, Sales Territory Region (shown in Figure 14-10).

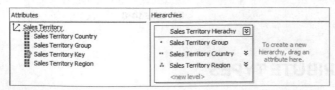

FIGURE 14-10

4. Go to the Attribute Relationships tab and drag Sales Territory Region onto Sales Territory Country and then Sales Territory Country onto Sales Territory Group (see Figure 14-11).

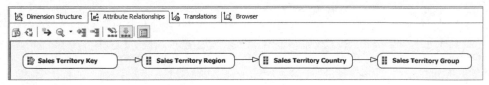

FIGURE 14-11

5. Go back to the Dimension Structure tab and select the Sales Territory Key attribute. In the Properties pane change the `AttributeHierarchyVisible` flag to `false`.

6. While selecting the Sales Territory Group and Sales Territory Region levels in the Hierarchies pane, you'll want to go to the Properties pane and change the HideMemberIf property to `Parent`. This gives you the option of hiding the level if the member matches the parent. For example, France has no regions and the member would just be the word France over again. Instead of being displayed twice, the name could be skipped the second time.

7. Once you deploy the cube, you have successfully edited the cube and can repeat these steps against other dimensions.

 Please select Lesson 14 on the DVD to view the video that accompanies this lesson.

15

Editing Your Cube

With your dimensions now complete, to finish the base cube development you'll need to modify the measure groups. In this lesson you'll learn how to format the cube to make it more usable for your end users. You'll also see how to browse your cube using the simple browser built into the BIDS environment.

 The examples in this lesson start where we left off in Lesson 14. If you didn't do the last lesson, you can download the starting point (Lesson14Complete.zip) from this lesson's download on www.wrox.com.

CUBE EDITOR TOUR

To open the Cube Editor (Figure 15-1) double-click the .cube file from the Solution Explorer. Once it is open you'll see the Data Source View, which makes up the cube in the right pane. Yellow items are fact tables and blue items are dimensions. Green tables represent dimensions that are also fact tables.

On the bottom left you can find a list of the dimensions and their attributes. Finally, on the top left you can find the measure groups and each of the measures. In this pane you'll be able to set the measure properties, such as how the numbers should be rolled up.

You'll notice that in the Dimensions pane on the left there are multiple date dimensions (Order Date, Ship Date, and Due Date). These appear to the end user as three different dimensions with the same attributes, which they can drag over when querying. Each of these is called a *role-playing dimension*. Notice that in the Data Source View on the right there are three foreign keys going into the Date dimension table. Each foreign key creates a new role-playing dimension.

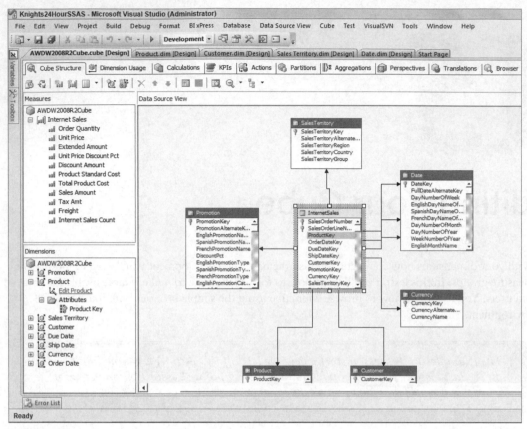

FIGURE 15-1

The brilliant thing about role-playing dimensions is that you'll have to maintain only a single dimension's properties. In other words, if you add a hierarchy to the date.dim dimension file, it will affect all dimensions using it. You can also access the dimension file by expanding the dimension and clicking "Edit *<dimension name>*." Role-playing dimensions will sometimes be named something lengthy and not user-friendly; the Dimensions pane is where you can rename them.

In the Measures pane you'll format each of the measures and define how they'll be rolled up. Start by selecting a measure, such as the Order Quantity measure, and going to the Properties window (F4 will open it if it's been closed). Then you can set the FormatString property to #,##0.00;-#,##0.00, which represents a positive or negative number that allows two places to the right of the decimal and has commas separating the thousands places. In our case, we want only whole numbers, so we can change the FormatString property to #,##0;-#,##0. Percent and currency formats are other common measure formats.

Many measure groups have dozens of measures or more inside them. If you want to set the formatting of multiple measures at once, you can right-click the measure group and select Show Measures In ⇨ Grid. Then you can multi-select the measures and go to the Properties pane.

Another symptom of having lots of measures in a measure group is data overload for your end users. They may spend too much time searching for a given measure while browsing for data. One usability feature in SSAS is to compartmentalize your measures into folders. To do this, simply select the measure and type in the DisplayFolder property the name of the folder into which you wish to place the measure. Once it's been typed in the first time, you can select it from the drop-down box for any future measures. Now when users are looking at the cube's measures, they'll see a user-defined folder under the measure group name.

The most important measure property is the AggregateFunction property. This defines how SSAS will roll the data up. The default method for rolling up is to sum the data, but averaging and counting are also common. To average the data you must have a defined time (or date) dimension. (To see how to specify a type in a dimension, review Lesson 14 on using the Dimension Editor.) Another common problem that can be solved easily in SSAS with the AggregationFunction property is that of semi-additive measures. Imagine for example that you have the data shown in Table 15-1.

TABLE 15-1

MONTH	QUARTER	INVENTORY
January	1	15
February	1	10
March	1	100

In this table, how much product inventory would you say was on the shelf in Q1? The default answer from SSAS would be 125, but that would be incorrect. Inventory examples like this are also known as *snapshot fact tables*, in which you take a snapshot of inventory, a portfolio, or an account for some period of time. Some companies would choose to say that there was an average inventory of 42 during Q1. Some others would show the first number, 15, for Q1, while still others would show 100 for Q1. If you wish to show the first number, you can select FirstNonEmpty for the AggregateFunction, as shown in Figure 15-2. If you wish to show the last number, select LastNonEmpty. Either of these options will require a time dimension and will require the Enterprise Edition of SQL Server.

FIGURE 15-2

The last thing to point out in the cube structure table is the implicit measure that has been added, which will be called *Measure Group* Count, as in Internet Sales Count. This measure counts how many rows you have in a given slice of data and can come in handy later for creating calculations or MDX. For example, it can easily be used to determine how many customer orders you had in a given quarter, since the Order Quantity column contains the number of products in a given sale.

Now that your cube's measures are formatted in the Cube Structure default tab, we want to cover each of the tabs that you see in the Cube Editor. We'll go into each these tabs in much more depth in the rest of this section of the book, but a brief introduction is in order at this point.

➤ The first tab is the **Dimension Usage tab** (Figure 15-3). This tab shows you the relationships between your measure groups and your dimensions. In the columns area (or top row in Figure 15-3) you'll see your measure groups, and along the rows axis (left column) you'll see your dimensions.

➤ In the **Calculations tab** you can create custom measures, like one for profit, as shown in Figure 15-4. After you create a calculation here, the formula will be stored on the server and available to all applications and clients. You can also pre-filter your data with named sets.

➤ The **KPI tab** is where you can create server-side key performance indicators (KPIs). A KPI allows you to create a metric, like Profit Margin, by which you measure employees. If the Profit Margin KPI falls below a

FIGURE 15-3

percentage, like 10 percent, an indicator like a stoplight will turn red. KPIs can be used in any type of scorecard in SSRS, Excel, or SharePoint. The advantage in putting them in SSAS on the server side is that no matter what client the user uses to view the data, he will see the same metric as everyone else.

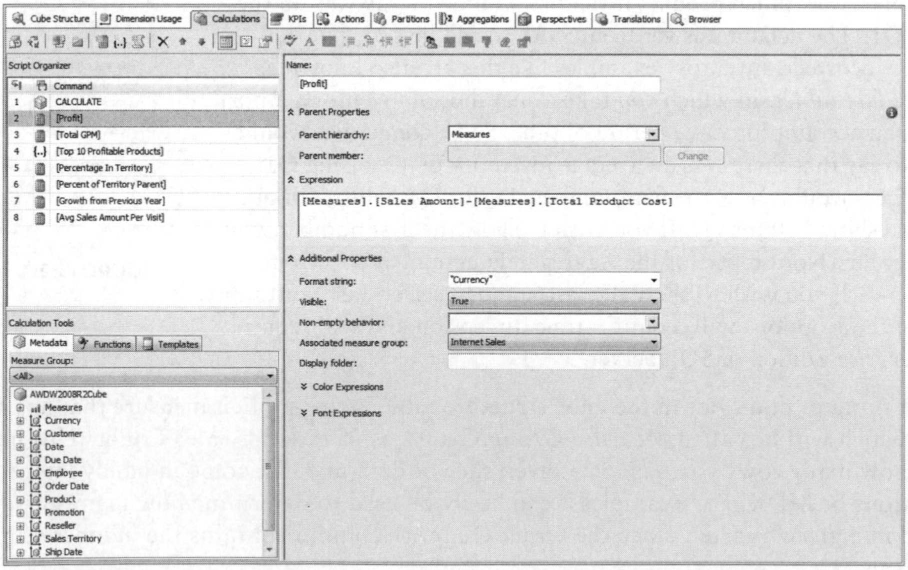

FIGURE 15-4

➤ The **Actions tab** in the Cube Editor allows you to create actions, which can give your users the ability to drill through to the underlying data from the cube or to open items like SSRS reports or web pages. Actions can make it much easier to QA your data or make the data your users are seeing actionable.

➤ The **Partitions** and **Aggregations tabs** are generally used by database administrators. The Partitions tab allows you to compartmentalize your data into separate files. As your data grows past 20 million rows in a given measure group, it should be split into multiple partitions to improve your query performance and scalability. In the Enterprise Edition of SQL Server you can slice the data into separate files — by year or client, for example. The Aggregations tab gives you control over how the data will be pre-aggregated. Pre-aggregating the data speeds up your queries and improves your end-user experience.

➤ A great usability feature in SSAS is the perspective feature. This allows you to create pared-down views of your dimensions, attributes, or any other measures for different roles in your company. For example, you can go to the **Perspectives tab** (shown in Figure 15-5) and right-click in the tab to create a new perspective. Once it's created, name it and uncheck objects you don't want showing up in the perspective. Users will see perspectives in most cube clients, or they can be set in the connection string. It's important to note that perspectives aren't a security mechanism to protect attributes that you don't want your users to see. Instead, they're solely a usability feature to prevent data overload.

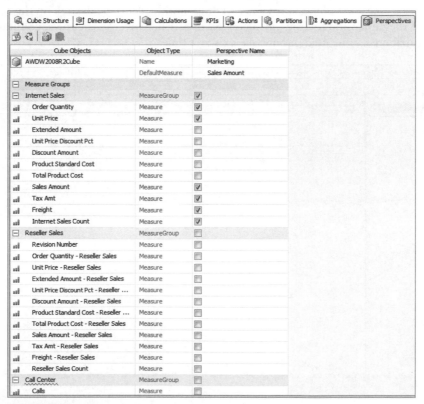

FIGURE 15-5

➤ The next tab is the **Translations tab,** which is not nearly as handy as it may appear at first. In this tab you can translate your measures and measure group names to nearly any language. When users connect to the cube, they can pass in their languages in the connection string; some browsers automatically detect a user's locale from Windows. SSAS will then return the measures and measure group names in the users' native languages. You can also perform a translation in each dimension to translate the attribute names and member names. The problem is that your data must support it with a new column like SpanishMonthName that SSAS will read from for member names. For attribute and measure names, you must enter the new translations manually.

The last tab, the Browser tab, is covered in the next section of this lesson.

BROWSING THE CUBE

The Browser tab in the Cube Editor will let you view the data of your cube and slice and dice it by the dimensions. Prior to using it, make sure any changes to your cube have been deployed by going to Build ⇨ Deploy *<Project Name>*. Once a deployment happens, you'll need to reconnect to the cube on the server by clicking the Reconnect icon on the top left icon bar.

As you can see in Figure 15-6, you start with a blank slate in the right pane. In the left pane, you can expand Measures to see a list of measures you can drag into the detail fields area on the right. You can also expand the dimension to drag any hierarchy or attribute over to the rows, columns, or filters areas. An attribute can be used in only one axis at a time.

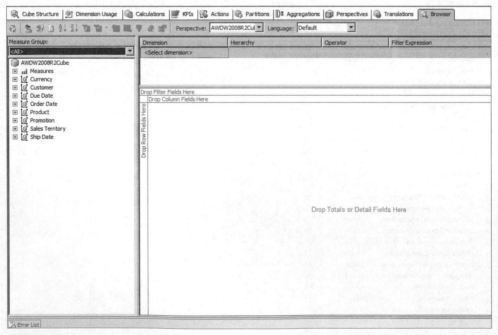

FIGURE 15-6

You can see in Figure 15-7 what the pane looks like once populated with data and sliced by Territory and Year. Since we dragged over a hierarchy, we can expand the Year level to see the Quarter level. If you want to filter on a given level or attribute, simply select the drop-down arrow for any attribute you've dragged over and select one or multiple members to filter.

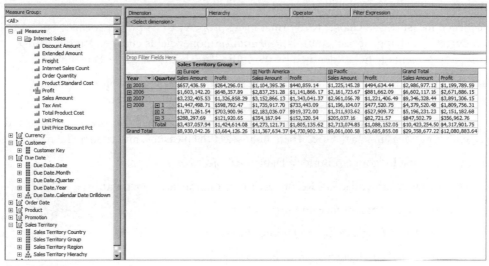

FIGURE 15-7

In the pane, you can also impersonate a given user by clicking the Change User icon at the top left. Then you can test any security roles. You can also select a given perspective or language from this same bar to get the complete user experience.

TRY IT

In this lesson so far you've seen how to format the measures in your cube and how to use the Cube Editor. In this Try It, you're going to explore the Cube Editor after fully formatting the measures using whichever method you like most.

Lesson Requirements

To complete this lesson, format each of the measures into its proper type. Place any measures related to cost and discount into a folder called Costs. Browse the cube to explore the data by the Year attribute in the Date dimension and Sales Territory dimensions.

Hints

➤ Use the Cube Editor to format the measures in the Cube Structure tab by setting the FormatString property.

➤ Place items into a folder by changing the DisplayFolder property.

➤ Lastly, browse the cube in the Browser tab of the Cube Editor.

Step-by-Step

1. Open the cube project that you created in the last project. If you didn't do the last example, download the project from www.wrox.com and deploy it.

2. Open the Cube Editor by double-clicking the .cube file.

3. Select each measure and change the FormatString property to its proper format. For numbers (non-currency), change it to #,##0;-#,##0 and for money fields change it to currency. Lastly, any percentage fields (denoted by the suffix Pct) should be set to Percentage.

4. Place the Product Standard Cost, Product Total Cost, Unit Price, Discounted Pct, and Discount Amount in the Cost folder by changing the DisplayFolder property to Costs.

5. You can optionally set multiple properties at once by right-clicking in the Measures pane and selecting Show Measures In ⇨ Grid. Then multi-select the measures and change them all at once.

6. Deploy your cube by going to Build ⇨ Deploy <Project Name>.

7. Go to the Browser tab and select Reconnect to refresh the latest metadata.

8. Drag over the Sales Amount measure into the details pane.

9. Drag over the Sales Territory hierarchy into the columns area.

10. Drag over the Due Date hierarchy into the Rows area.

11. Your project should look something like Figure 15-8 when complete.

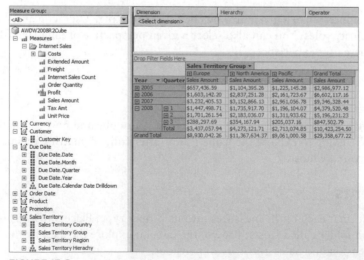

FIGURE 15-8

 Please select Lesson 15 on the DVD to view the video that accompanies this lesson.

16

Adding New Dimensions and Measure Groups

As is probably true of any project that you've been on, the requirements change as the project goes through its development cycle. In this lesson you'll learn how to develop your cube over time to add new measure groups, measures, and dimensions. You'll also learn about different ways to relate the dimensions to your measure groups.

 To start this lesson and make sure you have the same configuration for your cubes that we're working from, please download Lesson16Start.zip from this lesson's download on the Wrox website (www.wrox.com). After downloading the .zip file, make sure you can deploy it to your development SSAS instance. Lesson16Complete.zip shows you the complete solution.

ADDING A MEASURE GROUP AND MEASURES

In the example that you've been working on throughout this SSAS part of the book, you've been working on Internet-based sales only. Now the requirements have changed and you need to track sales to your resellers as well. To start, add the tables you'll need throughout this lesson to your Data Source View (DSV). For this lesson you'll need to add FactResellerSales, DimEmployee, DimReseller, DimProductCategory, and DimProductSubCategory (see the result in Figure 16-1). For the purpose of this and future examples, create a friendly name for each of the tables to lose the Dim and Fact prefixes (DimEmployee becomes Employee if you select the table and set the FriendlyName property). This will save time later as you create the dimensions.

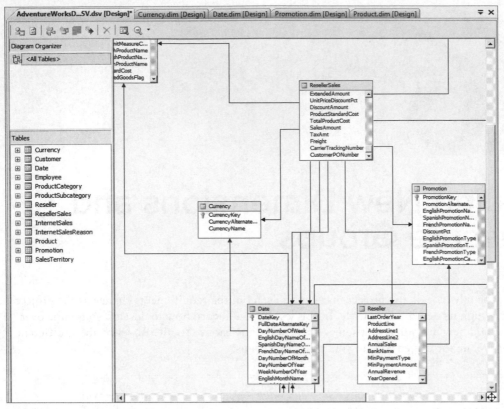

FIGURE 16-1

Now that the DSV has been saved, you're ready to add any measure and measure group. To add a measure group or measure, open the Cube Editor (discussed in Lesson 15) by double-clicking your .cube file in the Solution Explorer. You can add a new measure by right-clicking any measure group in the Cube Structure tab and selecting New Measure. When the New Measure dialog box opens (Figure 16-2), you select how you want the data to be aggregated with the Usage drop-down box. Then, select the column that you wish to have participate in this measure. We discussed how this data can be rolled up in Lesson 15.

> *You can have a measure used for more than one type of aggregation. For example, from the same SalesAmount measure column in the fact table, you could create Average Sales Amount and Total Sales Amount measures that roll the data up two different ways.*

To add a new fact table (measure group in SSAS) right-click in the Measures pane of the Cube Structure tab and select New Measure Group. This opens the New Measure Group dialog box (shown in Figure 16-3), in which you select the fact table to add. In our case, select the ResellerSales fact table.

FIGURE 16-2

FIGURE 16-3

As soon as you click OK, the Reseller Sales measure group is added, as shown in Figure 16-4. Where there are duplicate measure names, the measure group name is appended to the name. Measure groups must always be unique within a given cube.

FIGURE 16-4

ADDING A DIMENSION

Now that you have the new measure group added, you'll want to add new dimensions that relate to the Reseller Sales measure group so your users can slice by those pertinent attributes. To add a new dimension, right-click Dimensions in the Solution Explorer and select New Dimension. This opens the Dimension Wizard.

When you already have the table created in your database, you will select the Use Existing Table option in the first screen in the Dimension Wizard. This is the option we'll use to create the Reseller dimension. From this screen you can also create a time or other common types of dimensions, like customers or accounts, by following the templates provided in the wizard.

The next screen in the wizard (Figure 16-5) is where you specify the table to which you want to tie the SSAS dimension. For the "Main table" option, select Reseller as the table. The "Key columns" option is the primary key column or columns that represent a unique reseller. Lastly, the "Name column" property allows you to change what the end user will see when he or she drags over the Reseller Key attribute. For our example, select ResellerName for the Name Column.

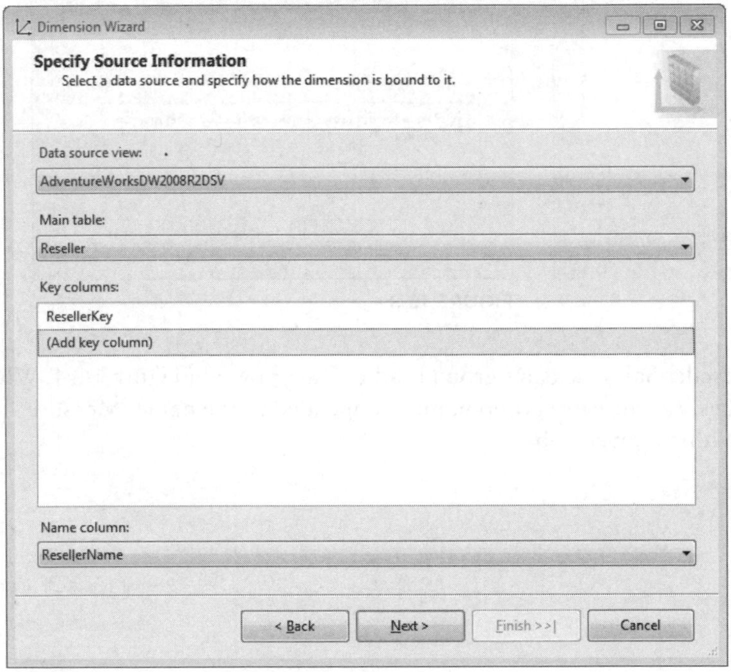

FIGURE 16-5

On the next screen (Figure 16-6) you're asked which attributes you want to add to the dimension. Simply check each of the attributes that you wish to add and specify whether you want it to be available for browsing. After you click Next you may be taken to an additional screen to add any snowflake tables. Finally, you'll be taken to a completion screen. Once you click Finish, the dimension will be created.

Although the dimension is added in the Solution Explorer, it is not yet participating in your cube. To arrange this you'll have to open the Cube Editor again. Right-click in the Dimensions pane (bottom left) and click Add Cube Dimension. Then select the newly created Reseller dimension. Next time you deploy your cube, the dimension will be included.

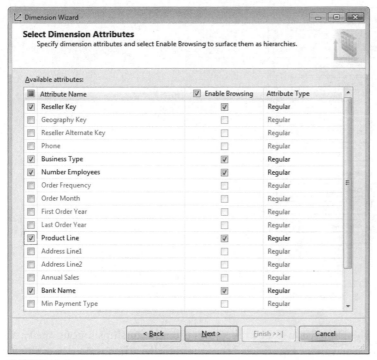

FIGURE 16-6

 Fact tables can also play the role of a measure group and dimension. You add a fact table to a cube by following the same process for adding a dimension. While this is not normal for most cubes, sometimes you may want to do it. For example, the information for an order may be a measure group and may also be a dimension for the order details.

One of the most important tabs in the Cube Editor is the Dimension Usage tab (Figure 16-7). This tab tells you which measure groups align with each dimension. For example, the new Reseller dimension relates to the Reseller Sales measure group but has no way to get to the Internet Sales measure group. If you were browsing the Internet Sales measures and dragged over an attribute from the Reseller dimension, you would get unpredictable answers (typically the number for the All level of the dimension repeated over and over again). Since this can be confusing for your users, it's a best practice to go to the Cube Structure tab and set the IgnoreUnrelatedDimensions property to `False` for each of the measure groups (yes, the property name is counterintuitive). After you set this property and redeploy, the measures will show NULL if you drag over an unrelated dimension.

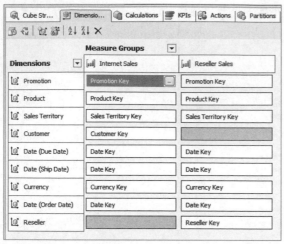

FIGURE 16-7

Relationship Types

In the last section you saw how the Dimension Usage tab shows the relationships among the various dimensions and measure groups. You saw in Figure 16-7 that the Reseller dimension doesn't relate to Internet Sales. You also saw how the dimensions were automatically related to the new measure group when you created the Reseller Sales measure group. What if the automated logic makes a mistake or the Reseller dimension really has a relationship to the Internet Sales measure group?

As you saw in Figure 16-7, dimensions that don't relate to the measure group are denoted by a gray box. To create the relationship or change an existing relationship, click the ellipsis button in the gray box or where a relationship already exists. This opens the Define Relationship dialog box, where you can create relationships between measure groups and dimensions. The most simplistic relationship is a *one-to-many relationship*; in SSAS this is called a *regular relationship* and you can set it in the "Select relationship type" drop-down box shown in Figure 16-8. After you select this option, you pick the primary key for your "Granularity attribute" drop-down box and pick the column in the fact table that links the tables together. Don't actually save this example as this is an incorrect relationship.

Another relationship type that you may use often is a *referenced relationship*. This is one in which you have to go through one table to get to another. You can also use a *many-to-many relationship* to show things like the results of a survey in which a given question may have multiple answers.

Adding Snowflake Dimension Tables

So far you've been using strictly star schema tables, in which every table relates directly to the fact table. In some cases, though, you may have child tables that relate to a dimension. For example, in our example schema DimProduct has a DimProductSubcategory child table and a DimProductCategory table that relates to that child. For this particular dimension example and many others like it, you want SSAS to denormalize the dimensions and provide one flat view of your data.

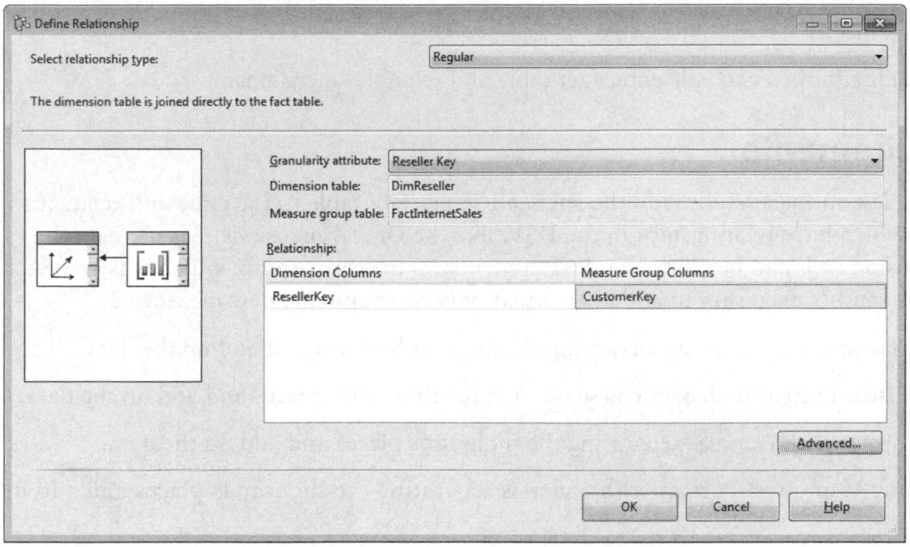

FIGURE 16-8

To arrange this, open the Product Dimension Editor. Right-click in the DSV pane to the right and select Show Tables. Then select the ProductCategory and ProductSubcategory tables in the Show Tables dialog box. You'll see that those two tables have relationships to the Product table but aren't actually being used (as denoted by the light blue color). To use these dimension tables also, simply drag the new attributes like EnglishProductCategoryName and EnglishProductSubcategoryName over to the Attributes pane. Then you can rename the attributes and create any hierarchies and attribute relationships that you wish. You'll notice that after you've dragged the columns over from the DSV pane on the right to the Attributes pane on the left, the tables on the DSV pane turn from light blue to dark blue, meaning that they're being used by this Product dimension (shown in Figure 16-9).

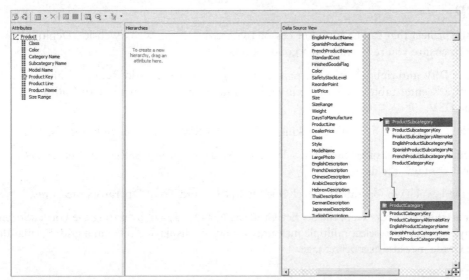

FIGURE 16-9

TRY IT

In this Try It you'll add the FactCallCenter fact table and related dimensions.

Lesson Requirements

To complete this lesson successfully, add the FactCallCenter fact table to the cube and relate it to the dimensions which have relationships in the DSV, like the Date dimensions. Also, create the Employee dimension so it can be related to the Reseller Sales measure group, which was created earlier in this lesson. It's necessary to add and format only the following new measures:

➤ **Orders:** Format with commas separating the thousands places and add up the data.

➤ **IssuesRaised:** Format with commas separating the thousands places and add up the data.

➤ **Calls:** Format with commas separating the thousands places and add up the data.

➤ **AutomaticResponses:** Format with commas separating the thousands places and add up the data.

➤ **ServiceGrade:** Format as a percentage and add up the data (for the time being).

➤ **AverageTimePerIssue:** Format with commas separating the thousands places and average the data.

Hints

➤ Start by adding the FactCallCenter fact table to the DSV.

➤ Then add the table in the measure group by clicking Add New Measure Group in the Cube Editor.

Step-by-Step

1. Open the project that can be found in Lesson16Start.zip on the Wrox website. Deploy the project to ensure you're starting on a good footing.

2. Open the DSV and right-click in the pane to the right and select Add Remove Tables. Add the FactCallCenter table. Change the FriendlyName property on the table to **CallCenter**. Save the DSV.

3. Open the Cube Editor by double-clicking AWDW2008RW.cube in the Solution Explorer.

4. Right-click in the Measures pane and select New Measure Group. Select CallCenter as the table that contains the data.

5. Delete the Level Two Operators, Level One Operators, and Total Operators measures.

6. Format all the measures except the Service Grade as `#,##0;-#,##0` by setting the FormatString property. You can also select multiple measures at once by displaying them in a grid. Format the Service Grade measure as a percentage.

7. Now you must add the Employee dimension. Do this by right-clicking Dimensions in the Solution Explorer and selecting New Dimension.

8. In the Dimension Wizard select "Use an existing table" and click Next.

9. In the Specify Source Information screen on the wizard, select the Employee table as the main table. The Key Column property should be set to EmployeeKey and the Name Column property should be set to LastName.

10. After clicking Next you'll be guided to add the related table (SalesTerritory). Ensure it is checked and click Next.

11. Check Gender, Marital Status, Salaried Flag, Last Name, and any column that may already be checked in the Select Dimension Attributes screen.

12. Click Finish to complete the wizard.

13. Back in the Cube Editor, right-click in the Dimensions pane at the bottom left and select Add Cube Dimension. Select Employee and click OK. This dimension will be used by the Reseller Sales measure group we created earlier.

In this example we added a CallCenter measure group that didn't relate to any dimension other than the Date dimension. Normally when there are no cross-measure group relationships you would create a new cube so it can process faster and make browsing easier.

Please select Lesson 16 on the DVD to view the video that accompanies this lesson.

17

Using MDX

In this lesson you'll learn the basics of the MultiDimensional eXpression language (MDX). MDX as a topic by itself has filled countless thousand-page books; here I'll condense the topic to give you a working knowledge of the language. You'll be using MDX for reports in clients like SSRS, to build KPIs, to perform calculations, and to do many other things.

 To start this lesson and make sure your cubes have the same configuration, please download Lesson16Complete.zip from this lesson's download on the Wrox website (www.wrox.com). After downloading, make sure you can deploy it to your development SSAS instance.

ANATOMY OF BASIC MDX

Knowing T-SQL is almost a liability when you're learning MDX because the two are fundamentally similar, but completely different in their details. As you specify measures or attributes that you want to see, you can place them on the columns area or rows area. You can also use them as filters. For example, the most rudimentary MDX statement would be the following:

```
SELECT
[Measure].[MeasureName] on columns,
[Dimension].[Attribute] on rows
FROM [Cube name]
```

A real example using our sample project would look like this:

```
SELECT
    [Measures].[Sales Amount] ON COLUMNS
FROM [AWDW2008R2Cube]
```

To run this statement you could use Management Studio and connect to the Analysis Services instance. Then you would click the New Query button. You can drag the columns over from the left pane into your query window to help you write the code faster. Object names must be in brackets if they have spaces, so it's just a good habit to keep them around all object names. The results from the previous query would look like Figure 17-1.

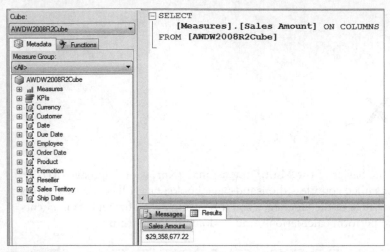

FIGURE 17-1

As you see, the MDX resulted in a single column with the equivalent of all sales in the fact table. The equivalent T-SQL statement would be SELECT SUM(SalesAmount) FROM FactInternetSales with no filtering WHERE clause. You could also see this sales data grouped by years by adding the dimension and attribute name, as shown in the following code snippet:

```
SELECT
    [Measures].[Sales Amount] ON COLUMNS,
[Due Date].[Year].Children on ROWS
FROM [AWDW2008R2Cube]
```

The results would look like Figure 17-2. By pointing to the .Children function of the Year attribute, you show all the members of that attribute. If you didn't include the .Children function, the results would show only the All member. You could create another variant of this statement by replacing .Children with .Members; then the results would return the members, as shown in Figure 17-2, as well as the All member. You could also have pointed to a user hierarchy. If you had done this, you wouldn't have needed to specify the .Children function.

FIGURE 17-2

Tuples and Sets

Do you remember in high school when you learned to refer to a spot on a graph using (x, y) coordinates? In MDX you use tuples in the same way. Tuples are a cross section or intersection of two areas in your cube. Multiple tuples are called *sets*. You'll see all of these in action in the upcoming examples.

To point to a set of (x, y) coordinates in a tuple, simply wrap the cross join in parentheses and separate the two items with a comma. For example, the following code will cross-join categories with the sales along the columns axis.

```
SELECT
([Product].[Category Name].Children,
[Measures].[Sales Amount]) ON COLUMNS,
[Due Date].[Year].Children on ROWS
FROM [AWDW2008R2Cube]
```

The results can be seen in Figure 17-3.

As you can see in the figure, there are a number of nulls in the data. If you wish to remove those nulls, you can use a NON EMPTY keyword to do it. If you run the following query, the nulls will be eliminated along whatever axis you request.

```
SELECT
NON EMPTY
([Product].[Category Name].Children,
[Measures].[Sales Amount]) ON COLUMNS,
NON EMPTY [Due Date].[Year].Children on ROWS
FROM [AWDW2008R2Cube]
```

In Figure 17-4 you can see the results of the null elimination. Notice that in 2005 and 2006, there is still null data. These nulls are showing because there were sales in 2005 for the Bikes category. If one column had data, the entire row must stay.

| | Accessories | Bikes | Clothing | Components |
	Sales Amount	Sales Amount	Sales Amount	Sales Amount
2005	(null)	$2,986,977.12	(null)	(null)
2006	(null)	$6,602,117.16	(null)	(null)
2007	$269,455.42	$8,950,122.54	$126,750.48	(null)
2008	$431,304.54	$9,778,927.83	$213,022.13	(null)
2010	(null)	(null)	(null)	(null)

FIGURE 17-3

| | Accessories | Bikes | Clothing |
	Sales Amount	Sales Amount	Sales Amount
2005	(null)	$2,986,977.12	(null)
2006	(null)	$6,602,117.16	(null)
2007	$269,455.42	$8,950,122.54	$126,750.48
2008	$431,304.54	$9,778,927.83	$213,022.13

FIGURE 17-4

You can also have multiple attributes and measures along the top columns axis or side rows axis in a tuple, as shown in the following code:

```
SELECT
NON EMPTY
(
[Product].[Category Name].Children,
[Product].[Subcategory Name].Children,
[Measures].[Sales Amount]
)

ON COLUMNS,
NON EMPTY
(
[Due Date].[Year].Children,
[Due Date].[Quarter].Children
) on ROWS
FROM [AWDW2008R2Cube]
```

Run this code and you'll get the result shown in Figure 17-5. Note that this screenshot takes only part of the results into account. The numbers you see next to the years are quarters in the rows axis.

		Accessories	Accessories	Accessories	Accessories	Accessories	Accessories	Accessories	Accessories	Bikes
		Bike Racks	Bike Stands	Bottles and Cages	Cleaners	Fenders	Helmets	Hydration Packs	Tires and Tubes	Mountain Bikes
		Sales Amount	Sales Amount	Sales Amount	Sales Amount	Sales Amount	Sales Amount	Sales Amount	Sales Amount	Sales Amount
2005	3	(null)	(null)	(null)	(null)	(null)	(null)	(null)	(null)	$240,574.29
2005	4	(null)	(null)	(null)	(null)	(null)	(null)	(null)	(null)	$304,799.10
2006	1	(null)	(null)	(null)	(null)	(null)	(null)	(null)	(null)	$308,149.09
2006	2	(null)	(null)	(null)	(null)	(null)	(null)	(null)	(null)	$419,898.76
2006	3	(null)	(null)	(null)	(null)	(null)	(null)	(null)	(null)	$366,247.61
2006	4	(null)	(null)	(null)	(null)	(null)	(null)	(null)	(null)	$422,297.27
2007	1	(null)	(null)	(null)	(null)	(null)	(null)	(null)	(null)	$642,622.21
2007	2	(null)	(null)	(null)	(null)	(null)	(null)	(null)	(null)	$741,782.49
2007	3	$6,480.00	$6,042.00	$7,979.74	$1,033.50	$6,440.14	$29,811.48	$5,718.96	$34,196.35	$1,048,763.76
2007	4	$8,520.00	$11,607.00	$13,166.51	$1,741.05	$11,451.58	$54,864.32	$9,678.24	$60,724.55	$1,403,213.28
2008	1	$9,000.00	$8,745.00	$15,162.71	$1,876.20	$11,715.34	$55,459.15	$10,833.03	$61,657.82	$1,675,527.86

FIGURE 17-5

Filtering Data

Filtering data in MDX can be done in two ways. The first uses a WHERE clause in the MDX statement itself. Doing this is a lot like doing the same thing in T-SQL, but with a twist. The second is to filter the data as you display it along the axis.

 One important rule about MDX is that the same attribute can be used on two axes. For example, the color attribute can't be used in the WHERE clause and be displayed along the rows axis. You'll get an error like the following if you attempt this: "The Gender hierarchy already appears in the Axis1 axis."

To filter data in a WHERE clause you use statements much like those you would use in T-SQL. The twist is that you point to the specific member or set of members for which you wish to filter. For example, to filter the last statement we used to show only the U.S.-based customers, you'd use a statement like this:

```
SELECT
NON EMPTY
([Product].[Category Name].Children,
[Measures].[Sales Amount]) ON COLUMNS,
NON EMPTY [Due Date].[Year].Children on ROWS
FROM [AWDW2008R2Cube]
WHERE [Sales Territory].[Sales Territory Country].&[United States]
```

You can also filter a set of members by placing the data in a set. A set is a collection of points or tuples to slice by. A set opens with a { and closes with a }, and you separate each of the tuples with a comma.

```
SELECT
NON EMPTY
([Product].[Category Name].Children,
[Measures].[Sales Amount]) ON COLUMNS,
NON EMPTY [Due Date].[Year].Children on ROWS
FROM [AWDW2008R2Cube]
WHERE
{
[Sales Territory].[Sales Territory Country].&[United States]
,[Sales Territory].[Sales Territory Country].&[United Kingdom]
}
```

Sets are handy throughout MDX to filter data out. Suppose you want to show only data for 2007 and 2008, but you also want to display the two years. You can filter these years in the WHERE clause and show them along the ROWS axis, as the previous statement shows. To do this you would employ a filter along the ROWS axis, as shown in the following code, by pointing to the specific set of members.

```
SELECT
NON EMPTY
([Product].[Category Name].Children,
[Measures].[Sales Amount]) ON COLUMNS,
NON EMPTY
{
[Due Date].[Year].&[2007],
[Due Date].[Year].&[2008]
}
  on ROWS
FROM [AWDW2008R2Cube]
WHERE
{[Sales Territory].[Sales Territory Country].&[United States]
,[Sales Territory].[Sales Territory Country].&[United Kingdom]}
```

NAVIGATION FUNCTIONS

Navigation functions are a key element to MDX that helps you navigate the hierarchies and attributes. I'll be discussing these at length here and again much more deeply in the next lesson, on calculations. One way to use navigation functions is to point to a specific member and then state you want its children, as shown in the following code snippet:

```
SELECT
[Measures].[Sales Amount] on 0,
[Due Date].[Calendar Date Drilldown].[Year].&[2007].Children on 1
FROM [AWDW2008R2Cube]
```

This will return all the quarters under the 2007 year, as shown in Figure 17-6. Notice that this time we're using a hierarchy to navigate to the next level.

FIGURE 17-6

The `.PrevMember` navigation function will allow you to step sideways in the hierarchy. For example, if you point to the 2007 member and state that you want `.PrevMember`, SSAS will take a step to the side and return 2006. You can also do the same thing with `.NextMember`:

```
SELECT
[Measures].[Sales Amount] on 0,
[Due Date].[Calendar Date Drilldown].[Year].&[2007].PrevMember.Children on 1
FROM [AWDW2008R2Cube]
```

Often you want to analyze the last *x* number of years of sales. In T-SQL you might use the `Getdate()` function and the `DateAdd` function to achieve this goal. One MDX method is to point to the [All] level of data and use the `.LastChild` navigation function. This returns the last member at that level. You can also use the `.Lag` function to navigate through years by passing in (1) to go back a year and (-1) to go forward a year, and so on, as shown in the following code:

```
SELECT
[Measures].[Sales Amount] on 0,
{

[Due Date].[Calendar Date Drilldown].[All].LastChild,
[Due Date].[Calendar Date Drilldown].[All].LastChild.Lag(1),
[Due Date].[Calendar Date Drilldown].[All].LastChild.Lag(2)
} on 1
FROM [AWDW2008R2Cube]
```

This code would return the data shown in Figure 17-7. Note that placing a Non Empty statement in front of the Year attribute would have eliminated the 2010 row.

FIGURE 17-7

In reports you may also want to sort the data by a given measure. To do this in MDX you wrap the tuple in an ORDER function and specify the measure by which you want to sort, as shown in the following syntax:

```
SELECT    [Measures].[Sales Amount]
  ON COLUMNS,
  NON EMPTY
  ORDER(
     ( [Customer].[Occupation].CHILDREN,
       [Product].[Subcategory Name].CHILDREN ),
                [Sales Amount],DESC)
                     ON ROWS
FROM [AWDW2008R2Cube]
```

As you can see in Figure 17-8, the data is sorted by Occupation first, then by Sales Amount.

If you want to sort by the Sales Amount measure regardless of the tuple, you can use BDESC instead of DESC as the operator. This breaks the tuple and sorts by the measure and does not order by the hierarchy or tuple. The result is shown in Figure 17-9.

As you can imagine, there are many other functions in MDX, and that's why there are entire books on the topic. We'll be covering the most practical applications for MDX next in the calculations lesson, and again in Section IV of this book.

FIGURE 17-8

FIGURE 17-9

TRY IT

In the next lesson you'll apply MDX to creating calculations. With what you've learned in this lesson, however, you can write complex SSRS dashboard reports or query the cube with your custom application, and that's what you'll do in this Try It.

Lesson Requirements

In this brief Try It, you will attempt to satisfy the requirements for a report in Management Studio. The final results should look like Figure 17-10. To fully meet the requirements for this section, you should accomplish the following:

➤ **Measures:** Show Product Internet sales and Order Quantity Rows: Show product categories and subcategories

➤ **Columns:** Show SHIP Years

➤ **Filter:** Show only men (from the customer dimension)

➤ Exclude null values

		2005	2006	2007	2008	2005	2006	2007	2008
		Sales Amount	Sales Amount	Sales Amount	Sales Amount	Order Quantity	Order Quantity	Order Quantity	Order Quantity
Accessories	Bike Racks	(null)	(null)	$8,160.00	$12,720.00	(null)	(null)	68	106
Accessories	Bike Stands	(null)	(null)	$7,314.00	$10,017.00	(null)	(null)	46	63
Accessories	Bottles and Cages	(null)	(null)	$11,088.41	$17,590.25	(null)	(null)	1,559	2,475
Accessories	Cleaners	(null)	(null)	$1,550.25	$2,186.25	(null)	(null)	195	275
Accessories	Fenders	(null)	(null)	$9,561.30	$14,111.16	(null)	(null)	435	642
Accessories	Helmets	(null)	(null)	$43,772.49	$68,440.44	(null)	(null)	1,251	1,956
Accessories	Hydration Packs	(null)	(null)	$8,028.54	$12,097.80	(null)	(null)	146	220
Accessories	Tires and Tubes	(null)	(null)	$49,773.84	$74,781.39	(null)	(null)	3,525	5,271
Bikes	Mountain Bikes	$267,574.21	$739,141.06	$1,867,010.98	$1,988,511.67	79	288	981	1,083
Bikes	Road Bikes	$1,302,361.59	$2,450,850.55	$2,006,603.49	$1,491,797.03	405	1,014	1,398	1,213

FIGURE 17-10

Hints

➤ Along the rows axis, use a tuple of [*Product*].[*Category Name*] and
[*Product*].[*Subcategory Name*].

➤ You will need a set to show multiple measures in the columns axis.

➤ You can filter on men by adding a WHERE clause and naming the exact member like this:
[Customer].[Gender].&[M].

Step-by-Step

1. Open Management Studio and connect to your SSAS instance.

2. Click New Query.

3. Run the following statement:

```
SELECT
NON EMPTY
{
(
[Ship Date].[Year].Children,
[Measures].[Sales Amount])
,
(
[Ship Date].[Year].Children,
[Measures].[Order Quantity]
)
}
ON COLUMNS,
NON EMPTY
(
[Product].[Category Name].Children,
[Product].[Subcategory Name].Children
)
on ROWS
FROM [AWDW2008R2Cube]
WHERE
[Customer].[Gender].&[M]
```

Congratulations! You've written your first MDX statement and learned a brand new language that
you can use throughout SSAS, SharePoint, and Reporting Services.

 *Please select Lesson 17 on the DVD to view the video that accompanies this
lesson.*

18

Creating Calculations

Now that you know the basics of MDX, this lesson will show you the most important application for it: creating custom calculations. Calculations are ways of deploying MDX code snippets to the server so that new measures show up when you're browsing the cube. When you create a calculation, only the formula is stored in SSAS and no new data is stored in the cube. This makes processing of these measures very fast; querying using them, however, is slower. In some cases, the only way to implement logic for your browsers easily is through calculations.

> To start this lesson and make sure you have the same configuration of your cube as we do, please download Lesson16Complete.zip, which is available as part of the download for this lesson from the Wrox website (www.wrox.com). After downloading, make sure you can deploy the file to your development SSAS instance.
>
> The download for this lesson also includes Lesson18Complete, which is the solution that includes the completed calculation code.

CALCULATION BASICS

To create a basic calculation, open the Cube Editor and go to the Calculations tab. Right-click the Script Organizer pane in the top left and select New Calculated Member. Type the calculation in brackets, like **[Total GPM]**. Brackets are required for any calculations that have spaces in them, so it's a good habit to add them to all calculations. In the Expression box, enter the MDX snippet of code that will be executed when people drag over this measure. In our case, we used the following code:

```
([Measures].[Sales Amount]-[Measures].[Total Product Cost]) / [Measures].[Sales Amount]
```

This MDX snippet will calculate the gross profit margin for Internet sales. It will be applied to any slice of data as long as it relates to the Internet Sales measure group. You should set the Format String property to its proper format such as currency, numeric, or percentage so it will properly appear to users. The last thing that should always be set is the Associated Measure Group, which specifies which measure group you wish to place this calculation into. You can see a completed calculation in Figure 18-1.

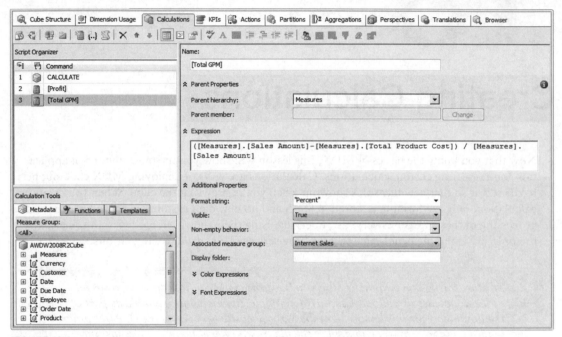

FIGURE 18-1

To aid in the creation of calculations, there are three tabs on the bottom left.

➤ The **Metadata tab** shows you a list of objects in SSAS that can be dragged over into the expression box for coding ease. After you deploy the cube, you'll need to click the reconnect button on the top left to see the new objects in the Metadata tab.

➤ You also can see a list of available MDX functions in the **Functions tab**.

➤ The last tab is the **Templates tab**, which shows you canned templates of calculations. You can right-click any template and select Add Template to create a new calculation from a template.

COLOR-CODING MEASURES

Another fantastic way to increase data visibility is to color-code a given measure conditionally. For example, if you want to color-code the Total GPM calculation if it falls below 30 percent, expand the Color Expression group and set the fore color to the following expression:

```
IIF([Measures].[Total GPM] < .3, 255, 000)
```

Once you build and deploy the cube, you'll see the new red font color in the Browser tab under lower profit margin conditions (shown in Figure 18-2). Whether the cube browser complies with the colors is up to the client application. Excel 2007 and above, for example, will show the font colors and sizes. Reporting Services, on the other hand, will not. You can also adjust the background of the cell and the font, as well as the size and thickness of the font.

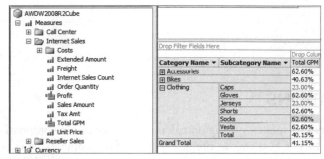

FIGURE 18-2

NAMED SETS

A *named set* is a type of calculation that allows you to filter or order your data automatically, among other things. To create one, right-click in the Script Organizer pane and select New Named Set. After naming it, write the MDX expression in the Expression pane. An example of a practical named set is one that finds the top 10 customers according to some metric. In the following formula you can see the top 10 products according to the previously created measure Total GPM.

```
TopCount
(
    [Product].[Product Name].Children,
    10,
    [Measures].[Total GPM]
)
```

To use the named set, drag it from the dimension onto the top sub-cube area, as shown in Figure 18-3.

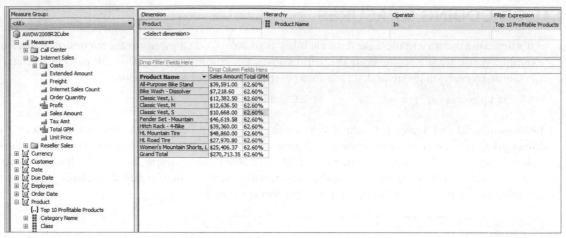

FIGURE 18-3

MORE ADVANCED CALCULATIONS

Much, if not most, of any SSAS project will be spent working on calculations, because it's impossible to create all the client measures in ETL. The best way to prepare yourself for a complex calculation is to go analog and write the mathematical formula on the whiteboard. Keep in mind while you create these calculations that you're storing only the formulas on the server side and that no data will be pre-aggregated for your newly created calculation. This section covers some calculations for common business scenarios you may encounter: use them as templates to model your own calculations after.

Percentage of All Level

One of the most common calculations is one that takes a measure and calculates how it relates to all sales. In other words, you want to be able to answer the question: "How much is Florida contributing to the bottom line?" Such a calculation could look much like Figure 18-4, with the Percentage in Territory measure.

Sales Territory Group ▾	Sales Territory Country	Sales Territory Region	Sales Amount	Percentage In Territory
⊞ Europe			$8,930,042.26	30.42%
⊟ North America	⊞ Canada		$1,977,844.86	6.74%
	⊟ United States	Central	$3,000.83	0.01%
		Northeast	$6,532.47	0.02%
		Northwest	$3,649,866.55	12.43%
		Southeast	$12,238.85	0.04%
		Southwest	$5,718,150.81	19.48%
		Total	$9,389,789.51	31.98%
	Total		$11,367,634.37	38.72%
⊞ Pacific			$9,061,000.58	30.86%
Grand Total			$29,358,677.22	100.00%

FIGURE 18-4

To set up this calculation, first you want to check for NULL data. This will make sure you don't have a divide-by-zero error when you run the calculation. You can perform this check with a simple WHEN statement, as shown in the following code snippet. The IsEmpty function will check for NULL data on any given statement.

```
Case
When IsEmpty
    (
        [Measures].[Sales Amount]
    )
Then Null
```

After that, you want to divide the tuple of the sales territory hierarchy by the All member of the same hierarchy:

```
Case
// Test to avoid division by zero.
When IsEmpty
    (
        [Measures].[Sales Amount]
    )
Then Null

Else ( [Sales Territory].[Sales Territory Hierarchy],
       [Measures].[Sales Amount] )
    /
    (
    // The Root function returns the (All) value for the target dimension.
       Root
       (
           [Sales Territory].[Sales Territory Hierarchy].[All]
       ),
    [Measures].[Sales Amount]
    )

End
```

Percentage of Parent

A similar calculation is one that determines the percentage of a given value's parent. For example, in Figure 18-5 you can see that the Central region accounts for only .03 percent of the United States sales. The calculation determines the value of the cell's data in relation to its parent in the hierarchy.

Sales Territory Group ▼	Sales Territory Country	Sales Territory Region	Sales Amount	Percentage In Territory	Percent of Territory Parent
⊟ Europe	⊞ France		$2,644,017.71	9.01%	29.61%
	⊞ Germany		$2,894,312.34	9.86%	32.41%
	⊞ United Kingdom		$3,391,712.21	11.55%	37.98%
	Total		$8,930,042.26	30.42%	30.42%
⊟ North America	⊞ Canada		$1,977,844.86	6.74%	17.40%
	⊟ United States	Central	$3,000.83	0.01%	0.03%
		Northeast	$6,532.47	0.02%	0.07%
		Northwest	$3,649,866.55	12.43%	38.87%
		Southeast	$12,238.85	0.04%	0.13%
		Southwest	$5,718,150.81	19.48%	60.90%
		Total	$9,389,789.51	31.98%	82.60%
	Total		$11,367,634.37	38.72%	38.72%
⊞ Pacific			$9,061,000.58	30.86%	30.86%
Grand Total			$29,358,677.22	100.00%	100.00%

FIGURE 18-5

The code for this calculation is similar to the previous code, with a few exceptions. The first exception is that you want to determine if the member you're looking at is at the All top level. To do this, you can use the `CurrentMember` function to point to the cell you're looking at presently; the Level suffix requests the level in the hierarchy that you're currently viewing in a given cell.

```
When [Sales Territory].[Sales Territory Hierarchy].CurrentMember.Level Is
    [Sales Territory].[Sales Territory Hierarchy].[(All)]
Then 1
```

You can also use the `CurrentMember` function to point to the member's parent for the mathematical calculation. The complete code is as follows:

```
Case
// Test to avoid division by zero.
When IsEmpty
    (
        [Measures].[Sales Amount]
    )
Then Null

// Test for current coordinate being on the (All) member.
When [Sales Territory].[Sales Territory Hierarchy].CurrentMember.Level Is
    [Sales Territory].[Sales Territory Hierarchy].[(All)]
Then 1

Else ( [Sales Territory].[Sales Territory Hierarchy].CurrentMember,
        [Measures].[Sales Amount]   )
    /
    ( [Sales Territory].[Sales Territory Hierarchy].CurrentMember.Parent,
      [Measures].[Sales Amount]   )

End
```

Year-over-Year Growth

One of the most common calculations is one that compares sales over one period to those over the same period in the previous year. For example, how do sales in January of 2008 compare to those in January 2009, or how do the sales on February 1st, 2009 compare to those on February 1st, 2008? Such a calculation is shown at work in Figure 18-6.

Year	Quarter	Month	Sales Amount	Growth from Previous Year
⊞ 2005			$3,266,373.66	
⊞ 2006			$6,530,343.53	$3,263,969.87
⊟ 2007	⊞ 1		$1,413,530.30	($378,168.15)
	⊞ 2		$1,623,971.06	($390,041.08)
	⊟ 3	⊞ July	$886,668.84	$386,303.68
		⊞ August	$847,413.51	$301,412.04
		⊞ September	$1,010,258.13	$659,791.14
		Total	$2,744,340.48	$1,347,506.86
	⊞ 4		$4,009,218.46	$2,681,419.14
	Total		$9,791,060.30	$3,260,716.77
⊞ 2008			$9,770,899.74	($20,160.56)
Grand Total			$29,358,677.22	

FIGURE 18-6

You can construct this calculation with the `ParallelPeriod` function, where you point to the Year level of the current member and pass in the number of units you want to go back (one unit of time in the following code):

```
Case
// Test to avoid division by zero.
When IsEmpty
    (
(ParallelPeriod([Order Date].[Calendar Date Drilldown].[Year], 1,
[Order Date].[Calendar Date Drilldown].CurrentMember),[Measures].[Sales Amount])
    )
Then Null

WHEN IsEmpty

    (
[Measures].[Sales Amount]
    )

THEN NULL

Else
([Order Date].[Calendar Date Drilldown].CurrentMember,
[Measures].[Sales Amount])
-
(ParallelPeriod([Order Date].[Calendar Date Drilldown].[Year], 1,
[Order Date].[Calendar Date Drilldown].CurrentMember),[Measures].[Sales Amount])

END
```

There is one major point to highlight before closing this lesson. When you bring a tuple into the calculation in which you're using a given hierarchy or attribute, the query will generally need to have that attribute dragged over into the browser pane as a row or column to use the calculation. For example, if you tried to drag over the Year-over-Year growth calculation but didn't have the accompanying Order Date attributes dragged over, the calculation would show 100 percent or an error.

TRY IT

In this Try It you will work on a more common business problem. Calculations are used to solve common problems like year to year comparisons or profit calculations. In this Try It section, you'll try to determine an average.

Lesson Requirements

Your executives want to see what the average sale per customer visit is. Create a calculation that determines how much the order was for each individual visit. Change the color to red if the average sale falls below $200 in a given category.

Hints

➤ The Internet Sales Count measure contains data about how many customer visits or invoices there are in a given slice of data. If you use it and the Sales Amount measure, you'll have the necessary data.

Step-by-Step

1. Create a new calculation in the Cube Editor in the Calculations tab.

2. Type [Avg Sales Amount Per Visit] in the Name property.

3. Type the following MDX code in the Expression box:

   ```
   [Measures].[Sales Amount] / [Measures].[Internet Sales Count]
   ```

4. Change the Format String property to Currency.

5. Select Internet Sales for the Associated Measure Group.

6. Change the Fore Color property to the following MDX statement:

   ```
   IIF([Avg Sales Amount Per Visit] < 200, 255, 000)
   ```

7. Deploy the new cube changes by selecting Build ➪ Deploy *<Project Name>*.

8. The finished solution should look like the one in Figure 18-7 in the Cube Browser. Notice that if your measure falls below $200, then the cell turns red (the red is not visible in this figure). Otherwise, it remains black.

Year	Quarter	Month	Date	Sales Amount	Avg Sales Amount Per Visit
⊞ 2005				$3,266,373.66	$3,224.46
⊟ 2006	⊞ 1			$1,791,698.45	$3,210.93
	⊟ 2	⊞ April		$663,692.29	$3,206.24
		⊞ May		$673,556.20	$3,147.46
		⊞ June		$676,763.65	$3,162.45
		Total		$2,014,012.13	$3,171.67
	⊟ 3	⊞ July		$500,365.16	$1,977.73
		⊞ August		$546,001.47	$1,943.07
		⊞ September		$350,466.99	$1,770.04
		Total		$1,396,833.62	$1,908.24
	⊟ 4	⊞ October		$415,390.23	$1,813.93
		⊞ November		$335,095.09	$1,736.24
		⊞ December		$577,314.00	$1,749.44
		Total		$1,327,799.32	$1,765.69
	Total			$6,530,343.53	$2,439.43
⊟ 2007	⊞ 1			$1,413,530.30	$1,793.82
	⊟ 2	⊞ April		$506,399.27	$1,722.45
		⊞ May		$562,772.56	$1,679.92
		⊞ June		$554,799.23	$1,728.35
		Total		$1,623,971.06	$1,709.44
	⊟ 3	⊞ July		$886,668.84	$628.40
		⊞ August		$847,413.51	$221.89
		⊞ September		$1,010,258.13	$260.04
		Total		$2,744,340.48	$301.08
	⊞ 4			$4,009,218.46	$295.01
	Total			$9,791,060.30	$400.57
⊞ 2008				$9,770,899.74	$302.83
Grand Total				$29,358,677.22	$486.09

FIGURE 18-7

 Please select Lesson 18 on the DVD to view the video that accompanies this lesson.

19

Data Mining

Data mining is one of the most exciting technologies in the Microsoft BI stack. Did you ever wonder how Amazon.com can recommend such good books for you and generally be right? In this lesson, you'll learn how to use data mining to make predictions, explore your data, and find patterns among your customers that you may not have been aware of.

INTRODUCTION TO DATA MINING

Data mining has been around for decades, but what Microsoft has revolutionized are its ease of use and development. Data mining can solve more grand problems than most technologies at a fairly minimal cost. SQL Server data mining ships with nine algorithms, and more can be added if you're feeling adventurous.

The first algorithm to highlight is the most common: the Decision Tree Algorithm. You can use this if your management wants to know who is classified as a good customer as opposed to a bad customer. While some old-timers in the organization may know this, it's very subjective. Data mining simplifies and automates that classification through the decision tree algorithm. The most practical application for this algorithm is to answer the question "Will this customer buy a product from me if I mail him a brochure?"

Data mining can also find fraud in insurance claims or applications for credit. In this case the Clustering Algorithm measures the insurance claim's distance from similar cases to see whether anything is out of bounds. If the claim is sizably different from its peers, it's flagged as potentially fraudulent.

Yet another application for data mining is the use of the time series algorithm. In this case you can predict what your sales, inventory, or staffing levels need to be three days from now. The Time Series Algorithm is fantastic at predicting a number, like the value of a home based on a trend over time.

A final common data-mining algorithm is the Association Rules Algorithm. Amazon uses something like this algorithm to make book recommendations. Simply put, the algorithm measures what you have in your shopping basket and analyzes what other products you may be interested in based on the shopping habits of your peers.

DATA-MINING PROCESS

The data-mining process consists of five major steps with varying degrees of difficulty. The rest of this lesson walks you through this process across a SQL Server platform, but generally speaking, the process is the same no matter the technology. For medium-complexity projects, you will be able to have the bulk of any data-mining project complete in about a month, but it's all going to come down to the shape of your data.

Understanding the Question

It may seem very simplistic, but it can't be taken for granted that the first step is to understand the question you're trying to answer with data mining. Many technicians want to experiment with data mining but don't have a firm understanding of what question they're trying to answer. Having a business analyst assist in this phase and the next may speed up your project.

It's All About the Data

Data mining is easiest if the data is in a flat table or view that has a single row for each case. A *case* is a row that states an individual incident that you're tracking. For example, you may have a single row per year per home that shows a home's value. You may also have a list of all your customers and a flag for each row that indicates whether he or she bought a certain product from you. There are many ways of structuring the data, and the ETL phase of your project is where you clean the data into an ideal structure.

A data warehouse or cube isn't even required for data mining! All you need is a table that has been denormalized (flattened). You can denormalize the table through views, T-SQL, or ETL. The trick is to get all the data in the table that can help you answer the question.

Data-Mining Model

In this phase of the project you open BIDS and work through creating the data-mining model. You may not get it right the first time. You will add columns that you think influence a buyer's decision, and you may miss data or add the wrong data altogether. Once you create the data-mining solution in BIDS, you can deploy it to the SSAS instance. After deploying the model, you're going to process it, which begins to train the system.

Evaluating the Model

Now that the model is deployed, you need to evaluate it to see whether it's accurate. To do this, you're going to hold back some of your rows before training the model. In SQL Server 2008 this is done automatically, but you can also do it manually through T-SQL or SSIS. After you identify the rows you've held back, you can test the model inside BIDS to determine its accuracy.

Productionalizing the Model

Once you've determined that the mining model is accurate, you can maintain the model by periodically retraining the model as client patterns change. You will also want to make sure the database is backed up with Management Studio.

CREATING A MINING MODEL

In this example you're going to mine the customers to see who is most likely to purchase a bike. After you've identified the problem you want to solve, you're ready to open BIDS and create an SSAS project. You can also use an existing SSAS project, which is what we do for this lesson. Either way, your first step will be to create a data source and a data source view (DSV). For this example you'll use AdventureWorksDW2008 R2 as your data source and include the following tables in the DSV: vTargetMail, vTimeSeries, vAssocSeqOrders, vAssocSecLineItems, ProspectiveBuyers.

> *Throughout this lesson you'll use Lesson18Complete.zip from the Wrox website (www.wrox.com) to start. After downloading it, please deploy the SSAS project to your development server to ensure you're on the same solution. You can also see the final solution in Lesson19Complete.zip.*

As you can see, in the case table vTargetMail the data is flattened, and the table contains a row for each customer with a bit column saying whether the customer bought a product. After you save the DSV, right-click Mining Structures in the Solution Explorer and select New Mining Structure. A *mining structure* is a container of many algorithms (also called *mining models*).

The Data Mining Wizard will create the first mining model and structure to store it. In the first screen you can select whether you want to train the mining model from a relational table or a cube. In our case, and in most cases, you'll select the table option.

The next screen (shown in Figure 19-1) is where you select the data-mining algorithm. There are nine built-in algorithms in SQL Server, but additional algorithms can be created in .NET. Decision Trees is a great one to start with if you're trying to predict who is a good customer. Clustering is a great algorithm for fraud detection, and Time Series is good for predicting a number like a home value or stock price.

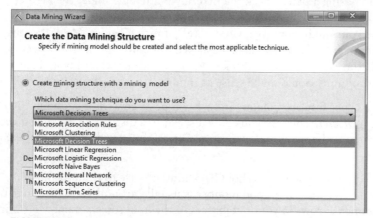

FIGURE 19-1

Once you click Next, you're taken to the screen (shown in Figure 19-2) where you must select the table that holds the data with which you wish to train. In this case select vTargetMail, which holds all your customers. If you had a one-to-many relationship, you could select a child table by checking the Nested option.

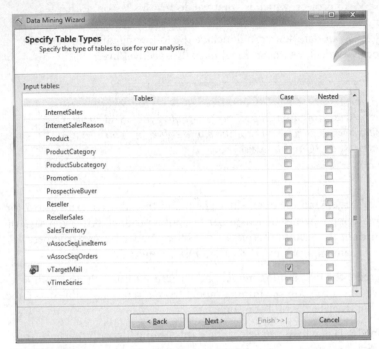

FIGURE 19-2

The next screen is the most important in the wizard. This is where you select the columns that you think will influence someone purchasing a bike. Check the BikeBuyer attribute under the Predict column. This is the column for which you wish to make a prediction. Then check the input columns on which you wish to base your prediction: Age, CommuteDistance, Gender, MaritalStatus, NumberCarsOwned, Region, TotalChildren, YearlyIncome (shown in Figure 19-3). After checking the BikeBuyer column as a predictor, you could have checked Suggest and the wizard would have made some guesses about which columns would make sense as inputs.

Next is where you select the data types for each column and what type of content is stored in each column (shown in Figure 19-4). A *discrete* column holds only a select few distinct values, like a gender column. A *continuous* column could have numerous values. Click Detect to detect which type is best for you automatically.

The next screen asks you how many rows you wish to hold back (and not use to train the model). These rows will later be used to test the model. A good number is usually around 20 to 30 percent, but it depends heavily on the number of rows in your database. On the final screen, name your mining structure **Target Customers**. The mining model should be named something easy that shows what algorithm is being used, like **DT**. You can also allow drilling through in your model if you wish to be able to allow your users to find interesting detail data after they find a pattern.

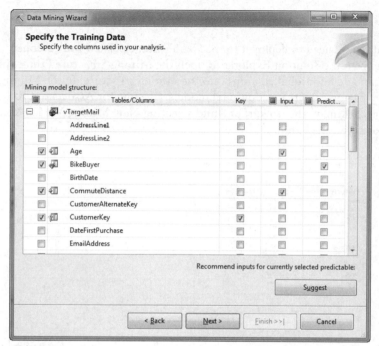

FIGURE 19-3

FIGURE 19-4

EXPLORING THE MODEL

With the structure now created, you'll need to deploy it to the SSAS instance. Then you can open the Target Customers.dmm file from the Solution Explorer to open the Mining Structure Editor. In the Mining Structure tab you can add additional columns into the mining structure. In the Mining Models tab (shown in Figure 19-5) you can create additional models, like one for Association Rules (as) and Clustering (cl), by right-clicking in the background and selecting New Mining Model. You can also set columns to be ignored the algorithm.

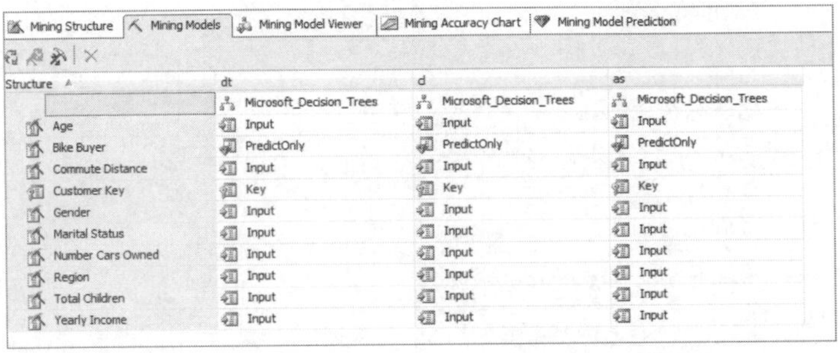

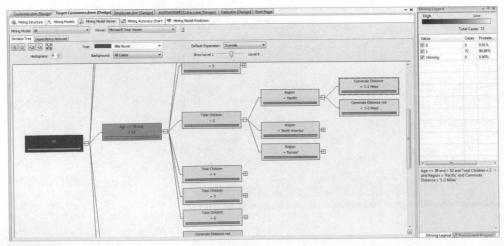

FIGURE 19-5

Once the new models are deployed, you can view them in the Mining Model Viewer tab (shown in Figure 19-6). If you have multiple algorithms, you can select the type of mining model you want to see from the Mining Model drop-down box. From the decision tree algorithm you can see why the mining model made the decisions it made. As you look at the model, you can see that the biggest reasons the mining model thinks a customer is good are on the far left, and as you branch deeper and deeper, the number of your customers who fit each particular condition becomes smaller.

For example, in Figure 19-6 you can see all the way to the right that the customers who fit this condition are 99 percent likely to buy a bike. These customers are between 39 and 53 years old, have two children, live in the Pacific region, and commute one to two miles. The percentage chance of a purchase can be seen in the Mining Legend area.

FIGURE 19-6

EVALUATING THE MODEL

The next phase of your project is to evaluate the model to see whether it's accurate. You can do this in the Mining Accuracy Chart tab shown in Figure 19-7. In the tab you can select the condition for which you're testing. For example, in Figure 19-7, we're trying to see how accurate our three mining models are at predicting the value of the Bike Buyer column's being set to 1, or true.

Select predictable mining model columns to show in the lift chart:

☑ Synchronize Prediction Columns and Values

Show	Mining Model	Predictable Column Name	Predict Value
☑	dt	Bike Buyer	1
☑	d	Bike Buyer	1
☑	as	Bike Buyer	1

FIGURE 19-7

Once you have it configured, you can select the Lift Chart tab to see how accurate the model is. You'll see at least three lines in the tab. The blue line (bottom line) shown in Figure 19-8 shows a coin toss, or a 45-degree angle through the graph. The red line shows the best-case scenario, in which you always predict correctly. The red line (top line) in our case is showing that if we guessed right 100 percent of the time, we'd have all our bike buyers in the first 49 percent of our customers. The yellow line (middle line) shows one of our mining models and how accurate it is. The goal is for the yellow line to be as close to the red line as possible for the best possible accuracy.

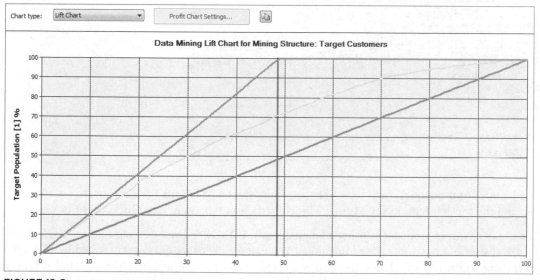

FIGURE 19-8

This tab can also show you how much money you would have made if you had selected each of the mining models by using what-if scenarios. To use that type of scenario planning, simply select Profit Chart from the Chart Type drop-down box.

QUERYING THE MODEL

Now that your model has been created, deployed, and tested, you're ready to start to query it in your application. You can query the model in applications like Reporting Services, Excel, or your own custom application. To query the model from BIDS, go to the Mining Model Prediction tab and click Select Case Table from the table on the right.

In our case we're going to select the vTargetMail table (and, yes, cheat a bit, using the same table for querying that we used for training). Notice that the lines are automatically drawn between the mining model on the left and the table that holds your unknown customers on the right, if the column names match. If they don't, just drag and drop the columns onto each other to create the joins. Double-click any column, like AddressLine1, to have it show in the report. From the left side double-click Bike Buyer to have the mining model predict whether that particular customer is a bike buyer.

Another important function is the prediction function. If you select that option from the grid at the bottom of the Mining Model Prediction tab (shown in Figure 19-9), you can select the PredictProbability function from the Field drop-down box. Then drag the Bike Buyer column into the Criteria/Argument area and add a comma followed by the number 1, or **[dt].[Bike Buyer],1**. In other words, you're asking the probability of the given customer's purchasing a bike.

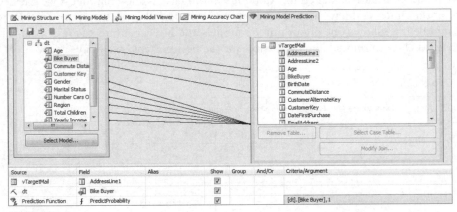

FIGURE 19-9

The results from the query will look like the results shown in Figure 19-10. You can see them by clicking the top-left icon in the Mining Model Prediction tab, Switch to Query Results View.

The query that was produced is using a language called DMX or Data Mining Extensions. It resembles T-SQL closely but has a few added functions. You can see the exact query you created by clicking the Query icon at the top left. This query can be altered to order the results or add additional advanced functions, but once you make changes, it may be impossible to go back to the query design view.

```
SELECT
    t.[AddressLine1],
    [dt].[Bike Buyer],
    PredictProbability([dt].[Bike Buyer],1)
From
    [dt]
PREDICTION JOIN
```

```
OPENQUERY([AdventureWorksDW2008R2],
    'SELECT
        [AddressLine1],
        [MaritalStatus],
        [Gender],
        [YearlyIncome],
        [TotalChildren],
        [NumberCarsOwned],
        [CommuteDistance],
        [Region],
        [Age],
        [BikeBuyer]
    FROM
        [dbo].[vTargetMail]
    ') AS t
ON
    [dt].[Marital Status] = t.[MaritalStatus] AND
    [dt].[Gender] = t.[Gender] AND
    [dt].[Yearly Income] = t.[YearlyIncome] AND
    [dt].[Total Children] = t.[TotalChildren] AND
    [dt].[Number Cars Owned] = t.[NumberCarsOwned] AND
    [dt].[Commute Distance] = t.[CommuteDistance] AND
    [dt].[Region] = t.[Region] AND
    [dt].[Age] = t.[Age] AND
    [dt].[Bike Buyer] = t.[BikeBuyer]
ORDER BY  PredictProbability([dt].[Bike Buyer],1) DESC
```

AddressLine1	Bike Buyer	Expression
3761 N. 14th St	1	0.9999338711...
2243 W St.	0	0.3509521061...
5844 Linden Land	0	0.3509521061...
1825 Village Pl.	1	0.6771825252...
7553 Harness ...	0	0.1973251994...
7305 Humphre...	0	0.4949507093...
2612 Berry Dr	0	0.4949507093...
942 Brook Street	0	0.3509521061...
624 Peabody R...	0	0.1257055153...
3839 Northgat...	0	0.4949507093...
7800 Corrinne ...	0	0.4949507093...
1224 Shoenic	0	0.1154204621...
4785 Scott Street	1	0.5889636640...
7902 Hudson A...	0	0.2607015457...
9011 Tank Drive	0	0.2607015457...

FIGURE 19-10

TRY IT

You've seen in this lesson how to create a mining structure to predict whether a customer was going to purchase a product from you. Now that you've seen that, it's time to explore a different type of algorithm. In this Try It you will predict a continuous number using time series analysis. You can use this type of algorithm to predict stock prices, inventory levels, sales figures, or staffing needs. It does this by doing technical analysis on trends in your numeric data to find dips and bumps in your chart.

Lesson Requirements

In this lesson, you need to build a new mining structure to analyze the vTimeSeries table in the AdventureWorksDWR2 database. Once you build the model, deploy it and review the model in the Data Mining Viewer tab. Lastly, for bonus credit, try to find out how many sales you're going to have in September of 2009 (the future in this table) for the ModelRegion of M200 Europe. The metrics to analyze are Amount and Quantity in the table. Use Region as an influencer.

Hints

➤ Create a new mining structure on vTimeSeries after adding it to the DSV.

➤ Your key should consist of TimeIndex and ModelRegion so you can analyze sales by month by region.

➤ Your Predict columns should be Amount and Quantity.

➤ You can use the PredictTimeSeries prediction function in TimeSeries to predict units of time in the future.

Step-by-Step

1. Make sure you've added vTimeSeries to the main DSV for your project.

2. Right-click Mining Structures and select New Mining Structure.

3. On the Select Definition Method, choose the "From existing relational database or data warehouse" option.

4. On the next screen, select Microsoft Time Series and click Next.

5. Choose the main DSV as your data source and click Next.

6. In the Specify Table Types screen of the wizard, check vTimeSeries and click Next.

7. In the Specify the Training Data screen, check TimeIndex and ModelRegion as your Key columns. Check Amount and Quantity as the Predict columns. The final screen should look like Figure 19-11.

8. Click Detect to determine the data types in the Specify Columns' Content and Data Type screen. This will determine if the values are continuous or discrete.

9. Call the mining structure **Forecast Sales** and the mining model **TS** (for time series). Click Finish and deploy the model to your development SSAS instance.

10. Go to the Mining Model Viewer tab to inspect the model (shown in Figure 19-12). Notice that you can select certain regions from the right-hand drop-down box to see their sales and the quantities that have been and will be sold. You can also see that the dotted line represents future sales and the solid line represents historical sales.

11. To run this particular query against a time series algorithm, you might find it's a little simpler to use Management Studio than it is to run it in BIDS. Open Management Studio and click

the Analysis Services DMX query icon at the top. When prompted, connect to your SSAS database and run the following query:

```
SELECT
[TS].[Model Region],
PredictTimeSeries([TS].[Quantity],6) AS PredictQty,
PredictTimeSeries ([TS].[Amount],6) AS PredictAmt
FROM
[TS]
      WHERE [Model Region] = 'M200 Europe'
```

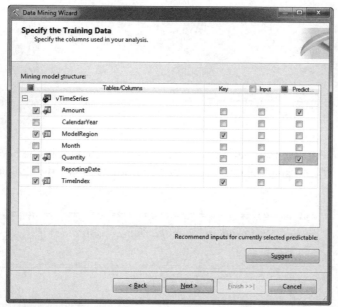

FIGURE 19-11

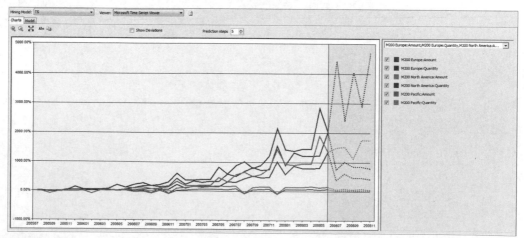

FIGURE 19-12

12. This query will return the results shown in Figure 19-13. The PredictTimeSeries prediction function is used to determine a given amount of units in the future. You passed in six units in the future. Congratulations! You have built your first TimeSeries algorithm.

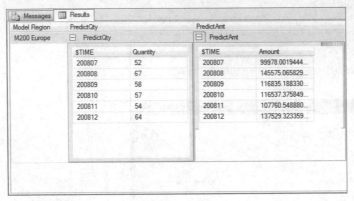

FIGURE 19-13

If you've been intrigued by this data-mining section, you can read more about it in the book *Data Mining with Microsoft SQL Server 2008* by Jamie McLennan, ZhaoHui Tang, and Bogdan Crivat (Wiley, 2008).

 Please select Lesson 19 on the DVD to view the video that accompanies this lesson.

20

Administering the SSAS Instance

In this SSAS section of the book you've seen how to create and browse a cube and mining models. Don't worry, we haven't forgotten the administrator who now has to manage and secure the SSAS instance. This lesson will show you how to secure and optimize the end-user experience. You'll also learn how to process the cube and keep it up to date.

 Throughout this lesson we'll be using Lesson19Complete.zip from the Wrox website (www.wrox.com) to start. After downloading it, please deploy the SSAS project to your development server to ensure you're on the same solution. You can also download the final solution by downloading Lesson20Complete.zip.

SECURING THE DATABASE

As you store more and more data in the cube, security will become a concern. In terms of security SSAS is much like SQL Server: you can secure objects like measures, attributes, cubes, and mining models. But in SSAS you can also secure row-level data so that, for example, the United States manager can see only his own sales. This security is implemented through Active Directory security and security roles on the SSAS database.

You can create security roles in BIDS as a developer or in Management Studio as a DBA. If you operate in Management Studio you must worry about becoming out of sync with the project and being overwritten by the developer. No matter the location, drill down to the Roles folder in BIDS in the Solution Explorer, or in Management Studio in the Object Browser, and select New Role. This creates a new role called Role that you can rename by renaming the Role.Role file in Solution Explorer to BikeViewer.role.

In the General tab you can set the database-wide roles like Full Control. In the Membership tab you can select the Active Directory logins or groups that will be part of this role. In the Cubes tab you can grant read and read/write access to the cube. You can also allow your users to check out the cube with a local cube permission.

In the Cell Data tab you can restrict the measures that can be seen by the user. You can also restrict the dimensions in the Dimensions tab. One of the coolest tabs is the Dimension Data tab (shown in Figure 20-1), where you can set row-level security. To do this, simply drill to the attribute you wish to lock down. Select "Deselect all members" on the left if you wish to remove security for attributes other than the one you check on the right. For example, Figure 20-1 shows you how to configure security to disallow access to all the Category Name attribute's members except Bikes. You can also go to the Advanced tab to create the security dynamically and disallow users from seeing the All total by checking "Enable Visual Totals."

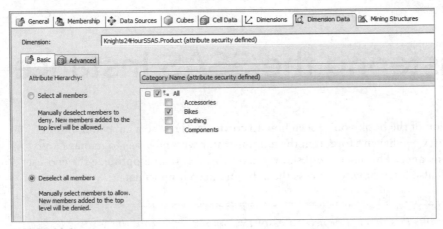

FIGURE 20-1

Once you've configured security you'll need to redeploy the cube to the SSAS instance. To see if your changes took effect, browse the cube and click the Change User icon on the top left. This opens the Security Context dialog box, where you can impersonate a different user by selecting "Other user" or a specific role by selecting the Roles option and choosing the role (as shown in Figure 20-2). You will then see the data that your end users would see if they connected with that account or role. Roles can also be passed into the connection string with the Roles keyword.

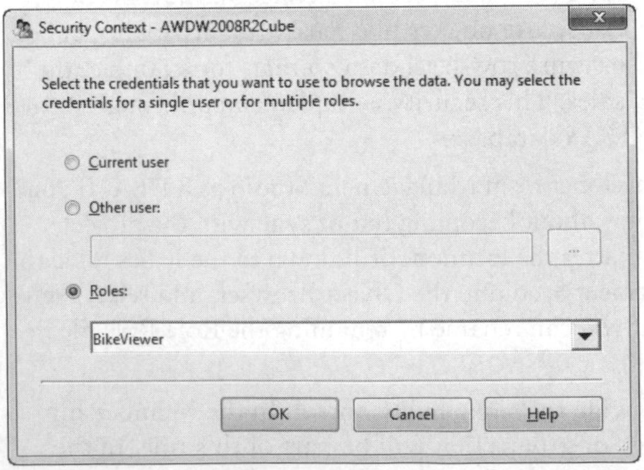

FIGURE 20-2

PARTITIONING THE DATA

As your measure group grows past 20 million rows, it becomes critical for performance to partition the data. There's not a magic number to tell you when to partition, but if you feel performance is beginning to suffer, it's a tool in your toolbox to scale SSAS. You can partition properly only in Enterprise Edition of SQL Server. Partitioning a measure group breaks the files into smaller files, which makes querying and processing much easier for SSAS. Querying SSAS against several partitions is seamless to the users.

To create a partition, open the Cube Editor and go to the Partitions tab. Typically people create partitions by year, quarter, or month. If you have multiple date-slicing columns in your measure group, you want to pick the date that's most popular in filtering.

Before creating a new partition, you must modify the existing one to change its binding type. By default each partition will be bound to a table. These tables can be given different names and then brought together with a partition. The alternative design is to query-bind the partition, as shown in Figure 20-3. In this mode you bind the partition to a query that has a WHERE clause in it that slices the data down to a reasonable number of rows. If you change the Binding type to Query Binding you will find that BIDS automatically converts to a select statement with an open-ended WHERE clause.

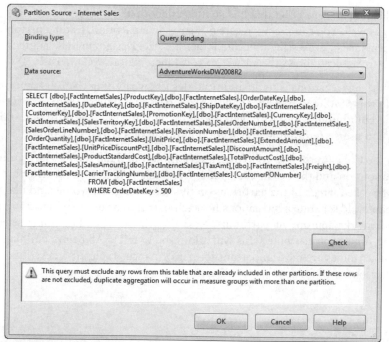

FIGURE 20-3

After restricting the rows of the original partition you are ready to create a new partition by clicking the hyperlink titled New Partition below the desired measure group. Check the table used for this new partition and then click Next. After clicking "Specify a query to restrict rows" you will again see a familiar query screen showing an empty WHERE clause.

Be very careful with how you restrict your rows in the WHERE clause. If an operator is incorrectly identified, it could provide inaccurate data. For example, on the old partition Where DueDateKey < 20071231 *and* Where DueDateKey > 20071231 *would be missing the sales for one day. The reverse mistake could be made as well.* DueDateKey <= 20071231 *and* DueDateKey >= 20071231 *will both duplicate sales for this one day.*

You can optionally store this new partition file on a separate disk if you choose. It is common not only for large measure groups to be partitioned but for those partitions to then be split across multiple disks. The last option you have before completing the partition is to begin an aggregation design, which will be discussed next. Aggregations are not mandatory at this point and you can choose to design them later.

AGGREGATIONS

You've probably built an application at some point that had so much data that you've pre-aggregated data. You can do this in SSAS as well. You can pre-aggregate measures in a partition, trading performance of query time for performance of processing time and larger file size. Designing these aggregations makes it seem as if Analysis Services knows the answer to your query before you even ask.

The best way to get started with aggregations is to do an initial design by running the Aggregation Design Wizard. When you do this SSAS will quickly analyze properties and structures to determine which aggregations should be built into the file. Although the Aggregation Design Wizard does not look at specific queries your end users are running, it is a good building block to start from.

To create aggregations, open the Cube Editor and go to the Aggregations tab. Find the measure group you wish to build the aggregations on and then right-click and select Design Aggregations. After the introduction screen you will be asked which of the partitions on this measure group you would like to build aggregations for. You can build separate aggregations for each partition or use the same design for both aggregations by checking the appropriate partitions. Next the wizard will allow you to select the aggregation to use for each dimension attribute. This will allow you to tell SSAS before building this aggregation design which attributes are most important for performance. Table 20-1 describes each of the possible usage selections.

TABLE 20-1

AGGREGATION USAGE	DESCRIPTION
Default	Runs the attribute through a set of complex rules to determine if it is ideal for aggregations
Full	Indicates that the attribute will be included in every aggregation created by your design. This selection should be used rarely, and only for attributes that are used in almost every query run by users. For example, if almost every query you run has an accounting year in it, fully aggregate the Year attribute in the Accounting Date dimension.

AGGREGATION USAGE	DESCRIPTION
None	Indicates that the attribute will not be included in any aggregations built by your design
Unrestricted	Indicates that no restrictions for this attribute are placed on the wizard. The wizard will determine whether the attribute is useful for aggregations or not.

After setting the aggregation usage you will generate object counts, which will ask you to return a count for each attribute and measure group. You can either hit the Count button to automatically count the rows or manually enter the counts. This is another aspect of determining how important an attribute is to the design.

The last choice you have before aggregation design begins is whether you want to restrict the file that is created by size or by percentage of performance gain. If you would rather watch the aggregation being built and stop the file size from growing at the click of a button you can pick "I click Stop," which means the file will continue to grow and add aggregations until you click the Stop button. Hit the Start button and watch for the design to begin. You will want to watch the red line to see if the line ever levels out while building the aggregations. This indication means you have likely reached a point of diminishing return with your design. Your file size continues to grow, but at what cost? Figure 20-4 shows a design that created a file until the performance gain was 30 percent. The chart shows file size on the horizontal axis and performance gain on the vertical axis.

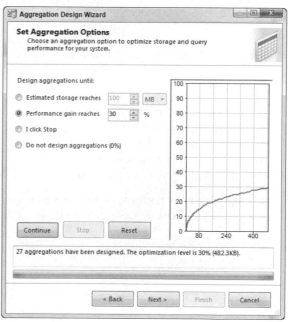

FIGURE 20-4

USAGE-BASED OPTIMIZATION

In addition to using the Aggregation Design Wizard to build your aggregations you can also choose to implement usage-based optimization. When configured, this feature will log specific queries that your users run. You can then build aggregations on those queries. This method not only has the benefit of creating aggregations from user queries, but enables you to filter out queries you don't want. For example, if you want only your CEO's queries to be tuned over everyone else's, you can select his user ID from a filter list. Or if the most important queries are run the last week of the month for end-of-month reporting, you can filter on a date range.

To create aggregations using usage-based optimization you must first do a little setup in Management Studio to capture your users' queries. After connecting to your instance of Analysis Services inside Management Studio, right-click the instance name and select Properties. The four properties you should be concerned with are listed in Table 20-2 along with their descriptions.

TABLE 20-2

PROPERTY	DESCRIPTION	DEFAULT VALUE
Log\QueryLog\CreateQueryLog Table	Determines whether the table is to be created	False
Log\QueryLog\QueryLogConnectionString	Connection string	
Log\QueryLog\QueryLogSampling	Number of queries to log (10 means every tenth query will be stored)	10
Log\QueryLog\QueryLogTableName	Name of the table that will be created	OLAPQueryLog

By changing these properties to create the log table you will be able to configure aggregations based on actual user queries. On the Aggregations tab in the cube designer you can then configure usage-based optimization as an aggregation design. Figure 20-5 shows the wizard and how you can configure it to filter based on dates, users, or query frequency. The rest of the usage-based optimization design is made in the same way as your initial design.

No matter which aggregation design you select, Analysis Services will allow you to merge a new design into an existing design if you desire. This way you get the best of both worlds.

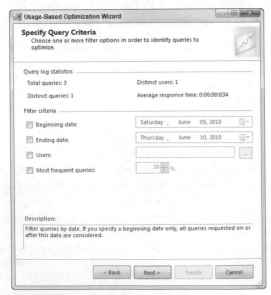

FIGURE 20-5

PROCESSING THE CUBE

Cubes are objects that must be refreshed periodically. In SSAS you can do this automatically with a feature called *proactive caching* if you have Enterprise Edition. Most people want to control the refreshing of the cube on their own schedule and do it manually through an SQL Server Agent job or in the ETL using SSIS.

When you select the cube you wish to process you will see many different processing options, as shown in Table 20-3. Depending on the options you select, different Analysis Services objects may be processed.

TABLE 20-3

PROCESSING OPTION	DESCRIPTION
Process Default	The server checks for all objects that haven't been processed and only processes those.
Process Full	The server processes structure, data, and aggregations.
Process Data	The server only processes data.
Process Structure	The server processes cube definitions without data.
Unprocess	The server clears the data in the cube.
Process Index	The server processes only aggregations.
Process Incremental	You provide a query that has the new fact data to be processed.

If you choose to process your cube in an SSIS package you will use the Analysis Services Processing task and then select one of the options shown in Table 20-3. Another common technique for refreshing cube data is to script the XMLA required for reprocessing. If you connect to the Analysis Services in Management Studio and right-click the desired cube you will see an option called Process. This option will walk you through the steps for processing your cube immediately, but you can also select the Script button, which produces the XMLA code needed for reprocessing. You can then use this script in a SQL Server Agent job with the SQL Server Analysis Services Command step type to schedule your processing at your convenience.

DEPLOYING CHANGE

As you continue to make changes to your cube during development you will frequently need to update your test and production environments with features that you have tirelessly added. Luckily, SSAS has many built-in tools for deploying changes to multiple environments. The Deployment Wizard and Synchronize Database Wizard will make life a little easier for you as you move through the development life cycle.

The Deployment Wizard is likely your first step when you make your first deployment to another machine. The wizard is the only item found under the Analysis Services folder if you navigate to the

Microsoft SQL Server 2008 R2 folder from your Start menu. Figure 20-6 shows it is expecting you to supply it with an .asdatabase file, which you can find by navigating to the bin folder of the project you have been working on.

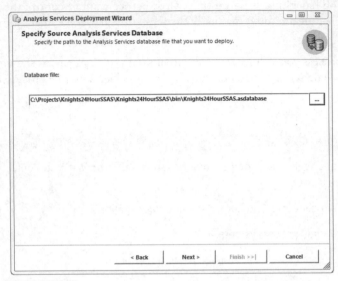

FIGURE 20-6

After you provide the .asdatabase file, the wizard will ask what server you wish to deploy to. A really nice feature of this tool is that it allows you to retain the roles and partitions that already exist if you are overwriting an existing SSAS database, so if you have a database administrator who manages security and partitions on the other server you will not overwrite the objects he or she has already created. You can also optionally change the data source connection before deployment. If the project you are working on is pointing to a development database you can change it to point to a production database before deploying.

The Synchronize Database Wizard has many of the same features as the Deployment Wizard. You will find this tool in Management Studio when connected to an instance of Analysis Services. By right-clicking the Databases folder in the Object Explorer you will find the Synchronize option. This will walk you through the steps of syncing an Analysis Services database on your current server with one on another server. You cannot use this wizard to sync databases on the same server. All the options you find here will be the same as the ones in the Deployment Wizard.

Now that you have learned about many of the tools that can be used for administering Analysis Services, try it in the next section by creating your own partitions and then designing aggregations to help increase performance.

TRY IT

In this Try It, you will learn how to manipulate a measure group so it is split into two partitions. Then you will build an aggregation design on both partitions to further improve query performance.

Lesson Requirements

For this example you will need the completed Lesson 19, which can be downloaded from www.wrox.com. Performance has become a concern as you have added more to your cube design. You will implement multiple partitions on the Internet Sales measure group. After the partitions are added you will build an aggregation design that will be shared across both partitions.

Hints

➤ Edit the original partition on the Internet Sales measure group to store all rows with an OrderDateKey less than or equal to 20071231.

➤ Create a new partition on the same measure group that stores all rows with an OrderDateKey greater than 20071231.

➤ Build an aggregation design that will provide 30 percent optimization.

Step-by-Step

1. Open the Knights24HourSSAS Analysis Services project that was developed in Lesson 19, or download the completed lesson from www.wrox.com.

2. In the Solution Explorer double-click AWDW2008R2Cube.cube to open the cube designer.

3. Navigate to the Partitions table and click the ellipsis in the Internet Sales measure group next to the source property to restrict the rows sent to the original partition.

4. Switch the binding type from Table Binding to Query Binding and add **OrderDateKey <= 20071231** after the WHERE clause, as shown in Figure 20-7. Click OK.

FIGURE 20-7

5. Click the New Partition link under the Internet Sales measure group to create the second partition.

6. After the intro screen select InternetSales from the "Available tables" list. (If you do not see it listed click Find Tables.) Click Next.

7. Check the "Specify a query to restrict rows" option, which will generate a select query with an empty WHERE clause, much like the first partition.

8. This time type **OrderDateKey > 20071231** after the WHERE clause and click Next. Be careful not to mix operator signs (greater than) with the first partition created. This could cause either duplicate or missing data for certain days.

9. Click Next to store the new partition in the default location.

10. Name the partition **Internet Sales New** before clicking Finish to start creating the aggregation design.

11. After clicking Next past the intro screen, ensure all attributes are set to build aggregations based on the default settings. Click Next.

12. Click the Count button on the Specify Object Counts page before clicking Next. This will generate a count for each dimension attribute.

13. Under the "Design aggregations until" option, click the "Performance gain reaches 30%" radio button. This means the aggregation file will continue to grow until there is a 30 percent performance gain.

14. Hit the Start button and watch the design being graphed, as shown in Figure 20-8.

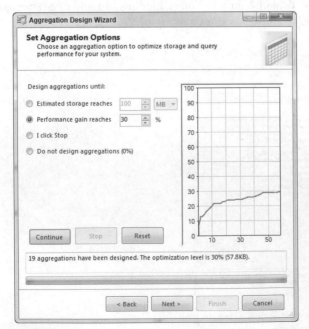

FIGURE 20-8

15. Click Next once the design is finished.

16. Rename the design **InitialAggDesign** and select "Deploy and process now" to go ahead and add these new features to the cube.

Congratulations! You have completed the Analysis Services section of this book. This book is designed to give you the luxury to jump around to any section you need. It will now focus on the presentation layers available in BI. These include Reporting Services, Excel, PowerPivot, SharePoint, and Performance Point. This SSAS section is complete, but that doesn't mean you've seen the last of SSAS in this book. Each of the presentation applications will use Analysis Services as the backend tool for displaying your data.

 Please select Lesson 20 on the DVD to view the video that accompanies this lesson.

SECTION IV
SQL Server Reporting Services

21

Understanding SSRS

In any business it is important to be able to view your data. SQL Server Reporting Services (SSRS) gives developers the tools needed to show data to the end users in a report format that is easy to understand. An end user can be anyone in a company, from a secretary to the CEO. When the end users have good data presented in an easy-to-understand format, it allows them to make informed business decisions. Questions often asked in a corporate boardroom can be answered by good reports — questions like "Which customers are most likely to close their accounts?" "Should we be open on Saturday?" and "How much should we spend on advertising?" Just taking a stab in the dark with these questions can be the death of a company. Having the right data in front of the company's decision-makers can avert costly mistakes.

Reports can also show predictions about whether profits will go up or down. This can help in determining staffing, in scheduling, and in predicting overhead cost. Predictions like this are based on algorithms built into tools like SQL Server Analysis Services. Reporting Services gives you a way to present these predictions in the form of tables, matrixes, maps, charts, and graphs. With these reports in hand, the end users will be confident they are making informed choices for the company.

As a report developer or a Business Intelligence consultant, you must create these reports. Therefore it is important to become familiar with the tools used in creating them. SQL Server Reporting Services 2008 R2 has many reporting tools to show the data. Before you get into showing the data to the users, you need to understand how to get this data into Reporting Services.

Some of the key concepts covered in this chapter include data sources, data sets, some of the Toolbox items, designing a basic table report, and finalizing reports. These concepts are the cornerstone of understanding and developing good reports in Reporting Services.

BUILDING YOUR FIRST REPORT

Assume your manager has asked you to build a report showing a list of your company's products. This product data is held in your product table. The columns your manager wants on the report are Product ID, Name, Color, List Price, Standard Cost, Sell Start Date, and Sell End Date. She wants the report to have a header showing the report title and the date on which the report ran. She also wants a page footer showing the page number and total page count.

The first step is to open Business Intelligence Development Studio (BIDS) and create a report project. The shortcut to BIDS can be found in your Start menu under SQL Server 2008 R2. After opening BIDS you can click File and then New Project to bring up the New Project window seen in Figure 21-1. In the left-hand pane select Business Intelligence Projects. In the right-hand pane select Report Server Project. Enter a name for the project in the bottom of the New Project window and click OK. You have created a Report Server Project.

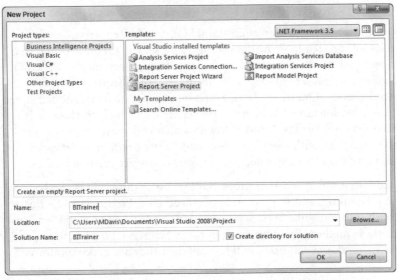

FIGURE 21-1

On the left-hand side of the screen you should see the Solution Explorer, as shown in Figure 21-2. If it is not visible, the window positions have been customized. The following chapters on Reporting Services will assume the windows in BIDS are in their default configuration. To reset the windows to their default positions you can click Reset Window Layout under the Window drop-down at the top of BIDS. You can also find the shortcut for many windows under the View menu, also at the top of BIDS.

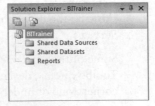

FIGURE 21-2

In the Solution Explorer you will find three folders:

➤ Shared Data Sources

➤ Shared Datasets

➤ Reports

The first item you need to create is a shared data source. A *shared data source* contains the server name and the name of the database where the report will query data. To create a shared data source, right-click the Shared Data Sources folder and select Add New Data Source. In the Name box type in **AW**. This represents the Adventure Works database. Make sure the type is set to Microsoft SQL Server. Click Edit and then select the name of your server from the Server drop-down menu. Or you may want to type in the name of the server. The drop-down menu tends to take a long time to render the server list. In the Database Name box enter **AdventureWorks2008R2**. Your windows should look similar to what is shown in Figure 21-3. (The server name may be different.) AdventureWorks2008R2 is the free sample database from Microsoft. You can download this database from www.codeplex.com.

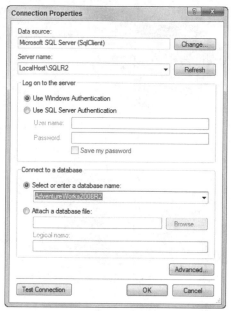

FIGURE 21-3

The *shared data set* is a new feature added to SQL Server R2. A shared data set will contain a query or call a stored procedure to retrieve data from a data source. To create a shared data set right-click the Shared Datasets folder and select Add New Data Set. Give the data set the name **Products**. Ensure that AW is selected in the Data Source drop-down menu. In this example, the following query is used:

```
Select ProductId, Name, ListPrice, StandardCost, SellEndDate, SellStartDate
From Production.Product
```

This query will retrieve the needed columns from the product table in our database. Your data set should look like the one shown in Figure 21-4. Click OK to close the data set and you will see the data set named Products under the Shared Datasets folder in the Solution Explorer. Shared data sources and shared data sets can be used by multiple reports in a project, hence *shared*.

This example will be a simple report that contains a table with the data from the shared data set created earlier. Right-click the Reports folder in the Solution Explorer on the right and select Add and then New Item. Select Report in the New Item window. Change the name of the report to **Products.rdl** and click Add. You have now created a blank report and the data set you want to show on the report. You will add these to the Products report.

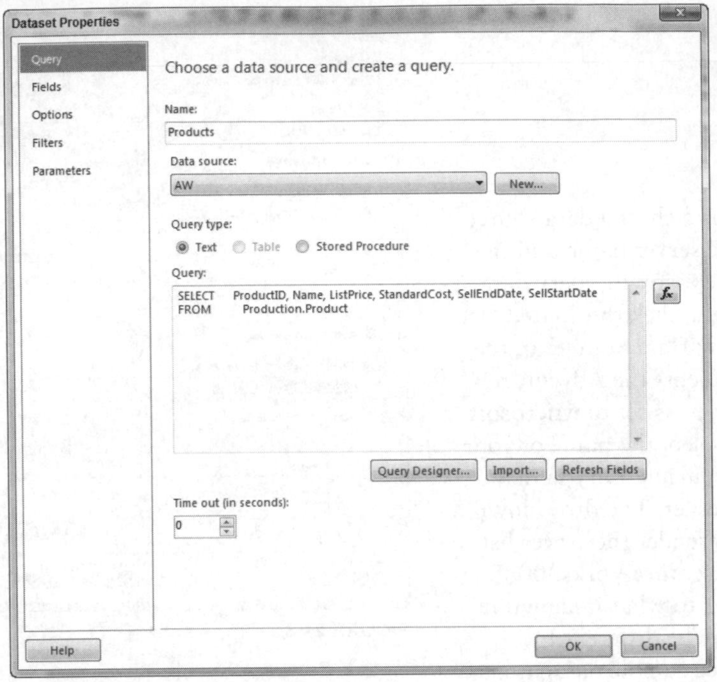

FIGURE 21-4

On the left-hand side of the screen you will see the Report Data window. This window will hold all the data sources and data sets the report will use. Right-click the Data Sources folder in the Report Data window and select Add Data Source. In the Data Source Properties window name the data source **AW**. Click the radio button next to "Use shared data source reference." Then select AW from the drop-down menu. The window should look like the one in Figure 21-5.

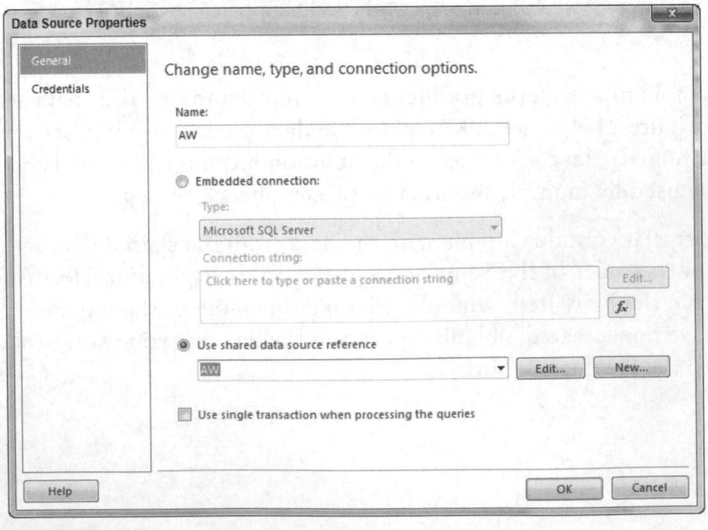

FIGURE 21-5

The next item for you to create is the data set. This example will use the shared data set you already created. Right-click the Datasets folder in the Report Data window and select Add Dataset. In the Dataset Properties window, name the data set **Products** and click the radio button next to "Use a shared dataset." Select the Products data set and click OK. This will create a data set on the report from the shared data set you created earlier. You will now see the data set and the columns in the data set in the Report Data window, as in Figure 21-6.

FIGURE 21-6

Putting Items on the Report

Now you are ready to put items on the report. The Toolbox should be showing on the left-hand side of the screen. You may see a tab at the bottom of the Report Data window for the Toolbox. If not, you can open the Toolbox by clicking View and then Toolbox in the menu at the top of BIDS. From the Toolbox drag over a table and drop it in the top left-hand corner of the *report body*. The report body is the white box in the center of the screen.

In the table you will see a header row and a data row. From the report data window we are going to drag each column onto the table. Drag ProductID into the first column on the left of the table. Then drag Name into the second column and ListPrice into the third column. You can continue adding columns to the report by dragging over the remaining columns. The table will automatically create the new columns. The trick is to watch for the "I

FIGURE 21-7

beam" that appears between columns and at the end of the table while dragging a column over it. Figure 21-7 shows this beam. When you see this beam, it indicates a new column will be created there. Continue dragging all the columns onto the table.

Previewing and Formatting the Report

You can now preview the report by clicking the Preview tab above the report body. Your report should look like the one in Figure 21-8.

Product ID	Name	List Price	Standard Cost	Sell End Date	Sell Start Date
1	Adjustable Race	0.0000	0.0000		6/1/2002 12:00:00 AM
2	Bearing Ball	0.0000	0.0000		6/1/2002 12:00:00 AM
3	BB Ball Bearing	0.0000	0.0000		6/1/2002 12:00:00 AM
4	Headset Ball Bearings	0.0000	0.0000		6/1/2002 12:00:00 AM
316	Blade	0.0000	0.0000		6/1/2002 12:00:00 AM
317	LL Crankarm	0.0000	0.0000		6/1/2002 12:00:00 AM

FIGURE 21-8

Notice that the report will need a few adjustments to fix the format of the data. For example, the List Price and Standard Cost columns are not formatted to look like currency, and the date columns show the time. Click the Design tab, which is next to the Preview tab, and you can fix some of these problems.

Right-click SellEndDate in the table. (Make sure you are clicking the data and not the header. The data is below the header and has square brackets around the label.) Select Text Box Properties. Click Number in the left-hand pane. Then click Date under Category and select the date format labeled 1/31/2000, shown in Figure 21-9. Click OK and repeat the same steps for SellStartDate.

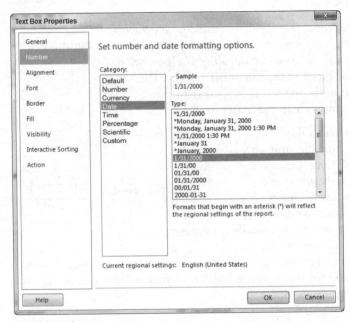

FIGURE 21-9

Right-click ListPrice and select Text Box Properties again. Click Number in the left-hand pane. Then click Currency under Category, leave the default settings, and click OK. Perform the same steps on StandardCost. Drag the right-hand side of the Name column to the right to increase the width of the columns. This will prevent the product names from word-wrapping on the report. Now preview the report and it should resemble the one in Figure 21-10.

You now know where the essential tools for report-building are in BIDS. The ability to query the needed data is crucial in creating reports. Each report you build in BIDS will start with a data source and a data set. These can be shared or just report-level items. If they are shared, they can be used by any other report in the project and by other reports on the report server once they are deployed.

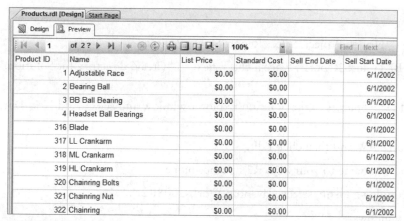

FIGURE 21-10

TRY IT

In this Try It you will learn to create your first report in BIDS. This will be a basic report consisting of one table and some simple formatting. Your manager wants to create a list of everyone in the Employee table. She wants to see the columns LoginID, JobTitle, BirthDate, HireDate, and VacationHours.

Lesson Requirements

In this lesson you will create a report project and a report. The report will contain the employee information from AdventureWorks2008R2. You will also create a data source and a shared data set and format the report to make it easier to read.

You will need the AdventureWorks2008R2 database. This database is free from www.codeplex.com. You will also need to know the name of your SQL Server R2 instance. If it is your default instance, you can use LocalHost as the server name.

 The download for this lesson available at www.wrox.com *includes the queries for this lesson.*

Hints

➤   Do not use the Report Wizard. This is covered in the next chapter.

➤   This report will have a single table.

➤   You will format the table using Text Box Properties.

Step-by-Step

1. In BIDS, click File ⇨ New ⇨ Project. Select Report Server Project.

2. Name the Project **BI Trainer Reports**. Place a check next to "Create directory for Solution." Click OK.

3. Right-click Shared Data Sources in the Solution Explorer window and select Add New Data Source.

4. Name the data source **AW** and then click Edit.

5. Set the server name box name to your SQL R2 instance name.

6. In the database drop-down menu, select AdventureWorks2008R2.

7. Click OK in both windows.

8. Right-click the Shared Datasets folder in the Solution Explorer and select Add New Dataset.

9. Name the data set **Employees** and use the following query in the data set:

```
SELECT      LoginID, JobTitle, BirthDate, HireDate, VacationHours
FROM        HumanResources.Employee
```

Click OK.

 The queries used in this lesson are available as part of the download available for this book at www.wrox.com.

10. Right-click the Reports folder in the Solution Explorer and select Add ⇨ New Item.

11. Select Report, name the report **Employees.rdl,** and click OK.

12. Right-click the Data Sources folder in the Report Data window on the right side of the screen and select Add Data Source.

13. Name the data source AW.

14. Click the radio button next to "Use shared data source reference."

15. Select AW from the Data Source drop-down menu and click OK.

16. Right-click the Data sets folder in the Report Data window and select Add Dataset.

17. Name the data set **Employees** and select the shared Employees data set in the bottom pane of the Dataset Properties window. Click OK.

18. Drag a table from the Toolbox onto the report body and place it in the top left of the report body.

19. From the Report Data window drag LoginID into the first column on the table.

20. Drag Job Title into the second column on the table.

21. Drag BirthDate into the third column.

22. Drag HireDate to the right of the third column and a colored bar will appear to the right of the last column; drop the column here to create a new column with HireDate.

23. Drag over vacation hours and create a new column to the right of the HireDate column using the method in the previous step.

24. Click the Preview tab and the report should resemble the one in Figure 21-11.

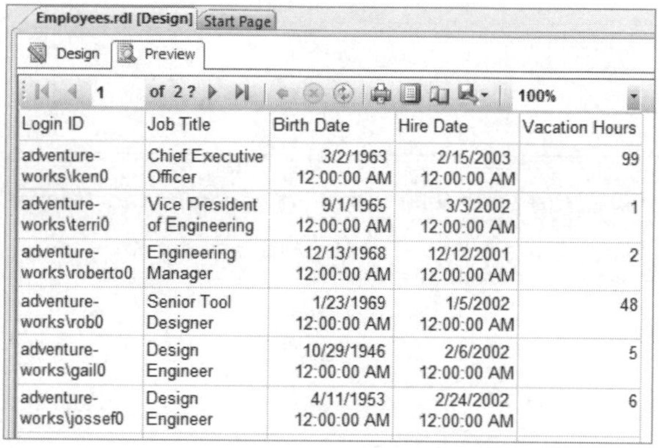

FIGURE 21-11

25. Click the Design tab.

26. Drag the right-hand side of the LoginID column to the right to increase the width of the column to about double the original width.

27. Repeat the previous step for the Job Title column.

28. Right-click BirthDate on the second row and select Text Box Properties.

29. Click Number in the left pane.

30. Select Date in the Category field.

31. Select the date format labeled 1/31/2000 and click OK.

32. Repeat the previous four steps for the HireDate Column.

33. Preview the report. It should resemble the one in Figure 21-12.

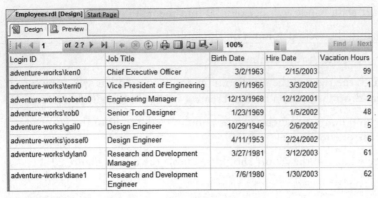

FIGURE 21-12

 Please select Lesson 21 on the DVD to view the video that accompanies this lesson.

22

Using Report Wizard

Building reports in BIDS manually — that is, without using the Report Wizard — gives you the ability to customize every property. This lets you control the appearance of the report down to the tiniest detail. Of course you may not need this level of control. If your manager wants a quick report and does not want to worry about the specifics of its appearance, the Report Wizard is the tool to use.

The Report Wizard is a walkthrough tool that asks several questions and automatically creates a report based on your answers. It does not enable you to make adjustments during the process. After you run the Report Wizard you can adjust the report, so the wizard can be used as a launching pad for your report, and you can finish the fine-tuning in BIDS manually.

The wizard can be launched in two ways.

If you are starting a new report project, launch the wizard by clicking File ⇨ New ⇨ Project and select Report Server Project Wizard.

If you already have a report project open, launch the wizard by right-clicking the Report folder in the Solution Explorer window and selecting Add New Report.

The first screen you see in the wizard is a welcome screen. (This screen offers you the option to hide it in the future.) The next screen is where you select the data source for your report. If you have a shared data source on your project, you will be able to select it from the Shared Data Sources drop-down menu. If not, select New Data Source and create a data source as described in the previous lesson. You can also check the option at the bottom of the screen to make the new data source a shared data source. Figure 22-1 shows the data source selection screen with the shared data source AW selected.

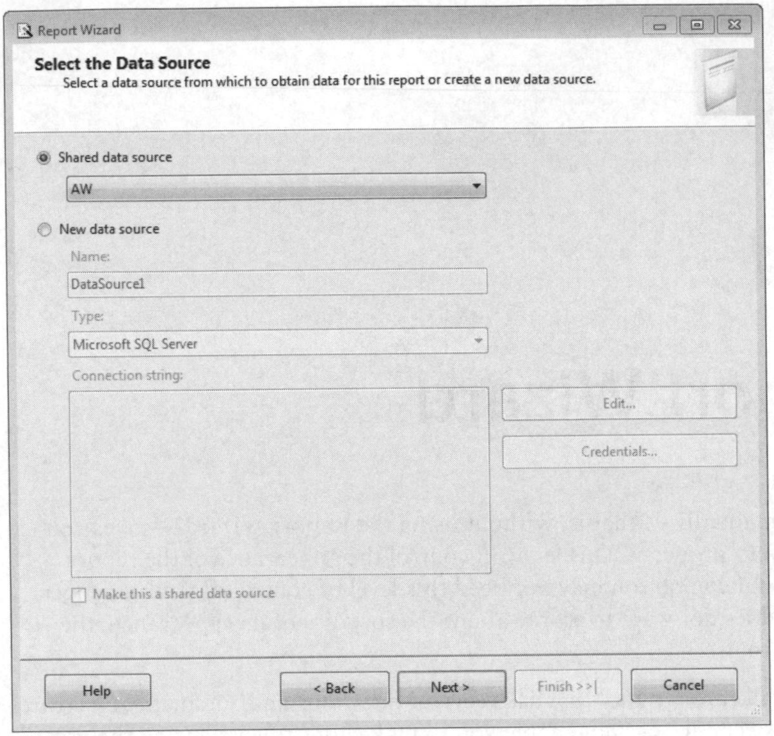

FIGURE 22-1

The next screen of the Report Wizard is the query design screen. You may also use the Query Builder to create the query. The Query Builder helps you graphically build a query. For this example the query will be as follows:

```
SELECT      ProductID, Name, ListPrice, StandardCost, SellStartDate,
            SellEndDate
FROM        Production.Product
```

This query will pull data about the products in the AdventureWorks database. The next screen prompts you to select either a tabular or a matrix report type. If you select tabular, the next screen will have the display fields for a table. If you select matrix, the next screen will show a Column option also. A table does not have column grouping, so that option is not shown when you select Tabular. In a later chapter you will learn about matrix reports.

The three display fields for tabular reports are Page, Group, and Details. Page separates the data by a field onto its own pages. Group groups the data by the selected field in individual row groups. Details shows the selected fields in the columns on the table. To add fields, highlight the field you want to add and click the Page, Group, or Details button. You can see in Figure 22-2 that all the fields have been added to the Details field.

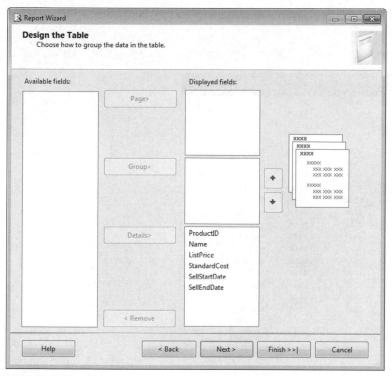

FIGURE 22-2

On the next screen you are able to select a color scheme to apply to the report. These are predefined color schemes that come with SQL Server 2008 R2. The table style choices are as follows:

➤ **Slate:** Blue and gray

➤ **Forest:** Light and dark green

➤ **Corporate:** Light and dark purple

➤ **Bold:** Maroon and red

➤ **Ocean:** Blue and light blue

➤ **Generic:** No colors

The last screen prompts you for a report name. This should be a name that describes what is going to be shown on the report. You may also click the Preview Report checkbox at the bottom. This will cause the report to jump directly to preview mode in BIDS once the report is created. Once you enter a name and click Next, the report will be created.

Previewing the report shows that it needs a few adjustments to clean up the presentation. The Date and Currency fields need to be formatted correctly and the column widths need to be increased. You learned how to do these things in the previous chapter. Figure 22-3 shows the report after all the adjustments have been completed. Notice that the wizard has placed a report title, "Products," at the top of the report in a text box.

Product ID	Name	List Price	Standard Cost	Sell Start Date	Sell End Date
1	Adjustable Race	$0.00	$0.00	6/1/2002	
2	Bearing Ball	$0.00	$0.00	6/1/2002	
3	BB Ball Bearing	$0.00	$0.00	6/1/2002	
4	Headset Ball Bearings	$0.00	$0.00	6/1/2002	
316	Blade	$0.00	$0.00	6/1/2002	
317	LL Crankarm	$0.00	$0.00	6/1/2002	
318	ML Crankarm	$0.00	$0.00	6/1/2002	
319	HL Crankarm	$0.00	$0.00	6/1/2002	
320	Chainring Bolts	$0.00	$0.00	6/1/2002	
321	Chainring Nut	$0.00	$0.00	6/1/2002	
322	Chainring	$0.00	$0.00	6/1/2002	
323	Crown Race	$0.00	$0.00	6/1/2002	
324	Chain Stays	$0.00	$0.00	6/1/2002	
325	Decal 1	$0.00	$0.00	6/1/2002	
326	Decal 2	$0.00	$0.00	6/1/2002	
327	Down Tube	$0.00	$0.00	6/1/2002	
328	Mountain End Caps	$0.00	$0.00	6/1/2002	
329	Road End Caps	$0.00	$0.00	6/1/2002	
330	Touring End Caps	$0.00	$0.00	6/1/2002	
331	Fork End	$0.00	$0.00	6/1/2002	

FIGURE 22-3

The dataset created by the wizard is given a generic name like Dataset1. Notice that the Report Wizard does not give you the option to select a shared dataset either. This is a limitation of the wizard, but you can rename and convert the dataset that was created by the wizard so that it is a shared dataset. Right-click the dataset in the Report Data window, select Data Properties, and change the name to a descriptive one. (The preceding example should probably be named Products.) After you close the Dataset Properties window, right-click the newly renamed dataset and click Convert to Shared Dataset. You will now see the dataset in the Shared Dataset folder in the Solution Explorer window.

Using the Report Wizard is a great way to get started quickly on a report. Just keep in mind that there will be a lot of cleanup needed after the wizard is run. The report needs to be adjusted and the dataset needs to be renamed. The wizard is not a good option if you have already created a shared dataset that you want to use in the report.

TRY IT

In this Try It you will learn to use the Report Wizard to create a tabular report showing all employees.

Lesson Requirements

In this lesson you will build a new report. You will use the Report Wizard. This report will contain the employee information from AdventureWorks.

You will need the AdventureWorks2008R2 database. This database is free from www.codeplex.com. You will also need to know the name of your SQL Server R2 instance. If it is your default instance, you can use LocalHost as the server name.

 The download for this lesson available at www.wrox.com *includes the queries for this lesson.*

Hints

➤ Use the Report Wizard; do not manually build the report.

➤ This report will have a single table.

➤ You will format the table using Text Box Properties.

Step-by-Step

FIGURE 22-4

1. Open the project BI Trainer Reports that you created in the previous chapter.

2. Right-click the Reports folder in the Solution Explorer.

3. Select Add New Report, shown in Figure 22-4.

4. Click Next on the welcome screen if it appears.

5. Select the shared data source named AW. Click Next.

6. Enter the following query into the Query window:

```
SELECT     LoginID, JobTitle, BirthDate, HireDate, VacationHours
FROM       HumanResources.Employee
```

Click Next.

7. Select Tabular as the report type and click Next.

8. Add all fields to the Details window by clicking the Details button five times. The end result will look like what is shown in Figure 22-5. Click Next.

9. Select Slate, then click Next.

10. Name the report **EmployeeList**. Then click Finish.

11. Click the Preview tab. The preview should look like what is shown in Figure 22-6.

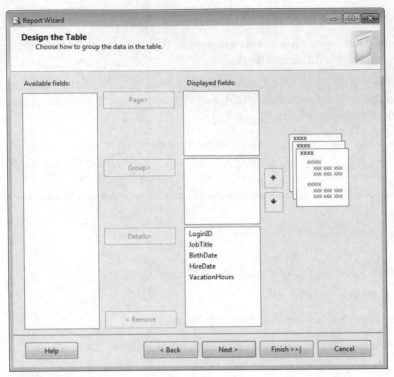

FIGURE 22-5

Login ID	Job Title	Birth Date	Hire Date	Vacation Hours
EmployeeList				
adventure-works\ken0	Chief Executive Officer	3/2/1963 12:00:00 AM	2/15/2003 12:00:00 AM	99
adventure-works\terri0	Vice President of Engineering	9/1/1965 12:00:00 AM	3/3/2002 12:00:00 AM	1
adventure-works\roberto0	Engineering Manager	12/13/1968 12:00:00 AM	12/12/2001 12:00:00 AM	2
adventure-works\rob0	Senior Tool Designer	1/23/1969 12:00:00 AM	1/5/2002 12:00:00 AM	48
adventure-works\gail0	Design Engineer	10/29/1946 12:00:00 AM	2/6/2002 12:00:00 AM	5
adventure-works\jossef0	Design Engineer	4/11/1953 12:00:00 AM	2/24/2002 12:00:00 AM	6
adventure-works\dylan0	Research and Development Manager	3/27/1981 12:00:00 AM	3/12/2003 12:00:00 AM	61
adventure-works\diane1	Research and Development Engineer	7/6/1980 12:00:00 AM	1/30/2003 12:00:00 AM	62
adventure-works\gigi0	Research and Development Engineer	2/21/1973 12:00:00 AM	2/17/2003 12:00:00 AM	63
adventure-works\michael6	Research and Development Manager	1/1/1979 12:00:00 AM	6/4/2003 12:00:00 AM	16
adventure-	Senior Tool	2/18/1972	1/5/2005	7

FIGURE 22-6

12. Click the Design tab.

13. Stretch the LoginID and Job Title columns by grabbing the right-hand side of each and stretching it to accommodate the data.

14. Right-click on the BirthDate text box and select Text Box Properties.

15. Select Number from the left-hand pane.

16. Select Date from the Category window and select the date formatted 1/31/2000. Then click OK.

17. Repeat the previous three steps for the HireDate field.

18. Click the Preview tab. The report should resemble the one in Figure 22-7.

EmployeeList

Login ID	Job Title	Birth Date	Hire Date	Vacation Hours
adventure-works\ken0	Chief Executive Officer	3/2/1963	2/15/2003	99
adventure-works\terri0	Vice President of Engineering	9/1/1965	3/3/2002	1
adventure-works\roberto0	Engineering Manager	12/13/1968	12/12/2001	2
adventure-works\rob0	Senior Tool Designer	1/23/1969	1/5/2002	48
adventure-works\gail0	Design Engineer	10/29/1946	2/6/2002	5
adventure-works\jossef0	Design Engineer	4/11/1953	2/24/2002	6
adventure-works\dylan0	Research and Development Manager	3/27/1981	3/12/2003	61
adventure-works\diane1	Research and Development Engineer	7/6/1980	1/30/2003	62
adventure-works\gigi0	Research and Development Engineer	2/21/1973	2/17/2003	63

FIGURE 22-7

 Please select Lesson 22 on the DVD to view the video that accompanies this lesson.

23

Building a Matrix Report

In the previous lessons you built reports using a table. This type of report is referred to as *tabular*. Tabular reports are good for displaying data that is not grouped or that may only have column groups. What if your reports need to be grouped by columns also? This is where the *matrix report* will be used. The matrix report allows row groups and column groups.

The matrix report is created in the same way as the table reports in the previous lessons. You will drag a matrix tool onto the report body instead of the table. The query will need to have enough data to allow grouping on columns and rows. If you are pulling sales data you might want to group the sales by store on the rows and by year on the columns.

Viewing the data in row and column groups like this is very typical for those querying a data warehouse or a cube. If you use the following query from the AdventureWorks data warehouse it will give you enough data to group on the columns and rows:

```
Select    e.EmployeeKey
   ,e.SalesTerritoryKey
   ,e.FirstName + ' '
+ e.LastName AS FullName
   ,d.CalendarYear as Year
   ,SUM(s.OrderQuantity) AS TotalQuantity
   ,SUM(s.SalesAmount) AS TotalSales
From DimEmployee e
   Join FactResellerSales s on
s.EmployeeKey = e.EmployeeKey
   Join DimDate d on
d.DateKey = s.OrderDateKey
Where e.EndDate is null
Group By e.EmployeeKey
   ,e.FirstName
   ,e.LastName
   ,e.SalesTerritoryKey
   ,d.CalendarYear
```

The preceding query gives you the total sales amount and quantity of sales. It also shows the year of the sales and the sales territory for the employee in question. We can now group this data by sales territory on the rows and year on the columns. The intersection of these column and row groups will be the sales data.

A report with a blank matrix is shown in Figure 23-1. This was created using the same procedures used in the previous two lessons. The only difference is that a matrix was placed on the report instead of a table and the data source connects to the database AdventureWorksDW2008. There is a dataset named Sales using the preceding query.

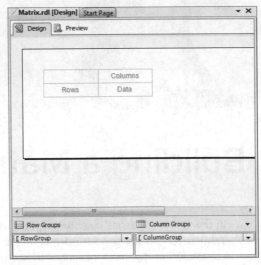

After you have the data source and dataset created and the blank matrix on the report body, you can start dragging the fields from the dataset onto the matrix. The matrix is made up of four sections. It has Columns in the top right, Rows in the bottom left, Data in the bottom right, and a blank header in the top left.

The Data section is used to display the measures or facts from the data warehouse. That is not to say the matrix is used only on data warehouses, but it does

FIGURE 23-1

fit nicely with dimension and fact tables. The facts are placed in the Data section of the matrix, and the dimensions are placed on the Row and Column sections. The facts or measures in the preceding query are Total Quantity and Total Sales. The rest of the fields will be the Column and Row groups.

In Figure 23-2 you can see that Total Sales has been placed in the Data section of the matrix. This has automatically placed the Total Sales header in the row above. The next step is to drag over the year above the Total Sales header. When you do this you will see a blue I beam appear above the Total Sales header field. When you see this beam you can release the mouse button. It indicates that the column group will be created.

Now you can create the row groups by dragging Employee Key into the Rows field. Then drag Sales Territory Key to the left of Employee Key. Again, you will see a blue bar appear to the left of Employee Key, indicating that the new row group will be created for Sales Territory Key. Figure 23-3 shows the completed matrix in design view.

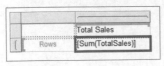

FIGURE 23-2

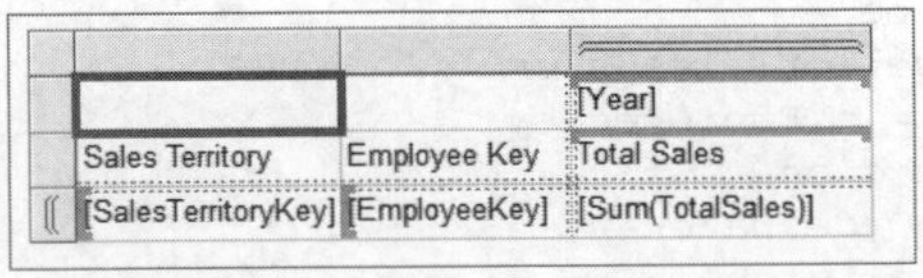

FIGURE 23-3

In the bottom of the BIDS environment you will see the row groups and column groups. Figure 23-4 shows these groups. They are created automatically when you drop the fields on the matrix. You can adjust the groups by right-clicking them and selecting Group Properties.

Row Groups	Column Groups	▼
[SalesTerritoryKey	[Year	▼
[EmployeeKey	[ColumnGroup	▼

FIGURE 23-4

The preview of this report will show the matrix with all the row and column groups along with all the total sales. The Total Sales numbers represent the sales for the intersection of the row to the left and the column above. Figure 23-5 is the preview of the report. You can see that Sales Territory Key is a parent group of Employee Key. You can tell this because there is more than one Employee Key for the Sales Territory Keys. The year group above does not have any child groups under it, but if the query had contained the months or quarters, these could have been child groups under the years.

		2001	2002
Sales Territory Key	Employee Key	Total Sales	Total Sales
1	286	607417.7473	1177732.7560
	289	506570.3840	1176251.4647
	293		256076.1559
2	281	751741.1054	3077197.9248
3	283	1247434.4374	3803368.3946
4	282	1143819.6543	3234995.6959
	287	887498.8259	2123969.1303
5	285	1380707.4422	2478985.1210

FIGURE 23-5

This report still needs a lot of cleanup. The sales numbers need to be formatted as currency, and the headers could use a little color. This format cleanup was explained in the previous two lessons. This example report will be cleaned up like the previous lesson's examples.

The data section of the matrix can show more than one measure. The Total Quantity field can be dragged over to the right side of the Total Sales field. If you drop the Total Quantity field when the blue beam appears, it will create a new column. In Figure 23-6 you can see Total Quantity to the right of Total Sales.

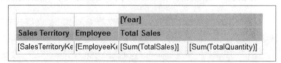

		[Year]	
Sales Territory	Employee	Total Sales	
[SalesTerritoryKe	[EmployeeK(	[Sum(TotalSales)]	[Sum(TotalQuantity)]

FIGURE 23-6

Notice that the header above the measures is one long field with only Total Sales as the header. This is not accurate, because you have two measures below. You can fix this by right-clicking the Total Sales header field and left-clicking Split Cells. Once the header is split you can then type **Total Quantity** in the blank field to the right. Now, when you preview the report it will look like what is shown in Figure 23-7. The measures are grouped under the appropriate years and Sales Territory still shows the Employee Key group to the right.

		2001		2002	
Sales Territory Key	Employee Key	Total Sales	Total Quantity	Total Sales	Total Quantity
1	286	$607,417.75	683	$1,177,732.76	2622
	289	$506,570.38	523	$1,176,251.46	2313
	293			$256,076.16	731
2	281	$751,741.11	1245	$3,077,197.92	7789
3	283	$1,247,434.44	1962	$3,803,368.39	8203
4	282	$1,143,819.65	1279	$3,234,995.70	8115
	287	$887,498.83	1160	$2,123,969.13	4726
5	285	$1,380,707.44	1550	$2,478,985.12	5145

FIGURE 23-7

The last bit of touch-up can be done to the Column and Row groups. This formatting is called *collapsible fields.* You can allow users to hide or show fields based on a clickable field on the report. The first thing to do is to create rows with totals. If the user hides a row, there needs to be something to show the aggregate of everything in the collapsed rows.

To create a total row for the Employee Key group, right-click this group in the Row Groups window at the bottom of BIDS and select Add Total ➪ Before. This will create a new Total row above the Employee Key group on the matrix, as seen in Figure 23-8.

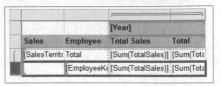

FIGURE 23-8

You will need to change the row visibility property of the Employee Key row below the newly created Total row. This is the bottom row in the example matrix. You can select this row by clicking the gray row-control border to the left of the row. If you do not see the gray border surrounding the matrix, click any field in the matrix and it will appear. This border can be seen in Figure 23-8. The bottom row is also selected in this figure. The highlight around the row indicates that it is selected. Click the small gray square to the left of the row to select the entire row. You can do this at the top of the matrix to select entire columns. The gray square at the top left of the matrix will select the entire matrix.

Right-click the gray box to the left of this row and select Row Visibility. Click the radio button next to Hide. Check the option "Display can be toggled by this report item," and then select SalesTerritoryKey from the drop-down menu below it. Once these options are selected the Row Visibility window should match the one shown in Figure 23-9. Then click OK to return to the report.

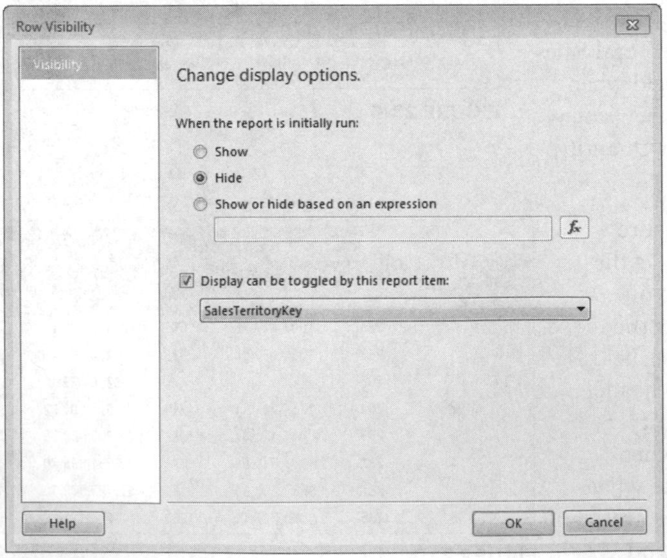

FIGURE 23-9

Preview the report again and it will have small boxes with plus signs in them in the first column and you will see the total for each sales territory and not for the individual employees. You can now click a plus box and this will expand the group to show the details of the total. Figure 23-10 shows the report with the collapsible fields and the first row expanded. The same steps can be performed to create collapsible columns too.

Matrix reports can be very useful for end users who need a way to view measures in a data warehouse. By placing a dimension on the row groups and another dimension on the column groups, and then using the collapsible rows and columns, you can easily drill down to see the details of a report. This will give you the ability to "slice and dice" the data in numerous ways.

Sales Territory Key	Employee Key		Total Sales	2001 Total Quantity	Total Sales	2002 Total Quantity
⊟	1	Total	$1,113,988.13	1206	$2,610,060.38	5666
		286	$607,417.75	683	$1,177,732.76	2622
		289	$506,570.38	523	$1,176,251.46	2313
		293			$256,076.16	731
⊞	2	Total	$751,741.11	1245	$3,077,197.92	7789
⊞	3	Total	$1,247,434.44	1962	$3,803,368.39	8203
⊞	4	Total	$2,031,318.48	2439	$5,358,964.83	12841
⊞	5	Total	$1,380,707.44	1550	$2,478,985.12	5145

FIGURE 23-10

TRY IT

In this Try It you will create a report using a matrix. You will set up row groups and column groups on the matrix. You will also create collapsible rows and columns on the report.

Lesson Requirements

In this lesson you build a matrix report. You will use the given query in the dataset for this report. You will need the AdventureWorksDW2008R2 database. This database is free from www.codeplex.com. You will also need to know the name of your SQL Server R2 instance. If it is your default instance you can use LocalHost as the server name.

> *The download for this lesson available at* www.wrox.com *includes the queries for this lesson.*

Hints

> ➤ Use a matrix on the report, not a table.

> ➤ You will be able to collapse rows and columns on the matrix.

Step-by-Step

1. Open the BI Trainer Reports project you created in the previous lessons.

2. Right-click the Shared Data Sources folder in the Solution Explorer and select Add New Data Source.

3. Enter **AWDW** in the name box and click Edit.

4. Type your server name in the Server Name box. If you are using a local default instance of SQL Server R2 you can use LocalHost as the server name.

5. Select AdventureWorksDW2008 from the database drop-down menu.

6. Click OK in both windows.

7. Right-click the Shared Datasets folder in the Solution Explorer and select Add New Dataset.

8. Name the dataset **SalesbyRegion**.

9. Select AWDW from the Data Source drop-down menu.

10. Use the following query in the Query window; this query is in the code files included with this book and can be copied from there.

```
SELECT FactResellerSales.OrderQuantity, FactResellerSales.SalesAmount,
DimReseller.ResellerName, DimGeography.City,
DimGeography.StateProvinceName, DimGeography.EnglishCountryRegionName,
DimDate.CalendarQuarter, DimDate.CalendarYear
FROM FactResellerSales
INNER JOIN
DimDate ON FactResellerSales.OrderDateKey = DimDate.DateKey
INNER JOIN
DimReseller ON FactResellerSales.ResellerKey = DimReseller.ResellerKey
INNER JOIN
DimGeography ON DimReseller.GeographyKey = DimGeography.GeographyKey
Where EnglishCountryRegionName = 'United States'
```

11. Click OK.

12. Right-click the Reports folder in the Solution Explorer and select Add ⇨ New Item.

13. Select Report and change the name to **SalesbyRegion.rdl**. Click OK.

14. Right-click the Data Sources folder in the Report Data window and select Add Data Source.

15. Name the data source **AWDW**.

16. Click the radio button next to "Use shared data source reference."

17. Select AWDW from the Shared Data Sources drop-down menu. Click OK.

18. Right-click the Datasets folder in the Report Data window and select Add Dataset.

19. Set the Name box to SalesbyRegion and select the shared dataset with this name in the window below. Click OK.

20. Drag a matrix from the toolbox to the report body.

21. Drag Sales Amount from the Report Data window into the Data field in the matrix.

22. Drag Order Quantity onto the matrix to the right of the Sales Amount. A blue beam will appear to the right, indicating the matrix will create a new row: drop the field when you see this beam.

23. Right-click the Sales Amount header above the data row and select Split Cells.

24. There will be two fields above the data now: in the blank right-hand field type **Quantity**.

25. Drag City onto the Rows field in the matrix.

26. Drag State Province Name to the left of City and drop it in a new column.

27. Change the header column from **State Province Name** to just **State**.

28. Drag Calendar Quarter above the Sales Amount and Quantity headers: when you see the blue beam appear above the headers, drop the field. This will create a new column above the header.

29. Drag Calendar Year above Calendar Quarter so it creates another row. The matrix should now look like the one in Figure 23-11.

		[CalendarYear]	
		[CalendarQuarter]	
State	City	Sales Amount	Quantity
[StateProvinceN	[City]	[Sum(SalesAmc	[Sum(OrderQua

FIGURE 23-11

30. Preview the report and you will see that it can use a lot of cleanup. The sales amount needs to be formatted as currency and the headers could use some color. Using the steps you learned in the previous two chapters, make these adjustments to the report. You can choose any colors you like. Companies usually like their reports to match the color scheme of the company logo.

31. Right-click the City group in the Row Groups window at the bottom of BIDS and select Add Total ⇨ Before.

32. Right-click the gray square to the left of the bottom row on the matrix and select Row Visibility. If the gray border is not visible around the matrix, click any field in the matrix to make it appear.

33. Select Hide and Check Display can be toggled by this report item.

34. Select StateProvinceName from the drop-down menu. Click OK.

35. Preview the report. You will see the states with a plus next to them.

36. Click a few of the pluses to see the work of the collapsible fields. Figure 23-12 shows an example.

					200
			3		
State	**City**	**Sales Amount**	**Quantity**	**Sales Amount**	**Quantity**
⊞ Alabama	Total				
⊟ Arizona	Total	$12,930.31	14	$5,202.64	
	Chandler				
	Gilbert				
	Mesa				
	Phoenix	$12,499.45	11	$5,202.64	
	Scottsdale	$419.46	1		
	Surprise				
	Tucson	$11.40	2		
⊞ California	Total	$486,774.40	624	$685,344.67	87
⊞ Colorado	Total	$52,277.11	74	$81,169.35	12
⊞ Connecticut	Total	$32,072.57	57	$58,748.37	9

FIGURE 23-12

37. Now you will make the columns collapsible too. Return to design view.

38. Right-click the CalendarQuarter group in the Columns Groups window at the bottom of BIDS, and select Add Total ⇨ After.

39. Right-click the CalendarQuarter group in the Columns Groups window and select Group Properties.

40. Select the Visibility node in the left pane.

41. Select Hide and Check Display can be toggled by this report item.

42. Select CalendarYear from the drop-down menu. Click OK.

43. Preview the report and you will see the columns are now collapsible and there is a plus next to each year, which allows you to expand and see the quarters in the year. The final report should look like the one in Figure 23-13.

		⊞	2001	⊞	2002
		Total		Total	
State	City	Sales Amount	Quantity	Sales Amount	Quantity
⊞ Alabama	Total			$3,110.04	9
⊞ Arizona	Total	$18,132.94	20	$259,845.42	878
⊞ California	Total	$1,172,119.07	1495	$3,394,071.80	8123
⊞ Colorado	Total	$133,446.46	196	$729,936.74	1908
⊞ Connecticut	Total	$90,820.94	151	$372,947.42	782
⊞ Florida	Total	$478,373.05	462	$701,181.74	1555
⊞ Georgia	Total	$155,523.18	286	$391,096.05	777
⊞ Idaho	Total			$7,848.64	18
⊞ Illinois	Total	$215,110.65	302	$279,705.12	532

FIGURE 23-13

 Please select Lesson 23 on the DVD to view the video that accompanies this lesson.

24

Parameterizing Your Reports

End users of your reports are always going to ask for changes to existing reports. Wouldn't it be nice if you could give them the ability to make changes to the reports themselves? With report parameters, you can. With parameters on a report, users can use drop-down menus and text fields to enter options to change a report to show different date ranges, hide columns, and choose a completely different set of data to show on the report.

These parameters can be available from a drop-down menu with a list of values or a free-form text box that allows the user to enter any value. The parameters can also have a default value that loads automatically when the report loads. These options give the report a lot of flexibility.

To create parameters on a report, you can alter the query on the report, choose a stored procedure that has parameters, or manually create parameters. The best practice is to use stored procedures for all your queries. This gives you the ability to make changes to the dataset of a report without having to re-deploy it. Now, with shared datasets, you have this ability inside reporting services. Several reports may use the same shared dataset and show the data in a different layout, maybe one with a matrix, one with a table, and one with a chart. This new feature will be discussed more in later lessons.

CREATING PARAMETERS

To show how to place parameters on a report, this lesson will use the matrix report from the previous lesson. The first example will be altering the query of the report to add parameters. This is a simple way to add them, but goes against the best practice of using stored procedures. Nevertheless, if your business does not like to use stored procedures for some reason, the report query option is available.

To place a query on the matrix report you will need to alter the query to match the following code:

```
SELECT       FactResellerSales.OrderQuantity, FactResellerSales.SalesAmount,
             DimReseller.ResellerName, DimGeography.City,
             DimGeography.StateProvinceName,
             DimGeography.EnglishCountryRegionName,
             DimDate.CalendarQuarter, DimDate.CalendarYear
```

```
FROM            FactResellerSales INNER JOIN
                    DimDate ON FactResellerSales.OrderDateKey =
                    DimDate.DateKey INNER JOIN
                    DimReseller ON FactResellerSales.ResellerKey =
                    DimReseller.ResellerKey INNER JOIN
                    DimGeography ON DimReseller.GeographyKey =
                    DimGeography.GeographyKey
WHERE           (DimGeography.EnglishCountryRegionName = 'United States') AND
                    DimDate.CalendarYear in (@Year) and
                    DimGeography.StateProvinceName in (@State)
```

Notice that at the bottom of the query are two extra where-clause comparisons. The state and the year now need to be entered into the parameters at the top of the report before the report will load. The report will show only the year and state the users enter. For this example the report is not using a shared dataset: that way the report can be altered easily. It is still using the AWDW shared data source, though. You could use the equals sign instead of the in comparison function in the where clause. Using the in function gives you the ability to change the parameter to a multi-value parameter, which gives users the ability to select more than one value in a single parameter.

When you enter the preceding query as the dataset in the report, it will automatically create the two parameters in the Parameters folder in the Report Data window, as shown in Figure 24-1.

At run time the report will load the preview screen, but you will see no data because the dataset is waiting for the parameters to be entered. You can see these two parameters at the top of the report. In this example the report has Florida entered as the state and 2001 as the year. In Figure 24-2 you can see what the report looks like and you can see the two parameters at the top of the report. Notice that only the data for 2001 and for Florida shows on the report.

FIGURE 24-1

FIGURE 24-2

DEFAULT PARAMETER VALUES

The end users are able to enter the year and the state they want to see on the report. Most users have a value they always use in a report, and, therefore, would like to have the report load with that value already in the parameter. To give your parameters default values, right-click the Year parameter in the Parameter folder in the Report Data window and select Parameter Properties. Click the Default

Values node on the left. Select the Specify Values option. Click the Add button and enter the value 2001 in the text box that appears. This window is the Report Parameter Properties window, and it is where you will make all the adjustments to your parameters. Repeat these steps to add Florida as the default for the State parameter.

When you preview the report, it loads automatically with the default values of 2001 and Florida. The users can still change the values of the parameters to show different sets of data. Change the year to 2002 and click the View Report button at the top right of the preview screen. Notice the value of the Sales Amount and Quantity change on the report. Now, change the year to 1990 and click View Report. There is no data on the report. This is because there is no data for that year. Your end users would have an easier time using the parameters if they had a list of the available years and states. That is where available values will help.

PARAMETER AVAILABLE VALUES

Now that you can change the report to show different years and states, it is time to give the report a list of available values from which the user will be able to choose. This list of values will come from two new queries added to the report. You will add two new datasets to the report. The first will be named StateParam, the second YearParam. It is a best practice to give your datasets names that indicate what they contain; when they are used by a parameter only, add Param to the name.

The query for the StateParam dataset will be as follows:

```
SELECT DISTINCT StateProvinceName
FROM            DimGeography
WHERE          (EnglishCountryRegionName = 'United States')
ORDER BY StateProvinceName
```

The query for the YearParam dataset will be as follows:

```
SELECT DISTINCT CalendarYear
FROM            DimDate
ORDER BY CalendarYear
```

Notice that each of these queries uses the DISTINCT function. This is because you do not need to show an option more than once in the drop-down menu for the parameters. If a user selects a state, all the rows that have that state will show. The same is true for year too.

Now you can add the preceding queries to the parameter Available Values properties. Right-click the Year parameter in the Parameter folder in the Report Data window and select Parameter Properties. Click the Available Values node in the left pane. Select "Get Values from a Query." Select YearParam in the Dataset drop-down Menu. Select CalendarYear in the Value and Label drop-down menus. The properties should look like those shown in Figure 24-3. The reason you select these separately is that in some cases the label the user sees on the report will differ from the value the query uses to pull the data. For example, you may have the query use a product ID to pull a certain product, but the user would rather see the product names in the parameter list. In this case the product ID would be in the Value field and the product name would be in the Label field.

Repeat these steps to add the StateParam query as the available values for the State parameter. Use StateParam as the dataset and StateProvinceName as the Value and Label fields. Preview the report and click the drop-down menu to see the list of available values. Figure 24-4 shows the drop-down menu with the available values. Change the values of the parameters and click View Report to see the data on the report change based on the selected values. Keep in mind that some of the states may not have any sales in some of the years.

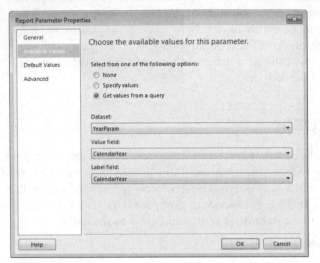

FIGURE 24-3

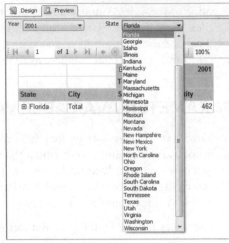

FIGURE 24-4

MULTI-VALUE PARAMETERS

This example report can show only one year and one state at a time. For the user to see all the years for a state or multiple states, you will need to change the report to allow multiple values. This is a simple change to the report parameter properties when the query is on the report.

Right-click the Year parameter and select Parameter Properties. On the General page, place a check next to "Allow multiple values." Click OK to close the Parameter Properties window and preview the report again. Click the Year Parameter drop-down menu. It should look like the one in Figure 24-5. Place a check next to a few of the years and click the View Report button. The report will show all the years selected. Repeat these steps for the State parameter to change it to multi-value also.

This example shows that setting up multi-value parameters is very easy if the query is on the report. If the report is using a stored procedure as the dataset, there is a little more work involved. The multi-value parameter passes the stored procedure a comma-separated list of the values. This means that if the user selects all the years the list will be 2001, 2002, 2003, 2004, 2005, 2006. The stored procedure does not know how to parse this string to get the individual years like the report query. The instructions to make stored procedures parse multi-value parameters are

FIGURE 24-5

beyond the scope of this book. Nevertheless, you can read about it at `http://www.bidn.com/blogs/MikeDavis/ssis/360/multi-value-parameters-from-stored-procedures-in-ssrs`.

ALTERING PROPERTIES WITH PARAMETERS

Parameters can be used for more than just selecting different sets of data. They can be used to control the properties of just about every report object. One of the most popular properties to control is the visibility of a column. This is simple to set up, but it is a manual process.

Using the preceding report, right-click the Parameter folder in the Report Data window and select Add Parameter. Name the parameter **ShowQuantity** and set the prompt to Show Quantity. Change the data type to Boolean. Click Available Values and select Specify Values. Click Add twice and set the label of the first value to Hide and the Value to True. Set the second label to Show and the Value to False. Once you have done all this the window should look like the one in Figure 24-6. Click OK to close this window and return to the report.

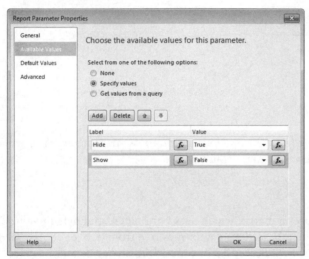

FIGURE 24-6

Right-click the gray control box at the top of the Quantity column and select Column Visibility. Select the option "Show or hide based on an expression." Click the function button (the button with the letters FX on it). This is the Expression Editor screen, which you will learn about in later lessons. For now, just click Parameters in the left-hand window. Then double-click ShowQuantity in the right-hand window. This will add the value of the ShowQuantity parameter to the top window, as shown in Figure 24-7.

When the user sets the parameter to Hide, the value of True will be passed to the Hidden property of the column. Repeat these steps for the Total Quantity column. Preview the report to see the new parameter. Change the ShowQuantity parameter value to see the Quantity columns hide and show on the report. You could also set a default value for this new parameter. The default value would need to be either True or False.

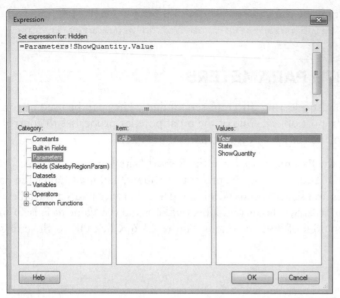

FIGURE 24-7

TRY IT

In this Try It you will alter the matrix report from the previous lesson to use parameters. You will also give these parameters a list of available values and default values.

Lesson Requirements

In this lesson you will create a report that uses a matrix which uses parameters and default values. You will need the AdventureWorks2008R2 database. This database is free from www.codeplex.com. You will also need to know the name of your SQL Server R2 instance. If it is your default instance you can use LocalHost as the server name. You will also need the matrix report from the previous lesson.

 The download for this lesson, available at www.wrox.com, *includes the queries you need for this Try It.*

Hints

➤ Make a copy of the matrix report.

➤ Do not use a shared dataset for this report.

➤ Alter the queries to use parameters.

Step-by-Step

1. Open the Project BI Trainer reports you created in the previous lesson.

2. Click the Sales by Region report in the Solution Explorer and press Ctrl+C and then Ctrl+V to paste a copy of the report. A new report will appear, named Copy of SalesbyRegion.

3. Right-click this new report and select Rename. Rename the report SalesbyState.

4. Double-click the SalesbyState report to open it.

5. Notice that the data source is named DataSource1. Right-click this and select Data Source Properties.

6. Change the name of the data source to **AWDW** and click OK.

7. Right-click the dataset SalesbyRegion and select Dataset Properties.

8. Select "Use a dataset embedded in my report."

9. Select AWDW as the data source.

10. Enter the following query into the Query box. (The code is included with the book as part of the download for this lesson and can be copied and pasted from there.)

```
SELECT FactResellerSales.OrderQuantity, FactResellerSales.SalesAmount,
DimReseller.ResellerName, DimGeography.City,
DimGeography.StateProvinceName, DimGeography.EnglishCountryRegionName,
DimDate.CalendarQuarter, DimDate.CalendarYear
FROM FactResellerSales INNER JOIN
DimDate ON FactResellerSales.OrderDateKey = DimDate.DateKey
INNER JOIN
DimReseller ON FactResellerSales.ResellerKey = DimReseller.ResellerKey
INNER JOIN
DimGeography ON DimReseller.GeographyKey = DimGeography.GeographyKey
WHERE (DimGeography.EnglishCountryRegionName = 'United States')
and DimDate.CalendarYear in (@Year)
and DimGeography.StateProvinceName in (@State)
```

    Click OK.

11. Click the plus sign next to the Parameters folder in the Report Data window. Notice that two parameters are automatically added to the report.

12. Right-click the Datasets folder and select Add Dataset.

13. Select "Use a dataset embedded in my report" and enter the following query:

```
SELECT DISTINCT StateProvinceName
FROM          DimGeography
WHERE      (EnglishCountryRegionName = 'United States')
ORDER BY StateProvinceName
```

14. Name the query **StateParam**.

15. Select AWDW as the data source and click OK.

16. Right-click the Datasets folder and select Add Dataset.

17. Select "Use a dataset embedded in my report" and enter the following query:

```
SELECT DISTINCT CalendarYear
FROM          DimDate
ORDER BY CalendarYear
```

18. Name the query **YearParam**.

19. Select AWDW as the data source and click OK.

20. Right-click the Year parameter in the Report Data window and select Parameter Properties.

21. Click Available Values and select "Get values from a query."

22. Select YearParam as the dataset and CalendarYear as the Value and Label fields and then click OK.

23. Right-click the State parameter in the Report Data window and select Parameter Properties.

24. Click Available Values and select "Get values from a query."

25. Select StateParam as the dataset and StateProvinceName as the Value and Label fields and then click OK.

26. Preview the report to see the finished report.

27. Select 2003 as the year and Florida as the state, and the report should look like the one in Figure 24-8.

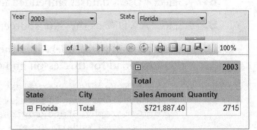

FIGURE 24-8

Congratulations, you have created a report with parameters and available values for the parameters.

 Please select Lesson 24 on the DVD to view the video that accompanies this lesson.

25

Building Reports on Your Cube

When you create a report that is querying a SQL database, you are using the SQL query language. When you report from an Analysis Services cube, you are using the MDX (Multidimensional Expressions) language. This language is very different from SQL and has a steep learning curve. The best way to learn MDX is to forget SQL and start with a clear head. Fortunately, you do not need to learn MDX to create reports from a cube.

Reporting from a cube can be accomplished with little or no MDX knowledge at all. The MDX Query Designer in BIDS is very efficient at creating the MDX query you need automatically. You may need a little MDX knowledge to understand how to modify the report.

The data source for cube reports will be an Analysis Services cube. In the previous lessons you learned how to create a shared data source. Those instructions still apply here, with one exception. The only difference is the type of connection. In the Type drop-down menu you will need to select Microsoft SQL Server Analysis Services. Figure 25-1 shows this selected with the connection string below the type. This shared data source will work just like any other. The big changes are in the dataset.

A dataset built on an Analysis Services data source will be significantly different from the regular SQL database datasets. You will notice the biggest difference in the Query Designer. In fact, when you create this dataset, you will notice the query box is grayed out. This is because you will not type any SQL in this dataset. You will not type in MDX either. You will use the Query Designer. Other than the query box's being grayed out, everything else should look the same as in other datasets.

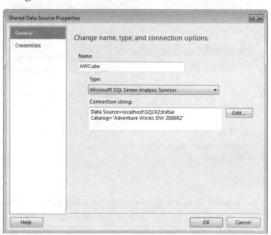

FIGURE 25-1

The MDX Query Designer will build the MDX query for you as you drag and drop the fields. After you click the Query Designer button in the dataset, the MDX Query Designer will open. In the left-hand window you will see a list of all the dimensions and measure groups in the Analysis Services database. Under this is the list of calculated members. In the right-hand window you will see the Parameter and Filter sections on the top and the query fields below.

To start building an MDX query, simply drag the fields you are going to use on the report into the Query Fields sections of the MDX Query Designer. It is helpful to drag over any measures you want to use first. This way you can see the measures change as you add dimensions. If you see the measures showing numbers that are not expected, it could indicate there is something wrong with the query you have designed. One example would involve unrelated dimensions. These wrong numbers occur when you drag over a dimension that is not associated with a measure at all. In the AdventureWorks database, the Reseller measures do not have any connection to the Customer dimension. This is because the customer information is kept for Internet sales, but not for sales in a reseller's store. In Figure 25-2, you can see the Cartesian product that occurs when you drag out unrelated dimensions and measures in the MDX Query Designer.

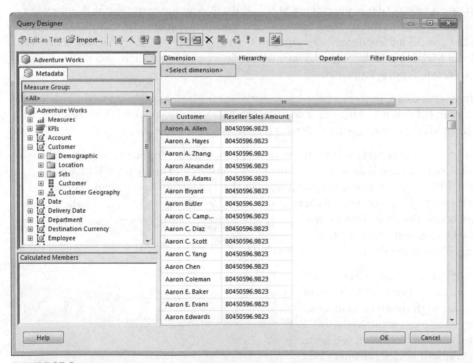

FIGURE 25-2

The easiest way to prevent these unwanted joins from happening is to use the Measure Group drop-down menu at the top of the list of dimensions and measure groups. Figure 25-3 shows this drop-down menu listing all the measure groups in AdventureWorks. Selecting the Reseller Sales measure group in this drop-down menu hides several dimensions, including the Customer dimension, because they have no relation to the Reseller Sales measures. Now you can safely drag over the dimensions and measures you want to see on the report.

If your report needs parameters or filters, these will go in the section above the fields you just dragged over to use on the report. There are five columns in this section. The first column is the name of the dimension associated with the field you dragged over. The second column is the name of the hierarchy you dragged over. Even dimensions that have only one level are called hierarchies.

FIGURE 25-3

The third column contains the operators. There are several different operators to choose from in this drop-down menu. Most of them are simple, like Equal and Not Equal. There are two range options, range-inclusive and range-exclusive. Selecting one of these options will cause the Parameters checkbox in the fifth column to become two checkboxes. These checkboxes give you the option to create a parameter on the report. When there are two checkboxes, you can create two parameters. One parameter is the starting value and the other the ending value.

The next column is Filter Expression. This column allows you to select the values by which you want to filter. If you do not check the Parameters checkbox this filter will be applied to the report and the user will not see it on the report, and therefore will not be able to change the value. In Figure 25-4 you can see a Country filter in the top line.

Dimension	Hierarchy	Operator	Filter Expression	Parameters
Geography	Country	Equal	{ United States }	☐
Date	Date.Calendar Year	Equal	{ CY 2008, CY 2010 }	☑
<Select dimension>				

FIGURE 25-4

Creating parameters on the report is easy. Just check the box under the last column, named Parameters. This will not only create a parameter on the report but also add the available values automatically. It will also set a default value for the value in the Filter Expression column. In Figure 25-4 you can see the year is being used as a parameter with the Equal operator. This field also has a default value of two years. This parameter will automatically be set up to handle multiple values on the report.

FIGURE 25-5

In the bottom sections you can drag over hierarchies you want to use on the report and, if the hierarchy has more than the desired number of columns, you can simply delete columns by right-clicking and selecting Delete. In Figure 25-5 you can see the Date.Calendar hierarchy. It includes Calendar Year, Calendar Semester, Calendar Quarter, Month, and Date. If you want to use all the items in this hierarchy except for Calendar Semester and Date, drag over the entire hierarchy, right-click the columns you do not need, and select Delete. In this example the report will use Calendar Year, Calendar Quarter, Month, Country, State-Province, City, and Reseller Sales Amount. It will also have a filter for the country United States and a range-inclusive parameter set for the Calendar Year, as seen in Figure 25-4. Even though we will not use Country on the report, it still has to remain on the query for the filter to function.

If you want to customize the MDX that is created by the Query Designer, there is a design button at the top of the designer. This turns the MDX Query Designer into the MDX text editor and allows you to create an MDX query manually. After you click OK in the Query Designer, you return to the Dataset Properties window. In the grayed-out query box you will see the MDX that was created by the designer.

Once you are done creating this new dataset, you will notice the parameter that has automatically been added to the report. The parameter name is DateCalendarYear. This is also the name of the hierarchy in the MDX Query Designer. Double-click this parameter and click the Available Values node. Here you can see the dataset and the fields selected for the label and the value. This dataset is not visible on the report yet.

To show the hidden dataset, close the parameter properties, right-click the Datasets folder and click Show Hidden Datasets. The DateCalendarYear query will appear in the Dataset list. Double-click this dataset, click Query Designer, and run the query to see the data brought back by the query. The ParameterValue column is the value that is passed into the query on the report. If you want to create a default value that is a changing value, for example the current year, you will need to know this information. The default value cannot just be the year value. It will need to include all of the hierarchy. Using expressions on MDX-driven reports is beyond the scope of this book, but you can see an example of how to do this at `http://www.bidn.com/blogs/DustinRyan/ssis/337/use-date-picker-control-with-mdx-based-reports`.

TRY IT

In this Try It you will build a report using the MDX Query Designer and pulling data from the AdventureWorks Cube. This report will use a matrix and have parameters with available and default values.

Lesson Requirements

In this lesson, you will build a report using a matrix. You will query an Analysis Services database and build the MDX query using the MDX Query Designer.

You will need the AdventureWorks2008R2 Analysis Services database. This database is free from `www.codeplex.com`. You will also need to know the name of your SQL Server R2 instance. If it is your default instance, you can use LocalHost as the server name.

Hints

➤ Connect to the Analysis Services database, not the SQL database.

➤ Use a matrix on the report.

➤ The parameter available and default values will be created automatically.

Step-by-Step

1. Open the Project BI Trainer reports you created in the previous chapter.

2. Right-click the Shared Data Source folder and select Add New Data Source.

3. Name the shared data source **AWCube**.

4. Select Microsoft SQL Server Analysis Services from the type drop-down menu and then click the Edit button.

5. Enter your SQL R2 server name.

6. Select AdventureWorksDW2008R2 from the Database drop-down menu.

7. Click OK in both windows.

8. Right-click the Shared Datasets folder and select Add New Dataset.

9. Name the dataset **SalesByGeography**.

10. Select AWCube as the data source.

11. Click the Query Designer button.

12. Select the Reseller Sales measure group from the Measure Group drop-down menu on the top left side of the designer.

13. Click the plus sign to expand the Measures menu and Reseller Sales.

14. Drag over Reseller Sales Amount into the bottom right section of the designer. You should see an amount appear as shown in Figure 25-6.

15. Expand the Date hierarchy and Calendar Date.

16. Drag the Date Calendar hierarchy into the same window with Reseller Sales Amount.

17. Right-click the Calendar Semester column in the right-hand window and click Delete Calendar Semester.

18. Delete the Month and Date columns as in Step 17. The designer should look like what is shown in Figure 25-7.

19. Expand the Geography dimension and drag over the Geography hierarchy.

20. Right-click the Postal Code column and click Delete Postal Code.

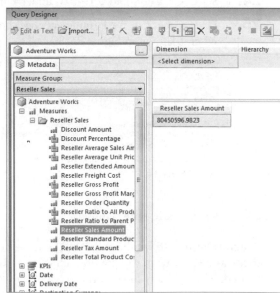

FIGURE 25-6

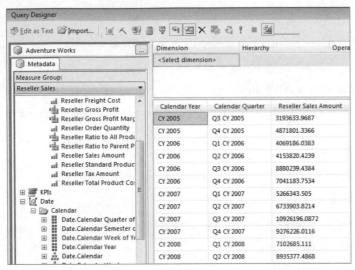

FIGURE 25-7

21. From the Geography dimension drag Country into the Parameter and Filter window at the top right.

22. Under the Filter Expression form next to Country select United States.

23. Drag Date Calendar Year into the Parameter and Filter window.

24. Select CY 2008 and CY 2010 under Filter Expression next to Year.

25. Place a check in the Parameters checkbox next to Year. The Query Designer should look like what is shown in Figure 25-8.

Dimension	Hierarchy	Operator	Filter Expression	Paramet..
Geography	Country	Equal	{ United States }	☐
Date	Date.Calendar Year	Equal	{ CY 2008, CY 2010 }	☑
<Select dimension>				

Calendar Year	Calendar Quarter	Country	State-Province	City	Reseller Sales Amount
CY 2008	Q1 CY 2008	United States	Alabama	Birmingham	4340.67
CY 2008	Q1 CY 2008	United States	Alabama	Huntsville	6502.35

FIGURE 25-8

26. Click OK in both windows.

Congratulations — you have created your first dataset from a cube. The rest of the build process is identical to the one in the previous chapter on building a matrix report. The parameters are already created. They already have available values and default values too.

 Please select Lesson 25 on the DVD to view the video that accompanies this lesson.

26

Using Maps in Your Report

Reports using tables and matrixes are good for presenting data to your users in a simple layout, but these are not always the best means of displaying data. If your company has stores in many different cities and states, it may be a better idea to show data on a map. The new map control in SQL Server R2 allows you to use the geospatial data type in SQL Server to show data on a map. This can be a map of the United States or a map of just a single state. As of the writing of this book, the United States is the only country available in this map feature.

In the AdventureWorks2008R2 sample database there is geospatial data in the Address.Person table. The following query will show the spatial data and can be seen in Figure 26-1 as it looks when run in SQL Server Management Studio (SSMS).

```
Select AddressLine1, City, SpatialLocation
from Person.Address
```

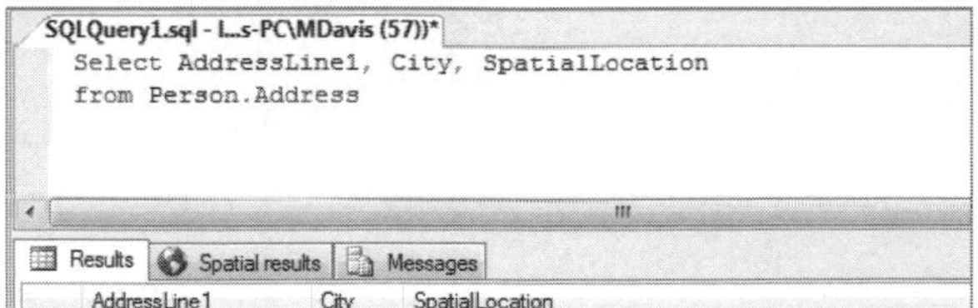

FIGURE 26-1

The Spatial Data column is not readable when queried from SQL Server Management Studio. Reporting Services can interpret this information as location information and show it on a map.

You can also show data on a map using just the state names or the county names. This comes in handy when you do not have spatial data in your database. If you have address data and want to convert it to spatial data, there are several websites available online that allow you to convert address data to spatial data. A list of these sites can be found at `http://TinyUrl.com/2dkf2o4`.

The easiest way to show map data is with the name of the state instead of the spatial data. Keep in mind that spatial data cannot be used in a cube. So, there will be some instances in which you are not going to be able to use spatial data, and the state or county names will be needed.

To create a map with state data you will need a query with the state names and some company measures to show, like sales counts. The following query will return a list of all the states with a count of how many people are in each state.

```
SELECT      Person.StateProvince.Name, Count(*) PersonCount
FROM        Person.Address INNER JOIN Person.StateProvince ON
Person.Address.StateProvinceID = Person.StateProvince.StateProvinceID
Where Person.StateProvince.CountryRegionCode = 'US'
Group by Person.StateProvince.Name
Order by Person.StateProvince.Name
```

Once you have a data set with this query, you can drag a map control from the toolbox onto the report and show this data on the map. The first window that appears when you drag a map from the toolbox onto the report is the New Map Layer window. In this window you can select a map gallery, ERSI shapefile, or SQL Server spatial query. The map gallery has a list of map options below it. ERSI shapefiles are a specialized file type. If your query has the spatial data, then you can use the SQL Server spatial query option. Our example query has the state names, so you will use the Map Gallery and choose USA by State from the menu, as seen in Figure 26-2.

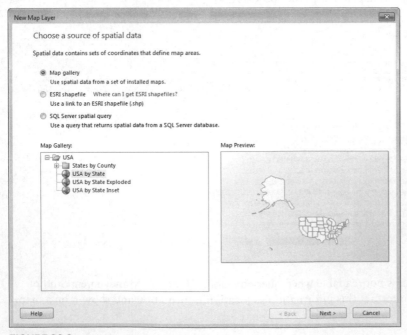

FIGURE 26-2

The next window gives you the ability to set the location of the map and to crop it if you desire. You can also add a Bing map layer to the map here. The map layer can be the road, aerial, or hybrid map type: road is just like a regular road map, aerial is a satellite view, and hybrid is a mix of road and aerial. There are two sliders in this window. The left slider allows you to change the size of the map and the arrows above the slider allow you to center the map as you choose. You can also click and drag the map to the desired location. The right-hand slider will change the resolution quality of the map. If your end users report that the map takes a long time to load, you can move the slider up to lower the quality of the map, which lowers the file size of the report and therefore can increase report performance.

The next window has three choices: Basic, Color Analytical, and Bubble.

➤ The **basic map** shows data on the states in the form of numbers.

➤ The **color analytical map** shows the states with different colors representing the amount in each state.

➤ The **bubble map** will show the map with bubbles on top representing the data. Bigger bubbles indicate larger amounts.

After you select Color Analytical, the next window will give you a list of the data sets on the report. This example is using the data set mentioned earlier, showing the states and giving a count of people in each state on the table. In this example the data set is named PersonByState and will be in the project files included with this book.

The next window is where you will match the fields to the states on the map. You need to match the State Name property to the state name in the data set. Select Name from the drop-down menu next to STATENAME, as shown in Figure 26-3.

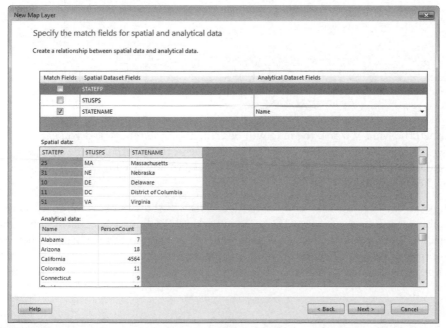

FIGURE 26-3

In the next window you can customize the colors shown on the map. The Theme drop-down menu has a list of different color options. The Theme options do not affect the colors on the map; rather, they affect the colors surrounding the map and the legend. Under "Field to visualize" select the field that you want the colors to represent on the map; in this case it is Sum(PersonCount). The "Color rule" option is a list of color choices that will represent the data. You can also check "Display labels" and select the desired field from the drop-down menu that appears, and this data will show up on the map. Figure 26-4 shows this window with the generic theme, Blue-White as the color rule, and "Display labels" selected and set to Sum(PersonCount).

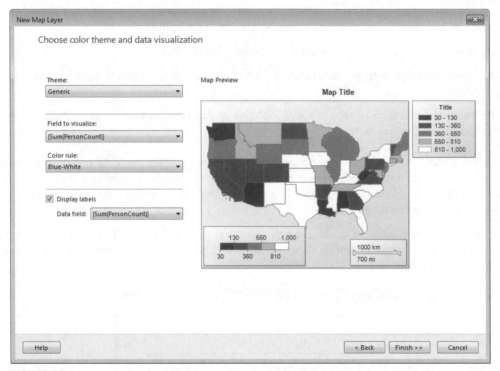

FIGURE 26-4

Once you have finished the Map Wizard, the map will be created on the report and you can preview it. Figure 26-5 shows the complete map in preview mode. Notice in this figure that the numbers over Rhode Island and New York overlap. If this occurs you may need to adjust your map either to zoom in further or not to show the labels.

Another type of map you can create is the bubble map type. This will show bubbles over each state. The size of each bubble represents the amount measured in the data. Walking back through the same steps above, but selecting Bubble Map instead, will get you to the last screen of the wizard, where you will have one new option: "Use polygon colors to visualize data." This will combine the bubble with colors just like the ones you saw in the color analytical map example. If you leave this option turned off and set all other options just like the ones in the previous example, the bubble map will look like Figure 26-6.

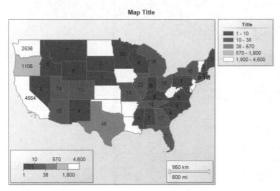

FIGURE 26-5

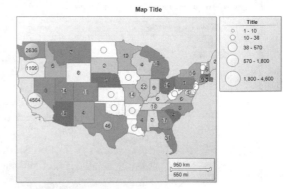

FIGURE 26-6

The spatial data works much like the state names. The only difference is that the data are specified by a point of latitude and longitude instead of referring to an entire state. The following query will show the data for the state of Florida and the total due for each location.

```
SELECT      Address_1.SpatialLocation, Address_1.AddressLine1,
                Address_1.City, Address_1.PostalCode,
                Person.StateProvince.StateProvinceCode,
                Sales.SalesOrderHeader.TotalDue
FROM        Person.Address AS Address_1 INNER JOIN
                Person.StateProvince ON Address_1.StateProvinceID =
                Person.StateProvince.StateProvinceID INNER JOIN
                Sales.SalesOrderHeader ON Address_1.AddressID =
                Sales.SalesOrderHeader.BillToAddressID
WHERE       (Person.StateProvince.StateProvinceCode = 'FL')
```

This time you will select "SQL Server spatial query" in the first window of the Map Wizard. This wizard starts when you drag a map control onto the report. If you want to run through the wizard again for an existing map, you can click the Layer menu that appears on the right side of the map on the report. Click the arrow to the right side of the layer you want to edit, and select Layer Wizard. A layer is a set of data that is represented on a map.

After you select the spatial query option, the next screen has the data sets. The data set in this example is named FloridaTotals. For this example assume you care only about the numbers in central Florida near Orlando. In the next screen you can zoom to the level shown in Figure 26-7. This figure also shows that the Bing road map layer has been added.

The bubble map would represent this data well and on the next screen you can select it. On the screen after that you will select the Florida Totals data set. The next window shows the analytical data and you can see the point information translated from the spatial data type to a form you can read. Figure 26-8 shows this screen, and you can see the point data in the bottom left corner of the window.

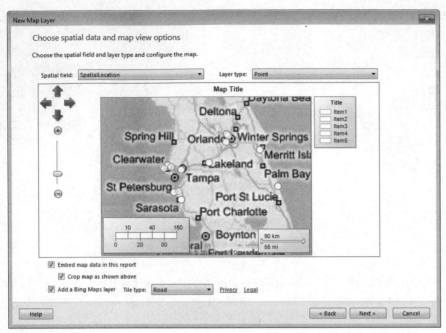

FIGURE 26-7

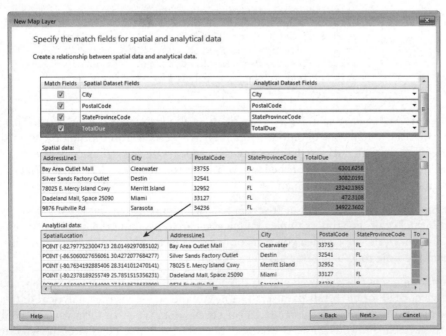

FIGURE 26-8

The last window of the Map Wizard has some of the same options discussed in the earlier examples. Now you can select TotalDue as the data field to represent on the map. The sizes of the bubbles and the colors of the bubbles can be used to show the value of the data. You can also use both to show the values if you desire. Figure 26-9 shows this map with the size used to indicate the TotalDue data. Notice how the roads can make it difficult to see the data on the map. This should be taken into consideration when you are creating maps for reporting. If your end users have a hard time seeing the data, then the map becomes useless to them.

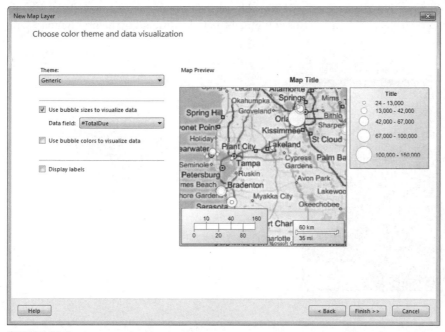

FIGURE 26-9

Now that you have created a map, you will need to know how to adjust the map in the future without running through the entire wizard again. You can do this with the map control on the right-hand side of the map in design view. Figure 26-10 shows this control and the following list explains each item.

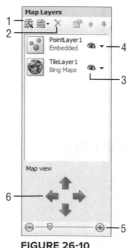

1. **New Layer Wizard:** Starts the wizard and will add a new layer of data to the map

2. **Add Layer:** A drop-down menu that adds a new data layer to the map

3. **Visibility:** Sets the layer to be visible or hidden on the map

4. **Layer Context menu:** A drop-down menu with the properties of the layer. When you are adjusting layers this menu will be your primary tool.

5. **Map Zoom Slider:** Adjusts the zoom level of the map

6. **Map Moving Arrows:** Move the map vertically or horizontally

FIGURE 26-10

Using the map you just created, you can adjust the properties of the layers to make it a little easier to read. Clicking the Layer Context menu next to the point layer and selecting Point Properties will open the properties window for that layer. There is a list of marker types at the bottom of the first screen and you can change the marker to a different shape, like that of a pushpin. In the Fill node you can change the color of the points to a color that will show on the map better, like yellow.

The Layer Context menu for the Bing map layer has the tile properties of the map. This allows you to change the look of the actual map layer. The map layer is not a point layer because it does not contain data. The tile layer has the map only. If you change the type of the map to hybrid, it will make the data on the map easier to read. After you make the preceding adjustments the map will look like Figure 26-11.

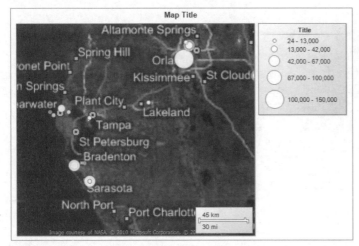

FIGURE 26-11

There is another set of properties that allow you to adjust the map. Right-click the map itself and select View Port Properties. This menu allows you to change the latitude and longitude lines on the map. The minimum and maximum latitude and longitude are set to Auto by default on the map. You can change these minimum and maximum values in this menu. You can also optimize the map to load faster under the Optimization node.

Three other items exist on the map: Title, Color Scale, and Distance Scale. You can right-click these items and select their properties. The properties for these items are basic formatting options like position and color. These will help you change the look and feel of the map.

TRY IT

In this Try It you will build a map on a report using the spatial data from a query.

Lesson Requirements

You will build a report with a map and show data on a map of Virginia. You will need the AdventureWorks2008R2 database. This database is free from www.codeplex.com. You will also need to know the name of your SQL Server R2 instance. If it is your default instance you can use LocalHost as the server name.

 The download for this lesson, available at www.wrox.com, *includes the queries you need for this Try It.*

Hints

➤   Walk through the Map Wizard.

➤   Use the query provided.

Step-by-Step

1.   Open the project BI Trainer Reports created in the previous lessons of this section (Section IV) of this book.

2.   Right-click the Reports folder in the Solution Explorer and select Add ➪ New Item.

3.   Select Report and name the report **VirginiaTotals.rdl**. Click Add.

4.   Right-click the Data Sources folder in the Report Data window and select Add Data Source.

5.   Name the data source **AW**.

6.   Select Use Shared Data Source Reference and select AW from the drop-down menu. Click OK.

7.   Right-click the Datasets folder and select Add Dataset.

8.   Name the data set **VirginiaTotals**.

9.   Select "Use a dataset embedded in my report."

10.   Select AW as the data source.

11.   Enter the following query into the query window. (This query is in the code included with this book, available at www.wrox.com, and can be copied and pasted from there. The query is named VirginiaTotals.)

```
SELECT       Address_1.SpatialLocation, Address_1.AddressLine1,
             Address_1.City, Address_1.PostalCode,
             Person.StateProvince.StateProvinceCode,
             Sales.SalesOrderHeader.TotalDue
FROM         Person.Address AS Address_1 INNER JOIN
             Person.StateProvince ON Address_1.StateProvinceID =
```

```
                              Person.StateProvince.StateProvinceID INNER JOIN
                              Sales.SalesOrderHeader ON Address_1.AddressID =
                              Sales.SalesOrderHeader.BillToAddressID
         WHERE         (Person.StateProvince.StateProvinceCode = 'VA')
```

12. Click OK.

13. Drag a map from the toolbox onto the report.

14. Select SQL Server Spatial Query and click Next.

15. Select the VirginiaTotals data set and click Next.

16. Place a check next to "Embed map data in the report."

17. Place a check next to "Add a Bing Maps layer."

18. Set the tile type to Hybrid and click Next.

19. Select Bubble Map and click Next.

20. Select the VirginiaTotals data set again and click Next.

21. Leave all the default settings on the Spatial to Analytical mapping window and click Next.

22. Select the Generic theme.

23. Set the data field to TotalDue and click Finish.

24. Preview the report and the map should look like Figure 26-12.

Congratulations! You have created your first map.

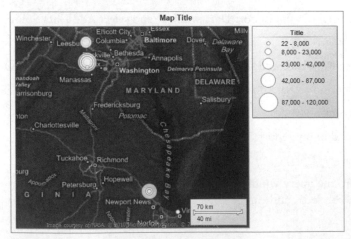

FIGURE 26-12

 Please select Lesson 26 on the DVD to view the video that accompanies this lesson.

27

Building a Dashboard

Reports are great at showing end users detailed information about your company, but sometimes that detail is too much information. The users just need an overview of how the company is doing. This is especially true of high-level executives. Most CEOs rarely need to see the data all the way down to the transaction level or even the individual level. These high-level users need to see the overall health of the company. This information is best displayed on a dashboard.

A dashboard shows the overview of the company in a way that makes it easy for users to get answers to the questions that are important to them. Such questions might be "What store is the best performing?" "Who are the top ten salespeople?" "What products are selling the best?" "Which managers have the best-performing staff?" These questions could be answered by reports, but reports may take several pages to supply the answers. A dashboard answers all these questions on one page.

Generally, a dashboard contains charts, gauges, and small tables. All of these items are at a high level and not very detailed. When a manager is viewing a dashboard and finds a number that stands out as very good or very bad, he or she may want to drill down to the details of that number. This drill-down capability can be added to a dashboard. The end user can simply click the row in question to open a detailed report based on where the user has clicked. These detailed reports are created and maintained separately from the dashboard.

TABLES AND FILTERS

Figure 27-1 is an example of a dashboard. The tables on this dashboard are using the same data set, but with different filters on each table. The chart is using the data set with no filter. This may not seem like a lot of data to show on a report, but keep in mind this is a single page and is a very high-level display of the data. You do not need to show a lot of details on the dashboard. This dashboard answers the question "Which states have the highest and lowest totals due?"

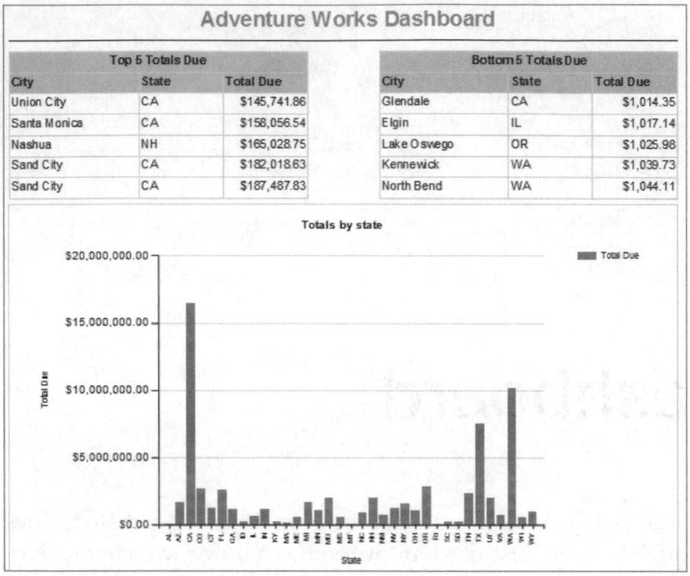

City	State	Total Due
Union City	CA	$145,741.86
Santa Monica	CA	$158,056.54
Nashua	NH	$165,028.75
Sand City	CA	$182,018.63
Sand City	CA	$187,487.83

City	State	Total Due
Glendale	CA	$1,014.35
Elgin	IL	$1,017.14
Lake Oswego	OR	$1,025.98
Kennewick	WA	$1,039.73
North Bend	WA	$1,044.11

FIGURE 27-1

In the previous chapters you learned how to create tables and populate them with data. Those same techniques apply here. The only difference is that tables have filters on them. The following is the query used by the dashboard in Figure 27-1.

```
SELECT Address_1.AddressLine1, Address_1.City, Address_1.PostalCode,
Person.StateProvince.StateProvinceCode AS State,
Sales.SalesOrderHeader.TotalDue, Person.StateProvince.CountryRegionCode
FROM Person.Address AS Address_1 INNER JOIN Person.StateProvince ON
Address_1.StateProvinceID = Person.StateProvince.StateProvinceID
INNER JOIN Sales.SalesOrderHeader ON
Address_1.AddressID = Sales.SalesOrderHeader.BillToAddressID
WHERE (Person.StateProvince.CountryRegionCode = 'US') AND
(Sales.SalesOrderHeader.TotalDue > 1010)
ORDER BY Sales.SalesOrderHeader.TotalDue
```

Notice that this query retrieves all the total-due amounts over $1,010. You can assume the end users do not want to see anything below this number. Even though the query has all the data, the tables are showing only the top and bottom five totals due. This is the result of a filter on each table. To create a filter on a table, click the table so that the gray control boxes appear around it, as in Figure 27-2.

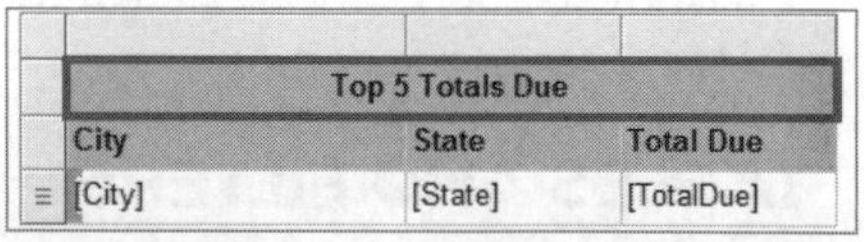

FIGURE 27-2

Right-click the gray box in the top left corner of the table, and select Tablix Properties. Then click the Filters node on the left to open the Filter menu. Click the Add button to add a filter to the table. In the Expressions drop-down menu select [TotalDue]. Select Top N as the operator. You want to filter the table to show only the top five, but you cannot just type the number five into the value field, because reporting services will interpret that as a string and not an integer. You will need to cast it as an integer. Click the "fx" button next to the Value field and enter **=cint(5)**, as shown in Figure 27-3. Afterward the value field will show <<Expr>> and it will be grayed out.

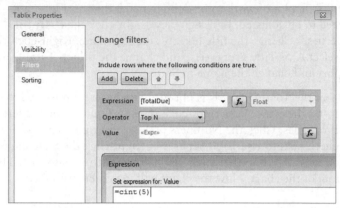

FIGURE 27-3

You will follow the same instructions to set up the other table to show the bottom five totals due. The only difference will be the operator. For the second table select Bottom N as the operator. The tables are now using the same data set and showing completely different data.

The chart will use the same data set as the tables and will not have a filter applied, so it will show all the states. The chart makes it easy to see any states that have a large total due. Even if a state does not appear in the top five, it is still easy for a user to determine the states with the highest numbers with a glance at the chart. In Figure 27-1 you can see that California has the highest number by far.

To create a chart, drag a Chart control over from the Toolbox onto the report body. Our example dashboard is using a column chart. This is the first option at the top left of the Chart Type Select window. Stretch the chart by dragging the edges to the desired locations. Click the chart once and the Chart Data window will appear on the right of the chart, as in Figure 27-4.

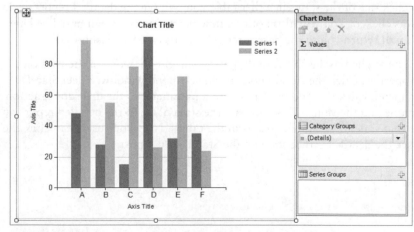

FIGURE 27-4

Click the plus button next to Values and select Total Due. The sum of the Total Due field will be added to the Values list and will be the data represented on the Chart. Click the plus next to Category Groups and select State. This will group the chart columns by state.

Previewing the chart shows that there is still a lot of work to be done to make the chart look polished. The titles, axis, and labels all need to be adjusted. In design view, right-click the chart title above the chart and select "Title properties." Change the title text to **Totals by State**. Right-click the axis title on the left side of the chart, select Axis Title Properties, and change the title to **Total Due**. Right-click the axis title below the report and change the name to State.

The report will have better titles now, but the Total Due axis is not formatted as a number and the State axis does not show every state. To fix these problems right-click the axis numbers on the left of the report and select Vertical Axis Properties. Click the Numbers node on the right. Then select Currency as the category and place a check next to Use 1000 Separator. Right-click the State names axis below the chart and select Horizontal Axis Properties. Change the interval from auto to 1. This will make every state show at the bottom of the chart. Now the chart will match Figure 27-1.

DRILL-DOWNS

One of the most requested features of a dashboard is the ability to drill down to a detailed report. This is easy to set up and can be done with the chart and tables on our example dashboard. The first thing you will need is a detailed report of the data. This is included with the code for this lesson, available at www.wrox.com. The report is named StateDetails. This report has the data down to the row level and has one parameter, that of the state. When the user clicks the drill-down link on the dashboard, he or she will be taken to the detailed report and will see the details of the state selected.

To set up drill-down on one of the dashboard tables, right-click the State text box and select Text Box Properties. Click the Action node in the left window. Click the radio button next to Go to Report. Select StateDetails on the report drop-down menu. This menu shows all the reports in the current project. Click the Add button to add a parameter to the drill-down action. Then select State as the name and the value. This will pass the state name to the detailed report and cause only the details for that state to be shown. Repeat these steps to add drill-down actions to the other table's State column. When you click one of the states in either table you will see the detailed report, as in Figure 27-5, where WA was clicked. You will also notice a new button on the menu bar. The blue arrow pointing to the left will return you to the parent report, in this case the dashboard.

This same drill-down can be applied to the chart. In design view, right-click one of the bars on the chart and select Series Properties. Click the Action node in the left-hand window. Select StateDetails on the report drop-down menu. Click the Add button to add a parameter to the drill-down action. Then select State as the name and the value. This will pass the state name to the detailed report and cause only the details for that state to be shown, just as in the tables. Now your users can click the bar above any state and see the details for that state on the StateDetail report.

Back to Parent Report

FIGURE 27-5

TRY IT

In this Try It you will build a chart on an existing dashboard and create drill-downs for the tables and the chart. This detailed report is already created and is part of the code you can download for this lesson.

 The download for this lesson, available at www.wrox.com, *also includes the SQL query needed for this Try It.*

Lesson Requirements

You will build a dashboard to display data from an overview level. You will also create drill-downs to open detailed reports. You will need the AdventureWorks2008R2 database. This database is free from www.codeplex.com. You will also need to know the name of your SQL Server R2 instance. If it is your default instance, you can use LocalHost as the server name.

Hints

➤ Start with the dashboard report that is already built in the code files.

➤ Add the chart to the dashboard.

➤ Create drill-downs on the tables and the chart.

Step-by-Step

1. Open the BI Trainer Reports project that you created in the previous chapters of this section of the book.

2. Right-click the Reports folder in the Solution Explorer and select Add ➪ Existing Item.

3. Select the Dashboard.rdl file included with the download for this lesson at www.wrox.com.

4. Right click the Reports folder in the Solution Explorer and select Add ➪ Existing Item again.

5. Select the StateDetails.rdl file included with the download for this lesson at www.wrox.com.

6. Double-click the DashBoard.rdl file in the Solution Explorer to open the report. Notice that the two tables are already completed because tables were covered in a previous chapter.

7. To add the drill-down to the table, right-click the State column data row in the left table and select Text Box Properties.

8. Click the Action node on the left.

9. Click the radio button next to Go to Report.

10. Select StateDetails from the Specify a Report drop-down menu.

11. Click Add.

12. Select State in the Name drop-down column.

13. Select [State] from the Value drop-down menu.

14. Click OK.

15. Repeat Steps 7 through 14 to add the same drill-down action to the table on the right. The screen should look like the one in Figure 27-6.

16. Drag a chart from the Toolbox to the space below the tables.

17. Select the column chart in the top left of the chart type list.

18. Click OK.

19. Drag the edges of the chart out until the chart fills most of the space below the tables.

20. Click the chart so the Chart Data window appears to the right of the chart.

21. Click the plus next to Values and select TotalDue.

22. Click the Plus next to Category Groups and select State.

23. Double-click the chart title and change it to **Total by State**.

24. Double-click the vertical axis title and change it to **Total Due**.

25. Double-click the horizontal axis title and change it to **State**.

26. Right-click the vertical axis numbers and select Vertical Axis Properties.

27. Select Number on the left and Currency under Category.

28. Place a check next to Use 1000 Separator.

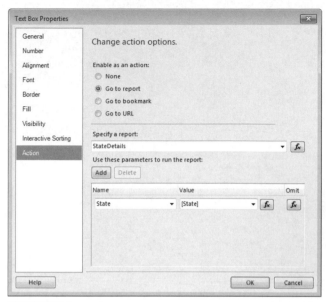

FIGURE 27-6

29. Click OK.

30. Right-click the horizontal axis labels and select Horizontal Axis Properties.

31. Change the interval to 1 and click OK.

32. Right-click one of the blue bars on the chart and select Series Properties.

33. Click Action on the left.

34. Click the radio button next to "Go to Report" and then select StateDetails from the Specify a Report drop-down menu.

35. Click Add.

36. Select State in the Name drop-down column.

37. Select [State] from the Value drop-down menu.

38. Click OK.

39. Click Preview to see the report.

40. Try drilling down on the three Action Spots on the report to see the StateDetails based on the state you select.

Congratulations! You have created your first dashboard.

 Please select Lesson 27 on the DVD to view the video that accompanies this lesson.

28

Deploying and Administering SSRS

After creating reports for your end users, you are ready to deploy them to the Report Server. Then your end users can view them in the Report Manager. The Report Manager is the location your end users can go to in order to view their reports and set up subscriptions to have the reports scheduled and delivered to them via email or the Windows file system.

Now you will need to deploy the reports. To do this you need to set the proper folders and server on the Report Server project properties in BIDS. To set these, click the project link at the top of BIDS and select the last option, Properties. This window is shown in Figure 28-1.

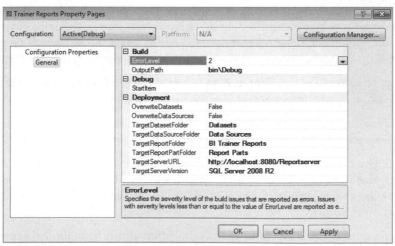

FIGURE 28-1

The properties you need to set in this window are listed under Deployment:

➤ **OverwriteDatasets:** If this property is set to true, the datasets in the project will be deployed even if a given dataset already exists in the Report Server.

➤ **OverwriteDataSources:** If this property is set to true, the data sources in the project will be deployed even if a given data source already exists in the Report Server, replacing the existing data source.

➤ **TargetDatasetFolder:** This is the name of the folder in which the datasets will be saved on the Report Server. If this folder does not exist, it will be created.

➤ **TargetDataSourceFolder:** Name of the folder in which the data sources will be saved on the Report Server. If this folder does not exist, it will be created.

➤ **TargetReportFolder:** Name of the folder in which the reports will be saved on the Report Server. If this folder does not exist, it will be created.

➤ **TargetReportPartFolder:** Name of the folder in which the report parts will be saved on the Report Server. If this folder does not exist, it will be created.

➤ **TargetServerURL:** This is the URL of the Report Server. If it is the local default instance it will usually be `http://localhost:8080/Reportserver`.

In Figure 28-1 you can see the settings for all the properties listed above. Notice that TargetServerURL has a port number of 8080. The port number is usually set to 80. If you have other settings on your server that are using port 80, you might need to change the port number to ensure that there is no conflict between the Report Server and any other services using that port. In this chapter we will use port 8080 for all the reporting examples.

To change the port settings and other configuration settings for your Report Server you will need to open the Reporting Services Configuration Manager. This is found in the Start menu under All Programs ➪ Microsoft SQL Server 2008 R2 ➪ Configuration Tools. The first window of the Reporting Services Configuration Manager is seen in Figure 28-2. In this window you can see the name of your SQL Server instance, the edition, version, Report Server database name, server mode, and whether the service is started or stopped. If your service is stopped you will need to click the Start button to start it.

On the left side of the Reporting Services Configuration Manager there is a list of windows that you will need to go through to ensure your Report Server is configured properly:

➤ **Service Account:** This is generally set to Network Service account to allow remote connections. If you prefer to use a specific account you can enter a username and password.

➤ **Web Service URL:** The Virtual Directory is usually named ReportServer. This is the location the reports are deployed to in BIDS. The TCP port is usually 80 but can be changed if another service is using this port already. The URL is the location entered in BIDS for the Report Server URL in the project properties.

➤ **Database:** These are the databases that hold all the supporting information for the Report Server, like the subscriptions and logs. The database credentials are usually set to NT AUTHORITY\NETWORKSERVICE.

➤ **Report Manager URL:** This is usually set to Reports. This URL is the location your users will go to in order to view their reports.

➤ **E-mail Settings:** The sender address is the address that will be used to send e-mails in the subscriptions from the Report Server. The SMTP server is the e-mail server used by your company.

➤ **Execution Account:** This is generally left empty unless you have a specific account that you need to use to access the report data on a remote server or to access external images used in the reports.

➤ **Encryption Keys:** These are used to protect sensitive information like connection strings and credentials. You can back them up so that if the server needs to be rebuilt, the sensitive information will not be lost.

➤ **Scale-out Deployment:** This window shows all the Report Servers used in the Report Server instance. The Report Server can be farmed out to multiple servers to improve performance.

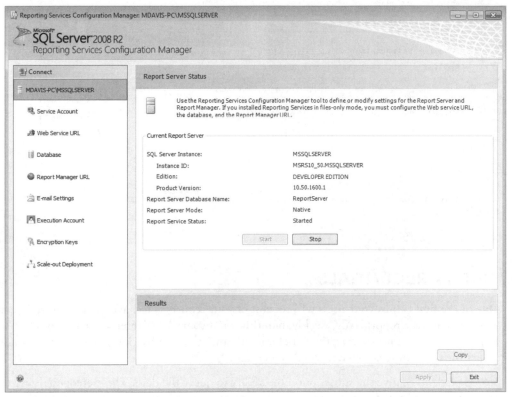

FIGURE 28-2

After you have the Reporting Services Configuration Manager set up properly you should be able to deploy reports from the projects in BIDS. To do this, right-click a report in the Solution Explorer in BIDS and select Deploy. This example will use one of the reports created in the previous chapters: the Sales by Region report. You will want to deploy the shared datasets used by the reports. Right-click the shared dataset SalesByRegion and select Deploy; then do the same for the report of the same name.

At the bottom of BIDS, the Output window will appear and show a message of either success or failure. Figure 28-3 shows the Output window with the success message you expect to see. You are looking

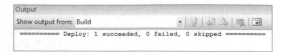

FIGURE 28-3

for the message "1 succeeded, 0 failed." If there was an error, it will read "0 succeeded, 1 failed" and an error will appear after this. This error is usually easy to understand and explains the problem. Generally, errors with deployment have to do with permissions.

After you have deployed the datasets and reports, you can open your browser and navigate to your Report Manager. If this is a local instance, the URL will probably be `http://localhost:8080/Reports`. You can see the Report Manager in Figure 28-4. Notice the folders shown in the Report Manager. These were created by the deployment performed in BIDS.

FIGURE 28-4

STORED CREDENTIALS

One of the first things your users will request of your reports is to have them delivered on a schedule. They may want a report daily, weekly, monthly, or at some other interval. You can set this up in the Report Manager with subscriptions. Before you can set up a subscription to a report, you need to adjust the data sources to have stored credentials.

Stored credentials give the subscription the ability to query the data. These credentials are usually a SQL user set up on the server with a security setting that gives the user the ability to query the data. In this example, the server has a user already created with the name reports. Click the Data Source folder in the Report Manager and you will see the data source AWDW, if it has been deployed already; if not, return to BIDS and deploy it.

Now you can enter the stored credentials into the data source. Click the radio button next to "Credentials stored securely in the report server" and enter the username and password of the SQL user you created. You can also click the Test Connection button at the bottom of the window to ensure that the credentials work. You can see the bottom half of this window in Figure 28-5. Click the Apply button to save the credentials for the data source.

Connect using:
- ○ Credentials supplied by the user running the report
  - Display the following text to prompt user for a user name and password:
  - `Type or enter a user name and password to access the data source`
  - ☐ Use as Windows credentials when connecting to the data source
- ● Credentials stored securely in the report server
  - User name: `reports`
  - Password: `••••••••`
  - ☐ Use as Windows credentials when connecting to the data source
  - ☐ Impersonate the authenticated user after a connection has been made to the data source
- ○ Windows integrated security
- ○ Credentials are not required

[Test Connection]
Connection created successfully.

FIGURE 28-5

SUBSCRIPTIONS

Now that you have stored credentials on each of your data sources you can create subscriptions on the reports. In the BI Trainer Reports folder you see the report name SalesByRegion. When you mouse over the report a drop-down menu will appear, and in this menu there is a Subscribe option, as shown in Figure 28-6.

Selecting Subscribe takes you to the Subscription window. The following is a list of all the menu options in the Subscriptions window and how they should be set up when Windows file share is selected.

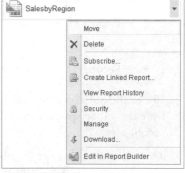

SalesbyRegion

- Move
- ✕ Delete
- Subscribe...
- Create Linked Report...
- View Report History
- Security
- Manage
- Download...
- Edit in Report Builder

FIGURE 28-6

➤ **Delivered by:** These options include Windows file share and e-mail. If you do not have the SMTP server information entered into the Reporting Services Configuration Manager, then the e-mail option will not show.

➤ **File Name:** This is the name of the file that is created by the subscription when it runs. The name does not include the extension of the file.

➤ **Path:** This is the Windows file share location where the report will be saved. This cannot be a drive-letter location. It must be a shared Windows location such as \\localhost\reports.

➤ **Render Format:** This is the type of file you want the subscription to create.

➤ **User name and Password:** These are the credentials used for writing the files to the Windows file share.

➤ **Overwrite options:** If this is set to "Do not overwrite" and the file already exists, the subscription will fail. The increment option will create a file and add a number to the file name so the original will not be overwritten.

➤ **Schedule:** A shared schedule can be used by several reports. Updating the shared schedule will affect all reports using it. The other option is an independent schedule used only by the created subscription.

After creating a subscription for a report, you will need a way to manage the subscriptions. Click the drop-down menu next to the report name again and select Manage, shown in Figure 28-6. The Report Management screen has several options on the left-hand side of the window. They include the following:

➤ **Properties:** Name and description of the report

➤ **Data Sources:** Data sources used by the report

➤ **Shared Datasets:** Shared datasets used by the report

➤ **Subscriptions:** Subscriptions set up on the report and the status of the last run for each subscription

➤ **Processing Options:** Cache and snapshot options

➤ **Cache Refresh Options:** Location of cache refresh plans

➤ **Report History:** Saved snapshots of the report

➤ **Snapshot Options:** Controls snapshot history options

➤ **Security:** Controls the security options and roles

Under the Subscriptions option you can see any subscription on the current report and the last time the subscription ran, along with the status of that run. You can delete the subscription in this screen also.

There is one other type of subscription available in Reporting Services. It is the data-driven subscription. This type of subscription is beyond the scope of this book, but you can learn more about it at www.bidn.com.

SHARED SCHEDULES

Subscriptions will deliver the reports you need, but the schedules for these subscriptions may change in the future and will need to be maintained. Imagine that you have dozens of reports running daily at 7 p.m., and you need to change this time to 8 p.m. Changing each of these reports' schedules would be very time-consuming. If they are all using the same shared schedule, you need to adjust only that one schedule, and all reports using it are updated.

Shared schedules can be found under the Site Settings in the Report Manager. This link is on the top right of the Report Manager. Under Site Settings is an option named Schedules, on the left. Under this option you can create all the shared schedules to use for all subscriptions. Figure 28-7 shows the Schedules screen with two schedules already created. These schedules are now available to anyone creating subscriptions.

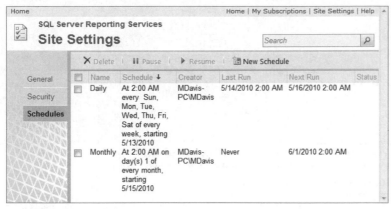

FIGURE 28-7

SECURITY

Security is a very important part of any Report Server. The Active Directory in Windows ties right into the security in Reporting Services. You can use the usernames and groups from Active Directory to control who can view, subscribe, edit, and delete reports.

To adjust the security for a report or the folder containing reports, click the drop-down menu next to the item and select Security, shown in Figure 28-6. To adjust the security, click the Edit Item Security link at the top of the window. You may receive a prompt asking whether you want to apply settings that are different from those of the parent item. You are asked this because the security for an item is inherited from the parent item. Clicking OK on this prompt will separate the security of this item from that of its parent. You can revert to this inheritance by clicking the Revert to Parent Security button, which appears after you remove the inheritance.

After you click the New Role Assignment button you see the window in Figure 28-8. The text box at the top is where you can enter the group name or username to assign to the current item. Below this are the different security levels you can give to the user.

- ➤ **Browser:** Allows the user to view folders and reports, and to set up subscriptions to the reports
- ➤ **Content Manager:** Allows the user to delete and create reports and folders
- ➤ **My Reports:** Allows the user to see the folders that have the My Reports access granted and to manage the content in these folders
- ➤ **Publisher:** Allows the user to deploy reports to the server
- ➤ **Report Builder:** Allows the user to create reports using Report Builder

The Data Sources and Datasets folders are not among the My Reports folders by default. If you want to allow a user access to these folders you will have to add My Reports access to them. This is not recommended and can be a security nightmare. If your users delete a data source or dataset that is being used by dozens of reports, all of those reports will fail to run, and each subscription for these reports will fail.

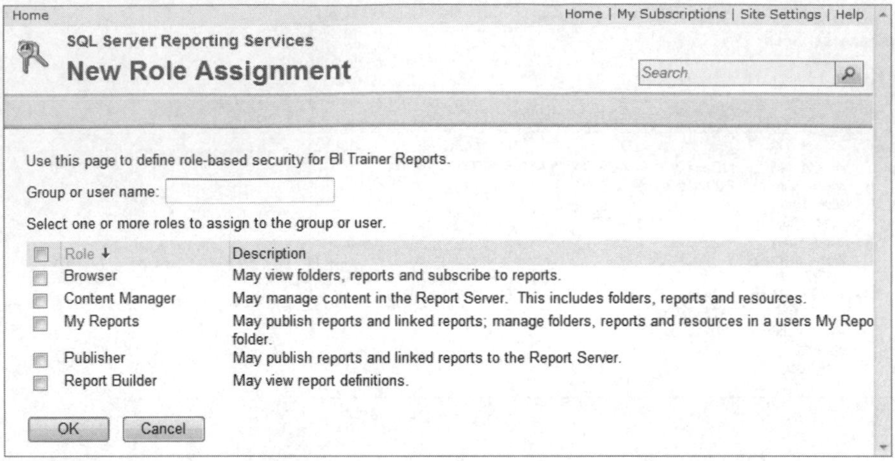

FIGURE 28-8

There is a Folder Settings button at the top of the Report Manager. This controls the overall security for the Report Manager. You can adjust the security for each folder separately by selecting Security from the drop-down menu next to each folder and report. If a user is set to Browser, several buttons will not show in the Report Manager for that user. Figure 28-9 shows the Report Manager with the user logged in as an administrator, and Figure 28-10 shows the Report Manager for a user logged in with Browser-level security. Notice the buttons and the folders that are missing in the second figure.

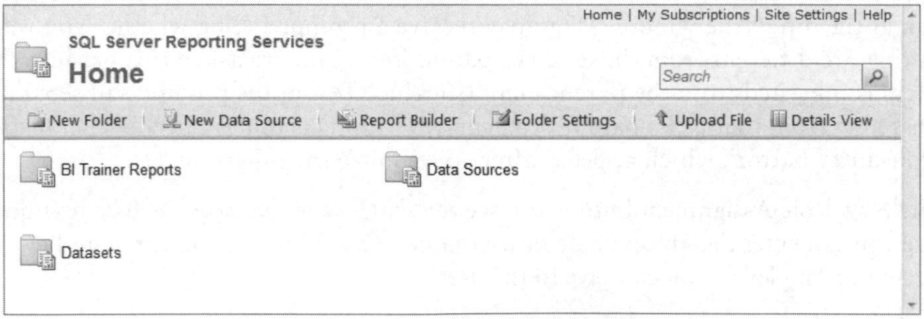

FIGURE 28-9

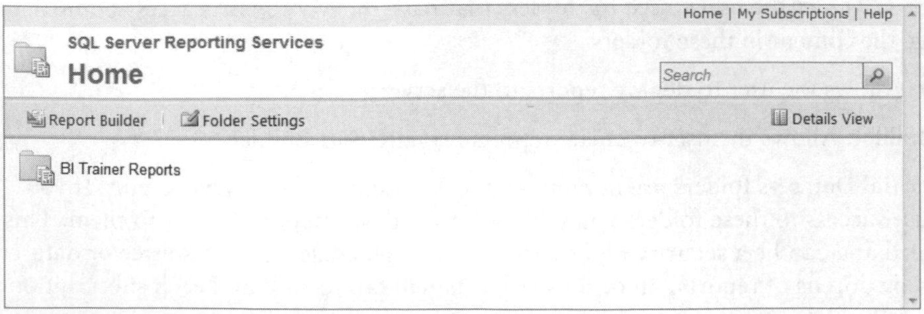

FIGURE 28-10

When logged in as a browser, the user will not have access to the security settings throughout the Report Manager. If the user clicks the drop-down menu next to a folder or report, he or she will see the security option in the menu. If the user clicks this link, he or she will see the message "You do not have permission to access this page."

These settings can be set up on a group basis also, but these groups may encompass users that need more access. For example, if you work at a financial institution and the lending department needs access to reports, you could give the lending group Browser access to the lending folder, so its members would be able to view reports, but not to manage the content in the folder. This would prevent the users from deleting reports. This works great for the entire department, except the manager. She needs to be able to create and delete reports and manage the content in the lending folder. In this case you would give the lending group Browser access, but the lending manager's individual login would get Content Manager access to the lending folder.

DATASETS AND CACHING

Shared datasets are a new feature in Reports Services 2008 R2. They allow reports to share queries used by multiple reports. There is also a caching option in the Report Manager that allows datasets to cache the data so that when the report is run it loads much faster. The data is stored in the Report Server database.

To manage the datasets and set up caching, click the drop-down menu next to the dataset, as shown in Figure 28-6, and select Manage. Then click the Caching option on the left side of the Report Manager. This window gives you the option to enable caching on a dataset. When you enable caching by checking Cache Shared Dataset, you can then select the number of minutes the dataset should remain in the cache. A common situation in which to use this option would be when you want a daily refresh of your data warehouse. If the data warehouse is refreshed nightly, it may make sense for you to set the number of minutes here to equal several hours. If the data is not going to be refreshed until tomorrow anyway, then there is no need to query the data source again. The first user to run the report will create the cache. The following users will see the report load much faster because it has been cached. There is also an option to expire the cache on a schedule. This could be set to a time right before the data warehouse load process starts.

Parameters can make dataset caching a little harder to manage. The cache that is saved will be based on the parameters the user selects. If subsequent users use a different set of parameters, then the cache cannot be used and the report will query the data source again. Caching can be improved by setting up a cache refresh plan.

Under the Caching option on the left, the next item down is Cache Refresh Options. In this window you can create a schedule for refreshing the cache and set the value of the parameters to be used in the schedule. The parameter settings should be the most popular parameter combinations to give the users the best use of the cache. The button at the top, New Cache Refresh Plan, will open the window to create the schedule. If you do not have caching enabled, you will receive a message telling you that caching is not enabled and asking whether you want to turn on caching with the default options. If you select OK here, caching will be turned on and set to the default time of 30 minutes. You can alter the time, if you desire.

Figure 28-11 shows the Cache Refresh Plan window for the report you created in Lesson 23, SalesByRegionParam. The datasets for this report have been converted to shared datasets and are not using any stored procedures. To convert a dataset to a shared dataset, right-click the dataset in BIDS and select Convert to Shared Dataset.

Notice the two parameters at the bottom of Figure 28-11. The year and state parameters need to be set to allow caching of this dataset. If the users typically use the current year and the state of Florida, then these should be the values entered. You can create several cache refresh plans if you have several combinations that are used frequently.

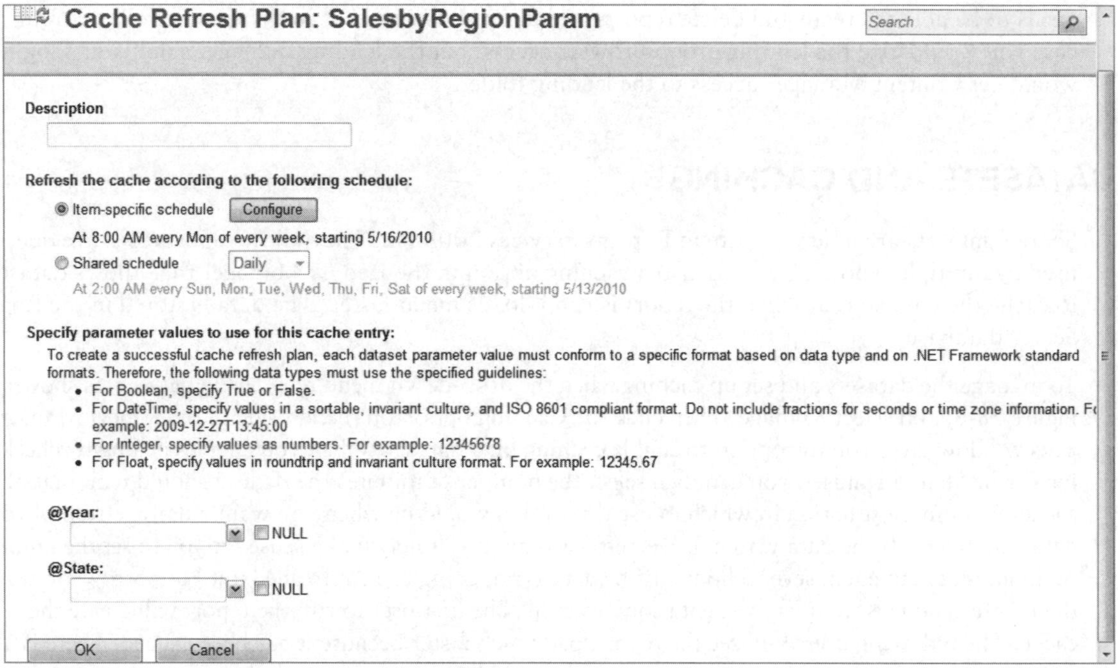

FIGURE 28-11

One word of caution: When you first set up caching of datasets, the size of the cache will not be a big concern, but after you have created many datasets, the caching size can become an issue. The Report Server database can grow very quickly. Check the database size after creating each new caching schedule to avoid this pitfall.

REPORT BUILDER 3.0

Some of your more advanced users may want to create their own reports. BIDS is not an option for this type of arrangement because it is expensive and hard to learn. Report Builder 3.0 is a great option for these users. This tool has the look and feel of Microsoft Office 2007 or later, with the ribbons across the top.

The Report Builder button in the Report Manager will open Report Builder 3.0. The first window is the wizard start-up screen. It gives you the option to start a table, matrix, chart, map, or just a blank report. On the left is the option to create a shared dataset. Although this tool is easier to use than BIDS, most users will need to receive a little training to get them started, especially if they have never created a report.

A blank report in Report Builder looks like the one in Figure 28-12. On the right side you see the link to connect to a Report Server. All the data sources and datasets in the Report Server will be available in the Report Builder. On the left is the Report Data window. This is the same window as in BIDS and works the same way. You can create data sources and datasets using the methods for BIDS described in previous lessons.

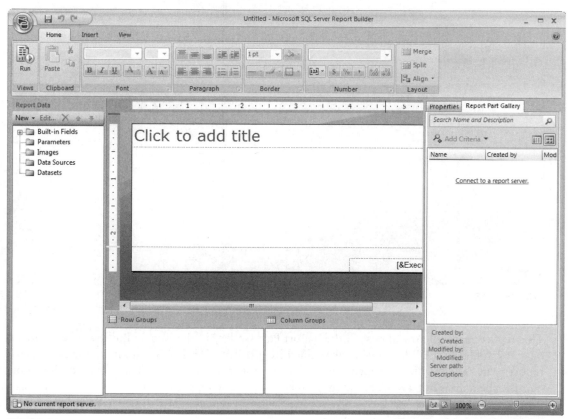

FIGURE 28-12

REPORT PARTS

On the right of the Report Builder is the Report Part Gallery. Users can create report parts and publish them to the Report Server for others to use. These can be tables, matrixes, charts or any item on a report. To publish a report part in Report Builder click the Ribbon button (the round button on the top left) and select Publish Report Parts. A window appears that asks whether you would like to publish all parts with the default settings or review and modify the report parts before publishing. When you select the review option a window will appear showing all the report parts that are going to be published. In this window you can change the names of the parts and add descriptions to them. Figure 28-13 shows this window with a matrix being published and the description.

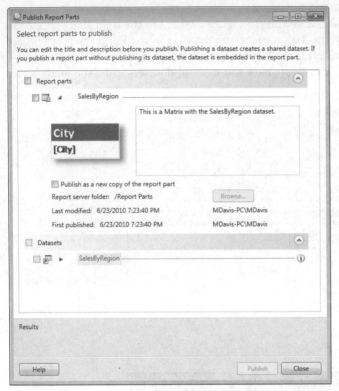

FIGURE 28-13

This report part will now appear in the Report Part Gallery in the Report Builder. There will also be a new folder in the Report Manager named Report Parts. This will contain all the published report parts. The only management option for report parts is Security. There are no caching options because the data is not associated with the report part. The report part is only an object that can be dropped onto a report. Any datasets associated with the report part will still need to be available in order for the report part to function.

VIEWING REPORTS

After the reports are published, the security set up, and the desired caching created, your users will be ready to start using the Report Manager to view their reports. They can do this by clicking the folder containing the reports and then clicking the report. If the report contains any parameters, they will appear at the top of the report viewer. Figure 28-14 shows the SalesByRegionParam report created in Lesson 23 in Report Manager. Notice the parameters above the report and the View Report button on the right.

FIGURE 28-14

If the user needs to run the report several times with different parameters, he or she can change the parameter values and click the View Report button again to refresh the report. In Figure 28-14 the matrix on the report has expandable fields. You can see a small plus next to the year and the state. These functions that you create in BIDS all transfer over to the Report Manager.

After you run a report in BIDS, you may want to export the report to save a copy of it in a file. The blue floppy disk button has a drop-down menu with the available options for export, as shown in Figure 28-15.

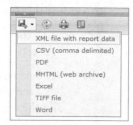

The export options have different effects on the pagination of the reports. In other words, you will get different page counts based on the export format you choose. The PDF option paginates based on the physical size of the page. The HTML option paginates based on the page break rules set up on the report.

FIGURE 28-15

You can also print from the Report Manager. The printer icon is on the same bar as the export icon. In the print window there is a Preview button that allows you to see what the report will look like before you print. It is always a good idea to check the printing of a report. Just because a report looks good on screen does not mean it will look good on paper. You can adjust the page layout in BIDS or Report Builder in the Report properties window.

TRY IT

In this Try It, you will deploy a data source, dataset, and report to the Report Server. Then you will view them in Report Manager. You will also export the report to Excel and PDF.

Lesson Requirements

Now, you will deploy reports to your report server. These reports will be available to users through the Report Manager portal. You will need the AdventureWorks2008 R2 database. This database is free from www.codeplex.com. You will also need to know the name of your SQL Server R2 instance. If it is your default instance, you can use LocalHost as the server name. You will also need to have rights to deploy reports to the Report Server. If you are using Report Server on your local machine you should have these rights.

The download for this lesson, available at www.wrox.com, *includes the complete BI Trainer Reports solution.*

Hints

➤   Use BIDS to deploy the report.

➤   Open the Report Manager using Internet Explorer.

➤   Look at the deployed fields to see the difference in pagination.

Step-by-Step

1.   Open the project BI Trainer Reports you created in the previous lessons. If you did not create them, you can use the BI Trainer Reports project available as part of the download for this book.

2.   Click the project menu at the top of BIDS, and select the last item, BI Trainer Reports Properties.

3.   Set the target server URL to your Report Server URL. If this is a local instance and the port has been changed to 8080, the URL will be `http://localhost:8080/Reportserver`. Leave all other options at the defaults, and click OK.

4.   Right-click the AWDW data source in the Solution Explorer and select Deploy. You should see a success message appear in the Output window.

5.   Right-click the SalesByRegion dataset in the Solution Explorer and select Deploy. You should see a success message appear in the Output window.

6.   Right-click the SalesByRegion report in the Solution Explorer and select Deploy. You should see a success message appear in the Output window.

7.   Open Internet Explorer and enter your Report Manager URL. If this is a local instance and the port has been changed to 8080, the URL will be `http://localhost:8080/Reports`. You can also find this URL in the Report Server Configuration tool under the Report Manager URL.

8.   Click the BI Trainer Reports folder in the Report Manager.

9.   Click the SalesByRegion report to see this report in the Report Manager.

10.   Click the Export drop-down menu, and select Excel.

11.   Click Open in the prompt that appears. View the report in Excel, and save the file to a local folder.

This next section requires a username to be set up in your SQL Server with the rights to query the AdventureWorksDW 2008 R2 database.

12. Return to the Home screen of the Report Manager. The home link is in the top left of the browser.

13. Open the Data Sources folder.

14. Click the AWDW data source.

15. Click the radio button next to "Credentials stored securely in the report server."

16. Enter the username and password that has rights to query the AdventureWorks data warehouse. You can click Test Connection to ensure the credentials are working.

17. Click Apply to save the credentials.

18. Return to the Home screen of the Report Manager. The home link is in the top left of the browser.

19. Open the Datasets folder.

20. Click the drop-down menu next to the SalesByRegion dataset and select Manage.

21. Click the Caching link on the left.

22. Place a check next to Cache Shared Dataset and click Apply. This will cache the report for 30 minutes when it is run.

23. Return to the BI Trainer Reports folder.

24. Open the drop-down menu next to the SalesByRegion report and select Manage.

25. Click Subscriptions on the left.

26. Click New Subscription at the top.

27. Select Windows File Share as the delivery method.

28. Enter in a Windows file share path that you have access to write files into. (This cannot be a drive-letter location.)

29. Select PDF and the Render type.

30. Select "Overwrite an existing file with a newer version."

31. Click Select Schedule, and select the option once and a time one or two minutes in the future; then click OK.

32. Enter the username and password that has the rights to write to the Windows file share. This can be your credentials in this exercise but will usually be a username set up for subscription use only. Check Figure 28-16, which shows the completed subscriptions window. Click OK to save the subscription.

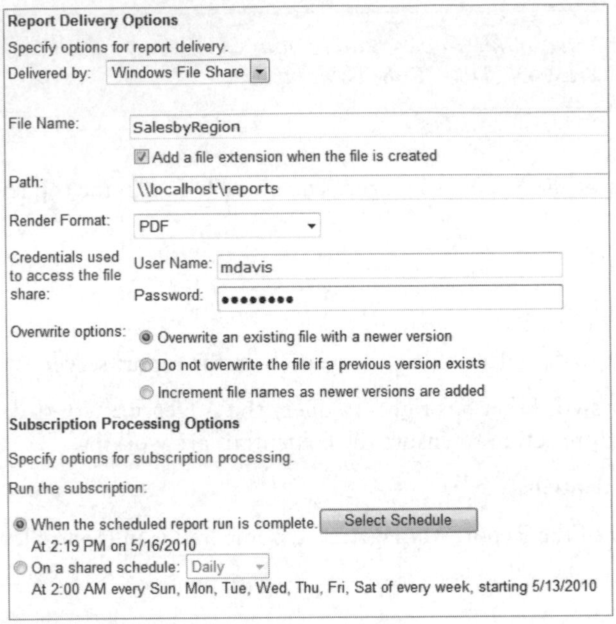

Report Delivery Options

Specify options for report delivery.

Delivered by: Windows File Share ▾

File Name: SalesbyRegion

☑ Add a file extension when the file is created

Path: \\localhost\reports

Render Format: PDF ▾

Credentials used to access the file share:
User Name: mdavis
Password: ••••••••

Overwrite options:
○ Overwrite an existing file with a newer version
○ Do not overwrite the file if a previous version exists
○ Increment file names as newer versions are added

Subscription Processing Options

Specify options for subscription processing.

Run the subscription:

○ When the scheduled report run is complete. [Select Schedule]
   At 2:19 PM on 5/16/2010
○ On a shared schedule: Daily ▾
   At 2:00 AM every Sun, Mon, Tue, Wed, Thu, Fri, Sat of every week, starting 5/13/2010

FIGURE 28-16

33. Wait for the needed time to pass for the subscription to run, then check the Windows file share. The report should be there in PDF format.

Congratulations! You have deployed and set up a subscription for a report.

 Please select Lesson 28 on the DVD to view the video that accompanies this lesson.

29

New Reporting Services Visualizations — Sparklines, Data Bars, and Indicators

SQL Server 2008 R2 Reporting Services (SSRS) includes many new visualization components. These components will help you display your data in a more appealing and graphical manner. *Sparklines* and *data bars*, two of the new components, provide in-row graphical depiction of the data. These require very little space, which allows them to fit in line with the data. You can offer your end users row-by-row visualizations of their data, allowing them to identify any inconsistencies or common trends quickly.

Other new features of SSRS 2008 R2 are *indicators*. Indicators are typically used to represent a single data value quickly. SSRS provides several different icons that can be used as indicators. These indicators can show how sales are trending through the use of the up, flat, and down trending arrows. They can also represent whether or not certain conditions are met.

ADDING SPARKLINES

Sparklines, although very similar to data bars (which we discuss later in this lesson) with regard to their configuration, have one very distinguishing characteristic. They can be placed only in a cell that is associated with an aggregation or grouping. Since sparklines represent aggregates they cannot be added to a detail row in a table. When placed, they represent each value in the corresponding line. As a result, a data point for each value is displayed in the sparkline.

Assume that you have created a matrix on a report from the AdventureWorks2008 R2 database. The matrix has an aggregated row for each country. In addition, each column in the matrix represents the total sales for each country for a given year. There is also a graph on the report that depicts the trends of the data. Figure 29-1 shows an example of this report.

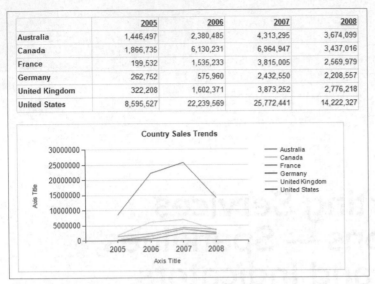

	2005	2006	2007	2008
Australia	1,446,497	2,380,485	4,313,295	3,674,099
Canada	1,866,735	6,130,231	6,964,947	3,437,016
France	199,532	1,535,233	3,815,005	2,569,979
Germany	262,752	575,960	2,432,550	2,208,557
United Kingdom	322,208	1,602,371	3,873,252	2,776,218
United States	8,595,527	22,239,569	25,772,441	14,222,327

FIGURE 29-1

This is a typical scenario. The challenge for the end user is correlating the data in the table with the data in the graph. Through the use of sparklines, a small graphical depiction of each row can now be included on the table.

To add a sparkline, right-click the year column and select Insert Column followed by Outside Group — Right. Then drag a sparkline from the toolbox into the new column. Double-click the sparkline and drag the value that you want to graph into the Values section. Finally, run the report (Figure 29-2).

	2005	2006	2007	2008	
Australia	1,446,497	2,380,485	4,313,295	3,674,099	
Canada	1,866,735	6,130,231	6,964,947	3,437,016	
France	199,532	1,535,233	3,815,005	2,569,979	
Germany	262,752	575,960	2,432,550	2,208,557	
United Kingdom	322,208	1,602,371	3,873,252	2,776,218	
United States	8,595,527	22,239,569	25,772,441	14,222,327	

FIGURE 29-2

USING DATA BARS

Data bars are also small graphs that can be included with each row displayed in a table or matrix. Unlike sparklines, data bars can be added to a detail grouping. Another difference is that a data bar typically illustrates one data point, but it can represent multiple points. Data bars are very similar to bar charts in that they can contain several different series and groupings. For example, a typical bar chart may represent quantity and sales, which are the series, and the data may be grouped by year. A data bar can be configured in the same way.

Assume that you have a table that contains a listing of countries and their corresponding sales (Figure 29-3).

You could easily add a regular bar graph to the report to enable better visualization of the data. However, you can also use data bars next to the data (Figure 29-4).

Name	Total Due
Australia	11,814,376
Canada	18,398,929
France	8,119,749
Germany	5,479,820
United Kingdom	8,574,049
United States	70,829,863

FIGURE 29-3

Name	Total Due	
Australia	11,814,376	
Canada	18,398,929	
France	8,119,749	
Germany	5,479,820	
United Kingdom	8,574,049	
United States	70,829,863	

FIGURE 29-4

The steps for adding a simple data bar are very similar to those you would follow to add a sparkline. The only difference is that you should select a data bar component from the toolbox instead of a sparkline. Once you have added the data bar to the table or matrix, double-click it and add the data point that you want to graph to the Values section.

CONFIGURING INDICATORS

Indicators are great components to use when you are trying to visualize trends, conditions, or some type of ranking or rating. For example, you could add a column containing an indicator to the table in Figure 29-4 (see Figure 29-5).

The steps for adding an indicator are similar to those you follow when adding a data bar or a sparkline. Instead of choosing either of the aforementioned items, you should select an indicator form the toolbox. Once you have added the indicator to the table or matrix, double-click it and click the properties icon in the Gauge Data window (Figure 29-6).

	Total Due	
Australia	11,814,376	
Canada	18,398,929	
France	8,119,749	
Germany	5,479,820	
United Kingdom	8,574,049	
United States	70,829,863	

FIGURE 29-5

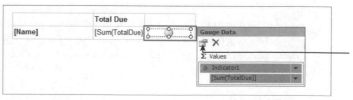

FIGURE 29-6

The Indicator Properties window appears (Figure 29-7). When configuring an indicator, you specify start and end values that will determine which indicator to display.

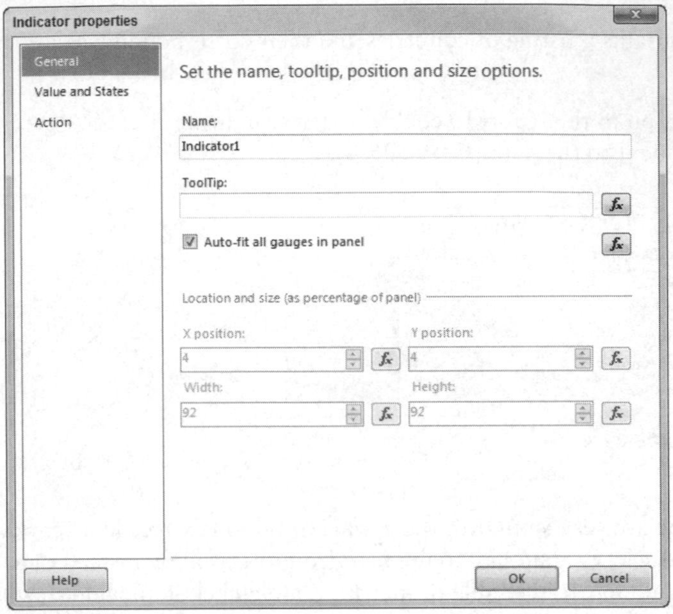

FIGURE 29-7

You can set your measurement unit states to be either percentages of the total or numerics (the values themselves). In addition, you can specify what image to display. You can choose either a built-in image or an external image.

TRY IT

In this Try It, you will learn how to create a SSRS 2008 R2 report that contains sparklines, data bars, and indicators. You will start with a report that can be downloaded from the Wrox web site. Use the ProductSales report contained within the project.

 The download for this lesson, available at www.wrox.com, *includes a Reporting Services project solution you can use with this Try It.*

Lesson Requirements

You will be using the Business Intelligence Development Studio (BIDS) to create a report. You will need the AdventureWorks2008 R2 database. You will modify a matrix report to include the new visualization components included with SSRS R2. In this example the report will show a sparkline that represents sales trends for particular products, a data bar that depicts the sales for each product, and an indicator that illustrates how sales are trending.

Hints

➤ Three columns will need to be added to the report.

➤ Add a sparkline to the grouping line of the report.

➤ Add a data bar to the detail group of the report.

➤ Finally, add two different indicators. One indicator will be added to the only grouping on the report and the other will be added to the detail row.

Step-by-Step

1. Open the BI Trainer Project 29 solution.

2. Double-click the report named ProductSales.

3. Ensure that the Design tab is active (Figure 29-8).

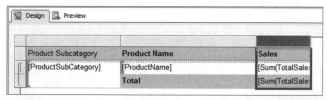

FIGURE 29-8

4. Right-click the column labeled Sales and select Insert Column, followed by Outside Group — Right. In the empty column next to the word Sales, type **Sales Trend**.

5. Drag a sparkline from the toolbox into the new column. Make sure that you drop the sparkline on the same row that contains the word Total.

6. Ensure that you select the first sparkline from the Line section of the Select Sparkline Type screen (Figure 29-9).

7. Click OK.

8. Double-click the sparkline.

9. Click the plus icon that is located to the right of the word Value and select Total Sales from the Column list.

10. Preview the report.

11. Drag a data bar into the column that is directly above the sparkline.

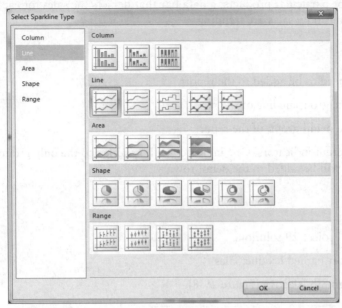

FIGURE 29-9

12. Ensure that you select the first data bar from the Data Bar section of the Select Data Bar Type screen (Figure 29-10).

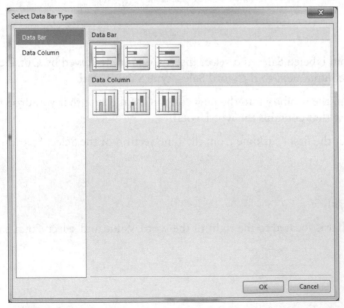

FIGURE 29-10

13. Click OK.

14. Double-click the data bar.

15. Click the plus icon that is located to the right of the word Value and select Total Sales from the column drop-down list (Figure 29-11).

16. Preview the report. Scroll down a little until to you see the Road Bikes subcategory. Expand it to see the data bars.

17. Return to design view and right-click the column labeled Sales Trend, select Insert Column, and then select Right.

18. Drag an indicator into the column next to the data bar.

19. Select the stoplight icons (Figure 29-12) from the Shapes section of the Select Indicator Type screen.

20. Click OK.

21. Double-click the indicator.

22. In the Values section, select Total Sales from the drop-down list that has Unspecified currently selected.

FIGURE 29-11

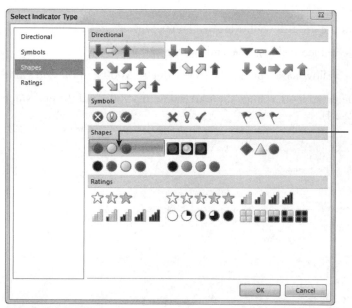

FIGURE 29-12

23. Click the properties icon and then select Value and States from the left navigation pane (Figure 29-13).

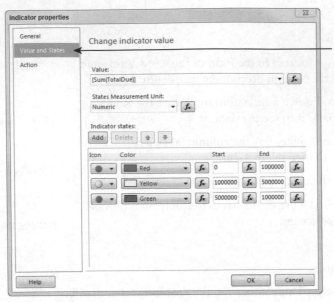

FIGURE 29-13

24. Select Numeric from the drop-down list labeled States Measurement Unit.

25. On the row with the red icon, change the end value to 5000.

26. On the row with the yellow icon, change the start value to **5000** and the end value to **10000**.

27. On the row with the green icon, change the start value to **10000** and the end value to **5000000** (Figure 29-14).

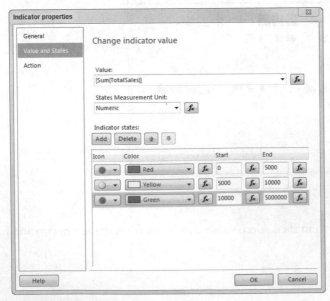

FIGURE 29-14

28. Click OK.

29. Drag an indicator into the column next to the sparkline.

30. Select the trending arrows (Figure 29-15) from the Directional section of the Select Indicator Type screen.

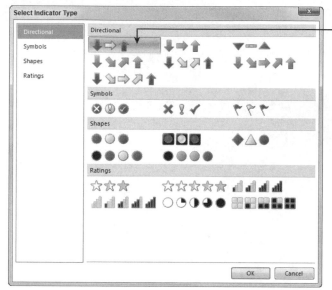

FIGURE 29-15

31. Click OK.

32. Double-click the indicator.

33. In the Values section select Total Sales from the drop-down list that has Unspecified currently selected.

34. Click the properties icon, and then select Value and States from the left navigation pane.

35. Select Numeric from the drop-down list labeled States Measurement Unit.

36. On the row with the red icon, change the end value to **20000**.

37. On the row with the yellow icon, change the start value to **20000** and the end value to **100000**.

38. On the row with the green icon, change the start value to **100000** and the end value to **50000000**.

39. Preview your report, and you will see trend lines on the Total sections and arrow indicators located directly next to them. If you expand a product subcategory, you will see a data bar for each product and a stoplight indicator next to the data bar.

 Please select Lesson 29 on the DVD to view the video that accompanies this lesson.

30

Using Report Builder

Report Builder 3.0 is a tool for designing, authoring, and publishing reports, designed for end users and business users. The tool allows users to create reports by:

➤ Starting from scratch

➤ Using a built-in wizard (table, matrix, or map)

➤ Using a shared dataset

➤ Using report parts

No matter the design method, once the report is complete it can be saved to the file system or published to the Report Manager. Choosing the latter allows those who have permissions to view the report. In addition, end users can open and edit reports in Report Builder from the Report Manager or SharePoint if they have permissions to access the report. Once open, the report can be modified and then published to the Report Manager. The users can either publish it as a new report or overwrite the existing report with the appropriate permissions.

Report Builder 3.0 is a tool that enables end users to perform several of the tasks that were the responsibility of the IT staff. They can now build new reports, modify existing reports, and leverage existing components that have been published to the Report Manager or SharePoint.

OPENING REPORT BUILDER

Report Builder can be opened from SharePoint or the Report Manager. You may also download it and install it on your machine. If you do this, you can open it from your Windows Start menu, though how you open it will often depend on what you are trying to do.

To open Report Builder 3.0 from the Report Manager, simply click the item labeled Report Builder (Figure 30-1).

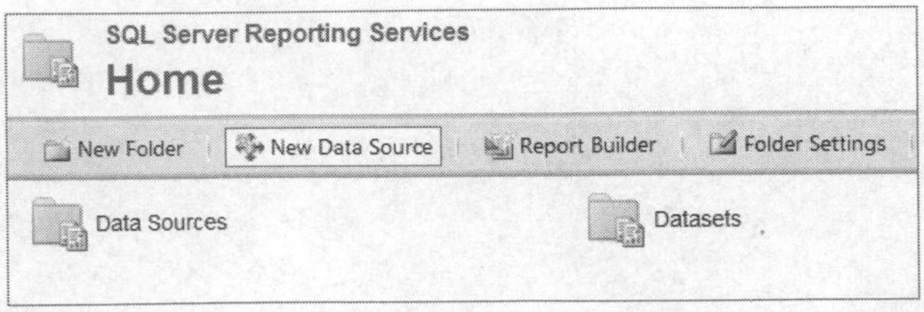

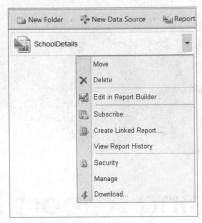

FIGURE 30-1

If you want to edit an existing report, click the drop-down list located next to the report in the Report Manager and select Edit in Report Builder (Figure 30-2).

You can also do this in SharePoint, if you have any reports that have been deployed to the server.

FIGURE 30-2

WORKING WITH THE TABLE, MATRIX, OR CHART WIZARD

Report Builder's wizards make it really easy for a person with a very limited technical background to create reports. When Report Builder is initially opened you are presented with a start-up screen that offers several choices (Figure 30-3).

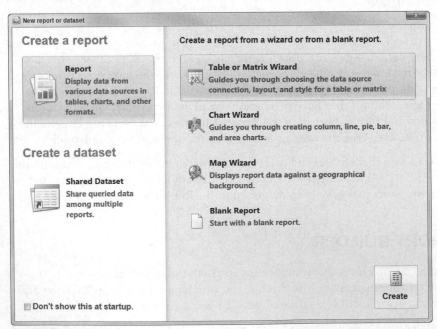

FIGURE 30-3

You can use three different wizards, Table/Matrix, Chart, or Map. You can also start with a blank report or create a shared dataset. (I'll discuss shared datasets a little later in this lesson.)

If you choose Table or Matrix Wizard and click the button in the lower right-hand corner of the window, labeled Create, the wizard will begin. On the first screen (Figure 30-4) you will choose or create a dataset.

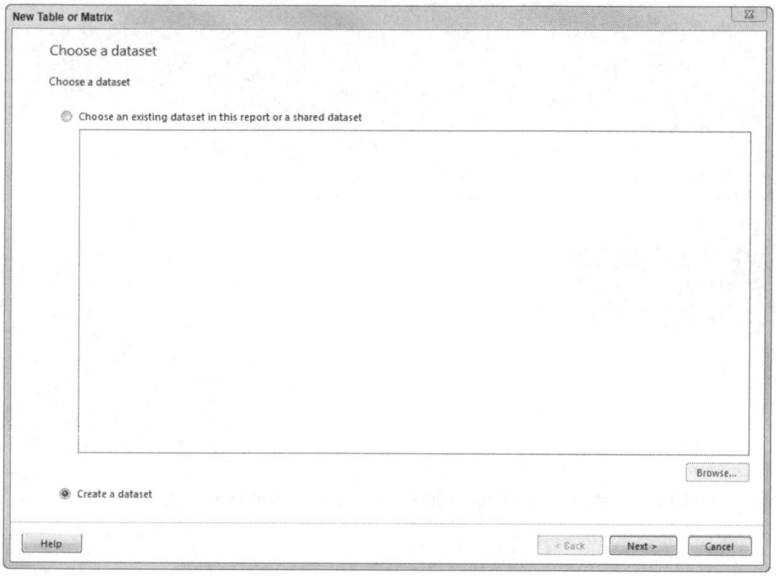

FIGURE 30-4

Clicking the button labeled Browse in the lower right-hand corner opens the Select Dataset window. This window allows you to browse the report server for any shared datasets. On the next screen you will arrange the fields from the dataset into columns, rows, and values (Figure 30-5).

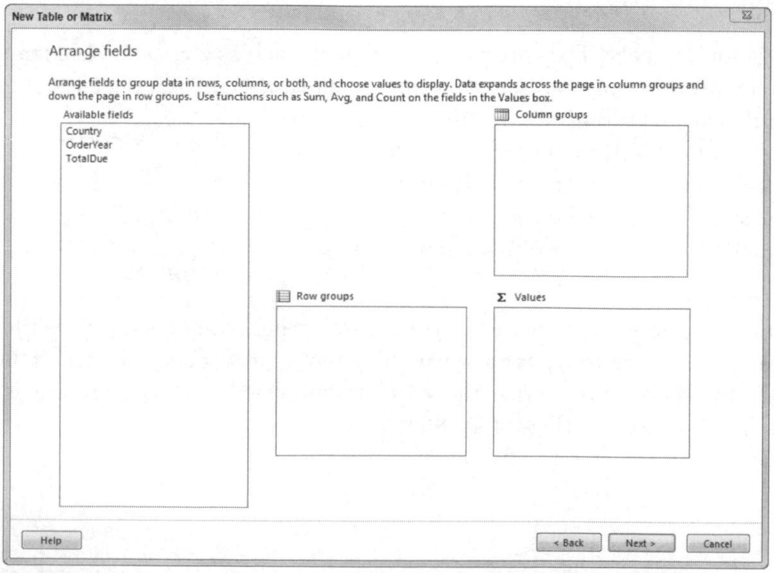

FIGURE 30-5

Finally, on the last two screens you select the layout and style of your report. Once you are done the report opens in design view (Figure 30-6).

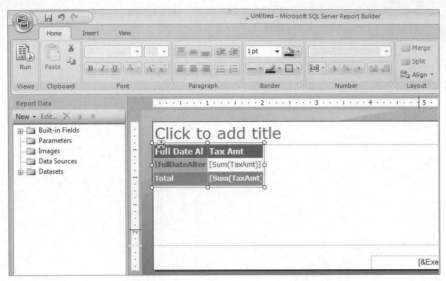

FIGURE 30-6

You can continue to make design changes to your report or save it to your report server. Click the icon at the top left-hand corner of the designer and select Save. The Save As Report screen will appear. Choose a location and click Save. The report is not published for viewing by others.

REPORT PARTS

Report parts are exactly what you'd expect. They are parts of a report, such as charts, tables, maps, and so on. In addition to the report part, any dataset or parameter on which the part depends accompanies it as metadata. What this means is that when a user selects a part and adds it to a report, any dataset, as well as the parameter that it needs, is automatically added. To use a report part, start the Report Builder, select Blank Report from the start screen, and click Create. On the right side of the tool is a section that allows you to search for report parts (Figure 30-7).

FIGURE 30-7

Click the tab labeled Report Part Gallery and either enter your search criteria and click the search button, which starts a search of the report server for any matching parts, or just click the search button, which will return all available report parts. Once the search is completed any matching entries will be displayed in the search results section (Figure 30-8).

Just double-click the report part or drag it onto the design surface and it, along with any accompanying datasets and parameters, will automatically be added to the report.

SHARED DATASETS

What if you want to allow your end users to design their reports from scratch, but they lack the technical skills to create the necessary datasets? With SSRS R2 you can publish only a dataset to the report server and allow your end users to use it in report design. Datasets contain preconfigured data that can be used as data sources for reports. Start Report Builder and choose Blank Report. In the object explorer on the left, right-click Datasets and select Add Dataset. The Dataset Properties window will appear (Figure 30-9).

FIGURE 30-8

FIGURE 30-9

Choose the radio button labeled "Use a shared dataset" and click Browse. You can now select datasets from the report server and use the dataset as a source for the report. If you drag a table, chart, or map onto the design surface you can use the columns included in the dataset as the source for the report.

TRY IT

In this Try It, you will learn to build a report using the Report Builder. You will leverage existing datasets and data parts.

Lesson Requirements

You will create a report using Report Builder 3.0. A report server must be running on your local machine or you must have access to a report server. You need the BI Trainer Project 30 project, which is included in this lesson's download available from www.wrox.com. Once you have downloaded the project, deploy it to your report server. You will also need the AdventureWorks2008 R2 database.

Hints

The report will include a report part named ProductSalesBarChart. The report will also use a shared dataset named CountrySales. Using the CountrySales dataset, you will create a matrix that has products as rows and years as columns.

Step-by-Step

1. Open the BI Trainer Project 30 solution.

2. Right-click the project in the Solution Explorer and select Properties; the Project Property Screen will appear (Figure 30-10).

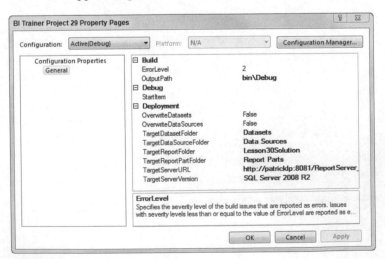

FIGURE 30-10

3. In the column labeled TargetServerURL, paste your report server URL.

4. Click OK.

5. Double click the ProductSalesBarChart report to open it. Click Report in the BIDS menu.

6. Select Publish Report Parts.

7. On the Publish Report Parts screen (Figure 30-11) select ProductSalesBarChart.

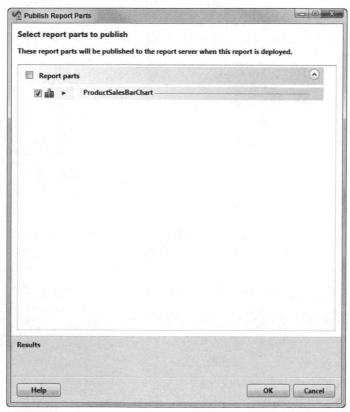

FIGURE 30-11

8. Click OK.

9. Right-click the project again and select Deploy.

10. Once the project is deployed, open Report Builder 3.0.

11. Select Create Blank Report.

12. Click the button labeled Create (Figure 30-12).

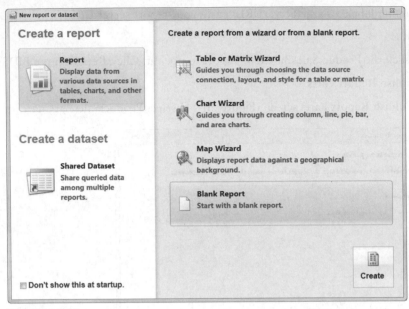

FIGURE 30-12

13. If Report Data section is not visible, click View in the main menu and select the checkbox labeled Report Data. Then right-click the Datasets folder in the Report Data section of the Report Builder.

14. Select Add Dataset and the Dataset Properties screen will appear. See Figure 30-13.

FIGURE 30-13

15. In the text box labeled Name, type **CountrySales**.

16. Click the button labeled Browse and the Select Dataset screen will appear (Figure 30-14).

FIGURE 30-14

17. Double-click the Datasets folder.

18. Select the CountrySales dataset.

19. Click Open.

20. Click OK.

21. Click Insert in the Report Builder menu bar.

22. Select Matrix ⇨ Insert Matrix.

23. Click on the design surface.

24. Drag the TotalDue column into the column labeled Data.

25. Drag the OrderYear column into the column labeled Columns.

26. Drag the Country into the column labeled Rows. Your report will resemble Figure 30-15.

27. Click Run to preview your report.

28. Click Design.

29. Click the Report Part Gallery tab.

30. Type **ProductSales** in the search box.

31. Double-click the ProductSales report part that is found.

32. Move it down so that it does not overlap with the matrix.

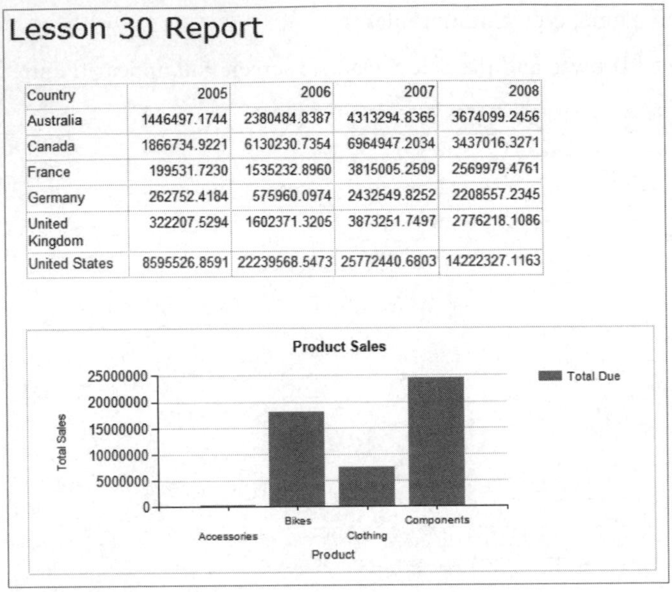

Lesson 30 Report

Country	2005	2006	2007	2008
Australia	1446497.1744	2380484.8387	4313294.8365	3674099.2456
Canada	1866734.9221	6130230.7354	6964947.2034	3437016.3271
France	199531.7230	1535232.8960	3815005.2509	2569979.4761
Germany	262752.4184	575960.0974	2432549.8252	2208557.2345
United Kingdom	322207.5294	1602371.3205	3873251.7497	2776218.1086
United States	8595526.8591	22239568.5473	25772440.6803	14222327.1163

Product Sales

FIGURE 30-15

33. Click the text box labeled "Click to add title."

34. Type **Lesson 30 Report**.

35. Run your report. It should resemble Figure 30-16.

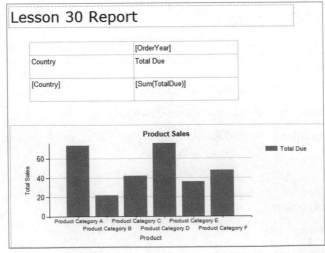

Lesson 30 Report

	[OrderYear]
Country	Total Due
[Country]	[Sum(TotalDue)]

Product Sales

FIGURE 30-16

 Please select Lesson 30 on the DVD to view the video that accompanies this lesson.

SECTION V
Containers

31

Reporting against a Cube with Excel

This lesson focuses on getting you ready to start using Excel to perform and deliver ad hoc analysis with data and features from your Analysis Services cubes. Excel is the most widely used client for business intelligence and ad hoc analysis because of its powerful features, rich formatting, and native integration with SQL Server and Analysis Services. In this lesson we will walk through accessing your data and performing common types of analysis.

We will be working with the Data tab in the Office ribbon menu at the top of your screen in Excel. Take a few minutes and get familiar with this tab: even if you don't know what the buttons do, just read through the captions to get an idea of the kinds of things you will be doing from here. You can connect to and retrieve data from data sources, sort and filter, implement grouping, and even perform some "what if" analysis using your cube data.

It's time to browse this AdventureWorks2008 cube together and see what you can do with it. You start with an empty worksheet and connect to your cube as shown in Figures 31-1, 31-2, 31-3, and 31-4.

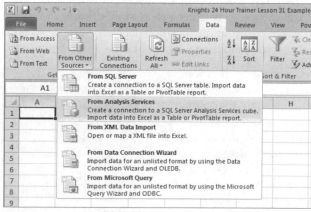

FIGURE 31-1

When you connect to a cube using Excel, you are making an ODBC connection that will be stored in an .odc file on the user's machine. By default, these files are stored here: C:\Users*User name*\Documents\ My Data Sources. The connection wizard is the standard ODBC Connection Wizard you have seen elsewhere in Microsoft Office and Visual Studio.

First you will need to decide what type of authentication to use (Figure 31-2). Since Analysis Services supports only integrated authentication, or Active Directory Windows-based authentication, this is the one we will choose. If you're running a typical installation of the AdventureWorks2008 sample database on your local machine, your server name will likely be <localhost>.

Click Next to pick the Analysis Services database and specific cube or perspective you want to connect to. You can see your options in Figure 31-3.

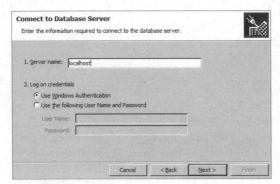

FIGURE 31-2

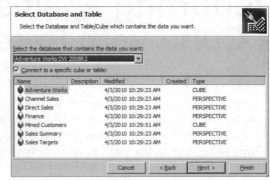

FIGURE 31-3

You will see a number of options to choose from. Here is not only the entire cube, but some individual perspectives that were created in the cube. Perspectives are non-security-bound views of the cube that limit the user to a selected number of dimensions and measures to make her analysis more concise and deliver it faster. For this analysis you want to have everything at your disposal so choose the Adventure Works Cube and click Finish. Next select PivotTable Report as in Figure 31-4.

Before you click OK there is one other thing you should look at.

Excel charts and tables are data-bound, so they have a number of settings to configure data refresh preferences. You can choose to refresh on file open; configuring either a set refresh schedule or completely manual refreshes is possible according to the needs of your organization. Click the Properties button in the lower left of the window in Figure 31-4 and you should get a dialog like the one in Figure 31-5.

This dialog is where you can configure some of the settings for the specific connection you are about to make. This connection will create the local .odc file to store the ODBC Connection information. Much of this will be based on user preference, and the connection can be configured not to automatically try to refresh in case you're away from the network, or don't have access to the data source. Here you can also choose to honor the extra features from the OLAP Server, including fill color, text color, and so on. You can control drill-through volume and specify a language preference if translations are set up in Analysis Services. This language feature means the LocaleID property is read from Windows and applied to any

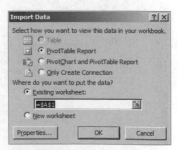

FIGURE 31-4

applicable language that is set up in the cube to help make the user's experience more transparent. For now, cancel out of this dialog and accept the defaults to keep this example straightforward.

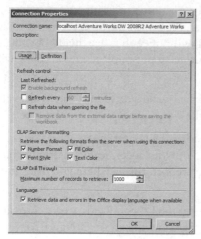

FIGURE 31-5

Once you click OK on the dialog in Figure 31-4, you have a connection to your cube and you can begin to explore the environment Excel gives you. Take a look at Figure 31-6. Once you understand what you can do with the environment and where the tools are, you will build an example report using this connection to the cube and its powerful analysis.

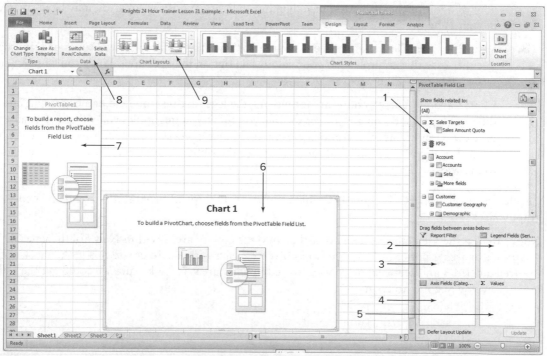

FIGURE 31-6

This is the main interface you'll be using in Excel. Moving clockwise from number one we'll review what each one does.

1. **PivotTable Field List:** This is the area or browser for all your dimensions, measures, KPIs, and so on from your cube. This is where you'll go to drag them into the boxes to make up your report and then refine them for your analysis. You will notice they are divided by measure group, dimension, and KPI. Any folder structure you have put in place in your cube will also be displayed here.

2. **Legend Fields:** Fields dropped into this area appear along the legend side of the chart. Each value in the field creates another line, column, or bar series on the chart, depending on chart type.

3. **Report Filter:** Fields here can act as a filter without affecting the layout in the actual report or pivot table. For instance, if you want to see sales data only for a certain demographic or client, but don't wish to include that information in your report, this is where you drag and drop that field and then filter it on the report.

4. **Axis Fields:** Values dropped here combine with the values in the Legend Fields area to provide the series of data across each axis field you have selected. See how this looks in Figure 31-7.

5. **Values:** This is where the measures themselves go: sales amount, tax, freight, cost, and so on.

6. **Chart area:** This will display the chart version of your creation. If your pivot table has too much complexity it can be difficult to fit it all into a chart, so make sure to balance your analysis if you need to visualize it in a chart. If the chart remains tied to the pivot table, it will adjust accordingly as you slice and dice.

7. **PivotTable area:** This is where the slicing and dicing begins. You can right-click here and get a lot of additional capabilities, including the ability to expose actions you may have created in your cube.

8. **Values or Data:** Depending on your version of Office this will say either Values or Data, but in either case this controls how your data is laid out on the axes and allows you to select subsets of data for further analysis.

9. **Chart Layouts:** These options are for moving the legend, title, and field names around into different layouts. If you hover over the one you think you might like you will get a quick preview without having to apply the formatting. Don't worry if you don't like it once you've applied it: there is always undo, or you can use the ribbon interface and set the layout back to the way it was.

Check out the example in Figure 31-7, which shows an analysis of profitability trends by geographic area.

Notice that in the area labeled 1 we are drilled into the county areas within New South Wales in Australia. In area 2 notice how the chart has pivoted along with us. To create this look, check out the area labeled 3 and see what fields we dropped in what areas to make sure we could get the right look. Now you're going to try it!

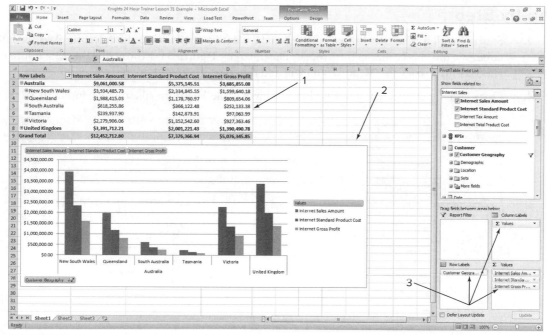

FIGURE 31-7

TRY IT

In this Try It you learn to analyze and report by browsing an Analysis Service cube in Excel. You will be given a typical analyst assignment, and you will complete it by leveraging the power of the cube's integration with Excel.

Lesson Requirements

For this lesson you will need access to the AdventureWorks2008 cube in Analysis Services. Excel 2007 or 2010 is required for the analysis and conditional formatting. You are going to analyze data from 2007 and 2008 to see what types of resellers are contributing to your sales and what products are selling the most.

Hints

➤ You will need to use a pivot table and a pivot chart to visualize the data.

➤ You will use data from three dimensions and one measure group in the cube to perform your analysis.

➤ You will add conditional formatting to your pivot table to enhance the at-a-glance analysis.

Step-by-Step

1. Starting with a clean worksheet in Excel, make a data connection to the AdventureWorks2008 cube. We did this earlier in the process, illustrated by Figures 31-1 through 31-4. Make sure to choose **only** PivotTable Report. You will add the chart after your analysis is set up.

2. Once you are connected, you should see a PivotTable Field List like the one in Figure 31-8.

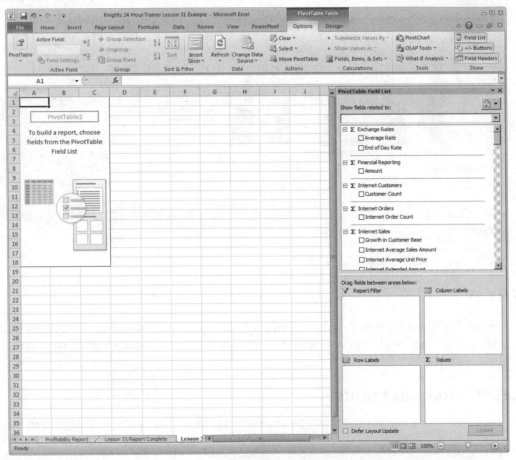

FIGURE 31-8

3. Now add the important measures and dimensions for your analysis. Drag Reseller Sales Amount to the Values area, Product Categories to the Column Labels area, and Date.Calendar and Reseller Type to the Row Labels area. Then explore your pivot table. Your matrix should look like the one in Figure 31-9.

4. Now that you have the right information in the pivot table, let's apply a great Excel feature called *conditional formatting*. Highlight the cells with numbers in them and select the type of conditional formatting you wish. You're going to use Data Bars ⇨ Solid Fill, as shown in Figure 31-10.

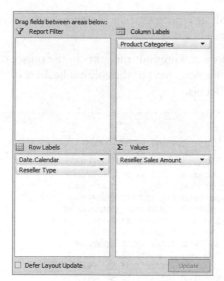

FIGURE 31-9

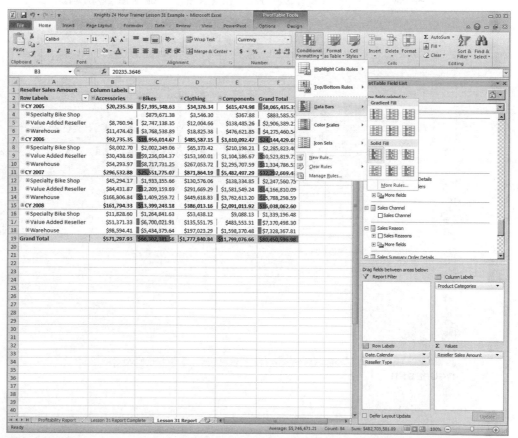

FIGURE 31-10

5. Now you can add the pivot chart to this analysis report. Click somewhere in the pivot table and then select Pivot Chart on the Options tab in Excel.

6. Position the chart so it fits neatly on the worksheet. Filter out the years until you see only 2007 and 2008. You can filter by clicking the down arrows next to the column headers in the pivot table. See Figures 31-11 and 31-12 for more details.

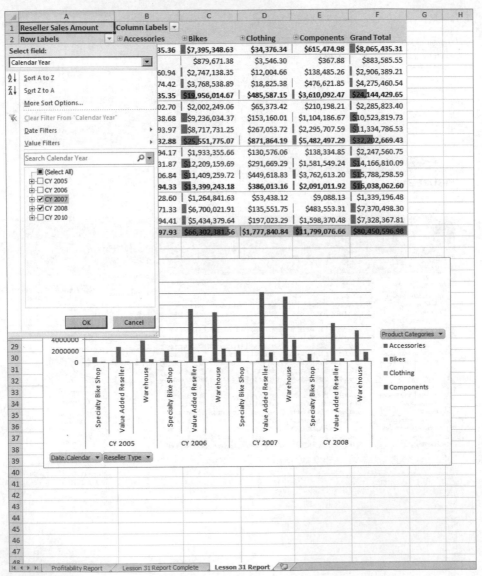

FIGURE 31-11

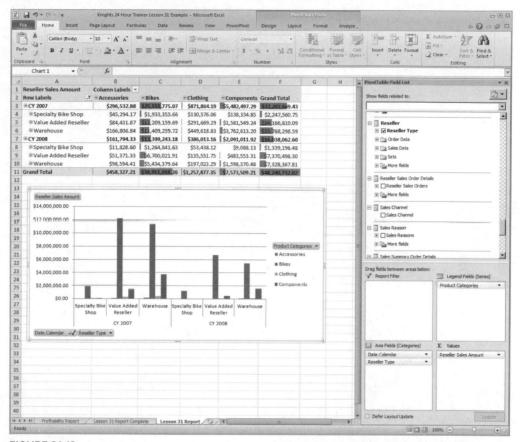

FIGURE 31-12

7. Notice that the chart formatting and filtering adjust automatically with your filtering selections.

Congratulations! You just created your first analytical report in Excel using a cube to quickly pivot and analyze data.

 Please select Lesson 31 on the DVD to view the video that accompanies this lesson.

32

Loading Data into a PowerPivot Workbook

This lesson will teach you about a new technology in Microsoft Office 2010 and SharePoint Enterprise 2010 called PowerPivot. PowerPivot is a new form of Analysis Services that integrates into Excel and SharePoint through some exciting new capabilities. In this lesson you will learn what this new environment is about and how to load data into it for analysis. We will cover reporting from this data in the next lesson, and cover the SharePoint integration later in the book, in Section VI.

WHAT IS POWERPIVOT?

PowerPivot is a powerful new free add-in for MS Excel and provides a new way to install Analysis Services in SQL Server to integrate with SharePoint 2010. In this lesson we will focus on Excel. The PowerPivot add-in is a free download from www.powerpivot.com, which is Microsoft's site devoted to this new technology. This add-in is essentially an encapsulated version of Analysis Services: It runs in memory as an add-in right from within Excel 2010 and gives you the ability to load very large amounts of data and work with them efficiently.

This ability to load large amounts of data now expands the power of Excel by combining it with the analytical capabilities of Analysis Services. This was previously limited by Excel's million-row limit. While Excel still has this limitation, through the PowerPivot add-in, users can drive more intelligent decisions based on the large amount of data they can now encapsulate in the workbook with this new technology.

PowerPivot delivers a new window in Excel 2010 in which you can load large amounts of data and do some really powerful things, such as the following:

➤ Use the new Data Access Expressions (DAX) formula engine to perform powerful cross-table calculations and analysis on our data

➤ Link data from multiple sources using common keys that we can create or import from the source systems

➤ Quickly build pivot tables and reporting

➤ Import data from a number of sources, including SQL Server and other RDBMSes, Reporting Services reports, data feeds from the Internet, and others

➤ Quickly sort and filter tens of millions of rows of data right from within Excel

So, how do you use it?

Step 1: Install the Add-In

First, you need to install the add-in. You can find it at `www.powerpivot.com/download.aspx`. The install process is very straightforward. You have the choice of a 32- or 64-bit version and there are some instructions on the site if you have trouble with the install. Remember, you need to be running Office 2010 for PowerPivot to install.

Step 2: Explore the Environment

Once you have the add-in installed, you can open Excel 2010 and notice the new tab you get, as shown in Figure 32-1.

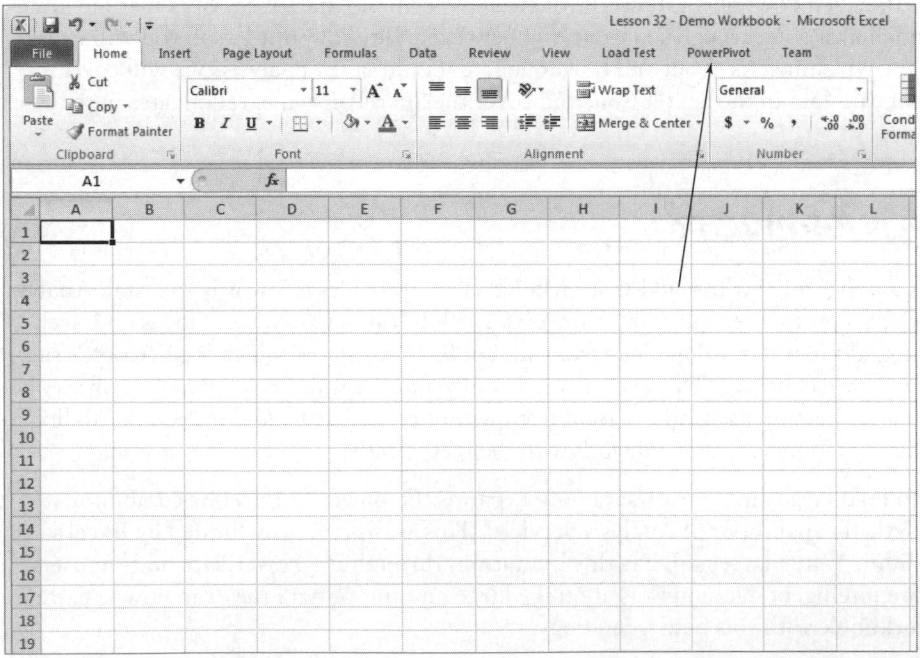

FIGURE 32-1

Click this and take a look at Figure 32-2.

From this tab you can launch the new PowerPivot window and change some settings that are important to the operation of the add-in. You can refresh linked tables in Excel and change whether PowerPivot automatically detects relationships in your data or if you will need to do all that manually.

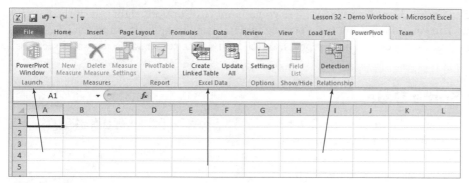

FIGURE 32-2

Launch the PowerPivot window by clicking the green icon at the top left of the ribbon. You should get something similar to Figure 32-3.

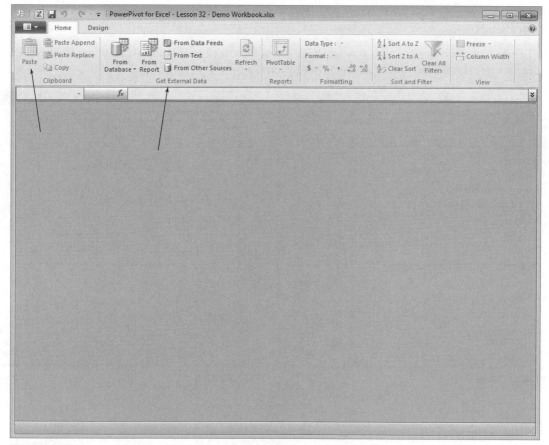

FIGURE 32-3

As you can see in Figure 32-3, PowerPivot gives you a number of options right out of the gate for importing data. You can do anything from pasting in data from an application to loading it from SQL Server, Analysis Services, flat files, reports, or feeds. It's time to get some data and see what you can do!

Step 3: Get Some Data

As you can see in Figures 32-4 through 32-7, for this example you are importing data from a SQL Server database. In Figure 32-4, you can select From Database and From SQL Server to enter your connection information to get your data.

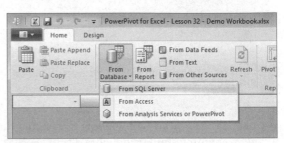

FIGURE 32-4

In Figure 32-5, you can connect to the server you need. In this example, it is my localhost, but you may have a different server name. You can also choose your database name here. You'll need the AdventureWorksDW2008R2 database. Then click Next.

In Figure 32-6, the example has you selecting the option to choose your tables rather than write a query so you can see exactly what we have to choose from.

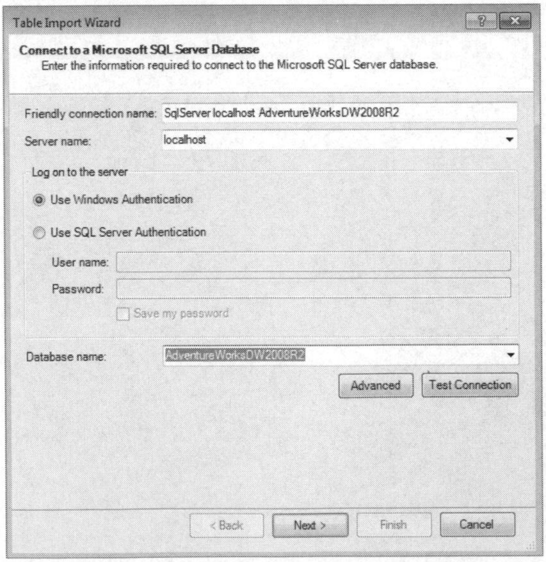

FIGURE 32-5

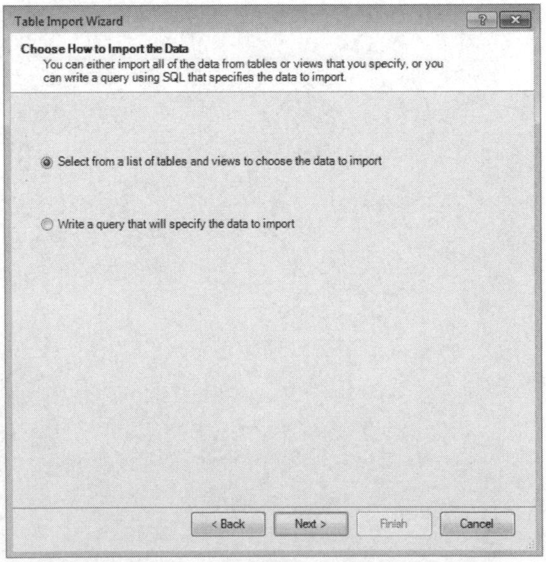

FIGURE 32-6

In Figure 32-7 you can select tables and then can preview and filter the data before importing. This is critical to avoiding over-importing. Even though you can work with huge amounts of data, you don't want unnecessary data. Now you'll see in Figure 32-8 that all the data is in place. You can now take a good look at what you have.

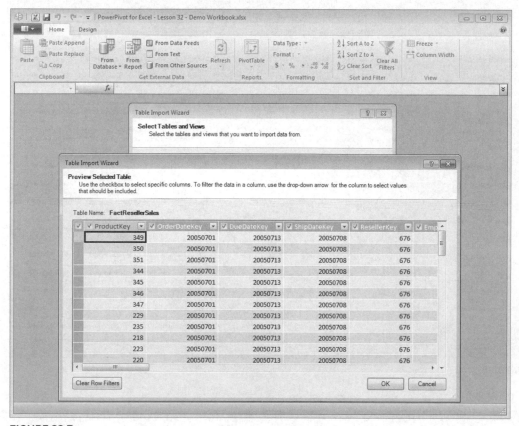

FIGURE 32-7

Now that you have your data, you can see that you have automatically found your relationships, and that all the data is in tables in PowerPivot. You can now jump out to create a pivot report if you want, but for this example we're going to do one last thing.

In Figure 32-9, we have used a new DAX expression to sum the sales by category. Check out the formula in Figure 32-9 to see the kind of syntax you have available to you. You'll notice it is very similar to your standard Excel formulas, but much more powerful. DAX is out of the scope of this lesson, but there are lots of good resources online for more information on the types of analysis you can perform with DAX.

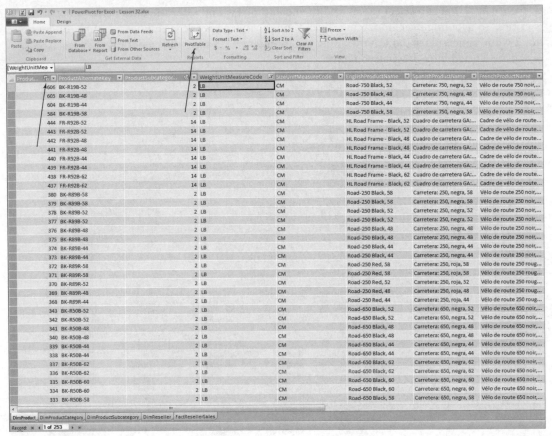

FIGURE 32-8

FIGURE 32-9

TRY IT

Now that we have loaded data and you have seen some of the power behind PowerPivot, in this Try It it's time for you to do it yourself. As usual, in this example we used the AdventureWorks2008DW R2 database from www.codeplex.com. You should do the same to make sure your results are consistent.

Lesson Requirements

In this lesson, you will load data into a PowerPivot workbook in Excel 2010 and verify the relationships within that data. You will also explore the data using PowerPivot's functionality. To complete this lesson you need to have a workbook loaded with AdventureWorks data for analysis.

Hints

➤ Remember to install the add-in first.

➤ Verify that it is installed by opening Excel 2010 and seeing if you have a PowerPivot tab.

➤ Import data from a SQL Server database.

Step-by-Step

1. Open a new Excel workbook and go to the PowerPivot tab.

2. Open the PowerPivot window by clicking the green icon at the top left section of the ribbon.

3. Select From Database and From SQL Server, as in Figure 32-10, to reach the screen where you enter your connection information to get your data. Click Next once you've entered your connection information.

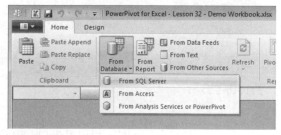

FIGURE 32-10

4. On the next screen, select "Choose tables and views to import." Click Next.

5. Select the tables and views you would like to import from the screen that appears. We recommend a small number to start.

6. Once you've previewed and filtered your data from the screen in Figure 32-11, click OK, which returns you to the "Select Tables and Views" screen, where you can click Finish to finish the import.

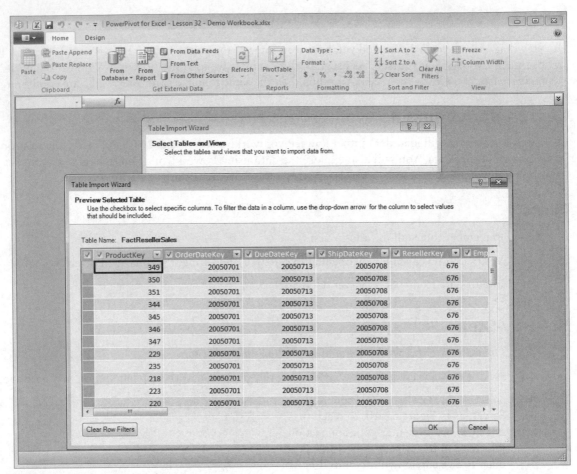

FIGURE 32-11

Congratulations! You have loaded data into PowerPivot for analysis. Experiment with the features and see what you want to try out in the next lesson on reporting from PowerPivot.

 Please select Lesson 32 on the DVD to view the video that accompanies this lesson.

33

Creating a PowerPivot Report

Now that you know how to load data into a PowerPivot workbook in Excel, you can begin to report on it. You can leverage some of the abilities of PowerPivot to deliver data quickly and efficiently to Excel, while using the visualization features of Excel to make your report useful to your end users.

Reporting is a powerful feature in Excel and now even more so with the addition of PowerPivot. PowerPivot has new capabilities for managing and building relational datasets right in Excel, and it does not need to use Access or complicated query strategies to get the end users the data on which they want to report. This lesson will teach you how to harness the power of Excel and the new PowerPivot add-in to make complicated and in-depth reporting simpler to deliver.

COMPONENTS OF A POWERPIVOT REPORT

A number of components make up your report. Major pieces include:

- ➤ Data source (we will be using PowerPivot data)
- ➤ PivotTable
- ➤ Pivot chart
- ➤ DAX (Data Access Expressions) formulas for analysis

You'll build these items piece by piece and then you'll have a visually appealing report for your end users.

BUILDING THE REPORT

First you need to import your data. You learned how to do this in the previous lesson. You're going to import the following tables from the AdventureWorks2008DW R2 database:

- DimDate
- DimProduct
- DimProductCategory
- DimGeography
- FactInternetSales

Now that your data is imported, you're going to add a simple DAX expression to allow you to get the total sales for each product category. The expression follows.

```
=SUMX(RELATEDTABLE('factinternetsales'), [SalesAmount])
```

It goes as a new column in the DimProductCategory and DimProductSubcategory tables in PowerPivot, as shown in Figure 33-1. You may need to create some relationships between those tables and FactInternetSales using the "create relationships" functionality in PowerPivot. Just right-click the header of the column in question and select Create Relationship.

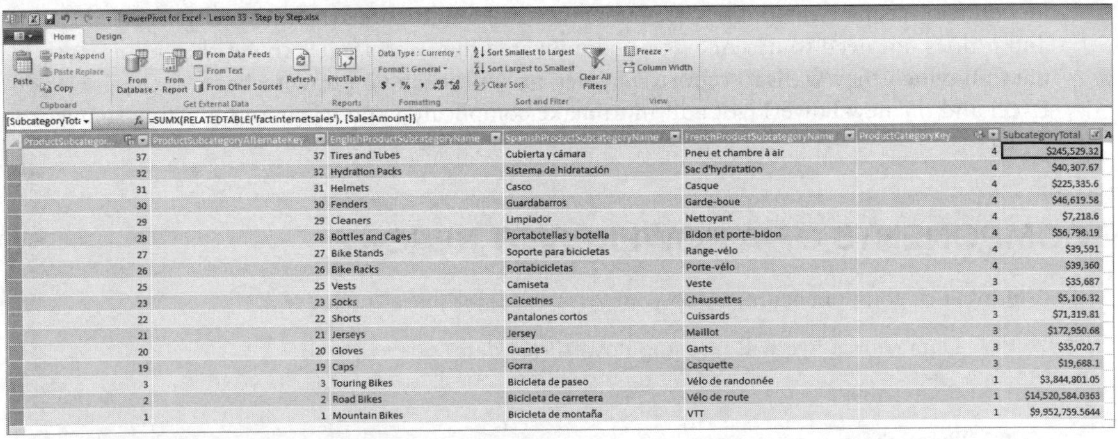

ProductSubcategor...	ProductSubcategoryAlternateKey	EnglishProductSubcategoryName	SpanishProductSubcategoryName	FrenchProductSubcategoryName	ProductCategoryKey	SubcategoryTotal
37	37	Tires and Tubes	Cubierta y cámara	Pneu et chambre à air	4	$245,529.32
32	32	Hydration Packs	Sistema de hidratación	Sac d'hydratation	4	$40,307.67
31	31	Helmets	Casco	Casque	4	$225,335.6
30	30	Fenders	Guardabarros	Garde-boue	4	$46,619.58
29	29	Cleaners	Limpiador	Nettoyant	4	$7,218.6
28	28	Bottles and Cages	Portabotellas y botella	Bidon et porte-bidon	4	$56,798.19
27	27	Bike Stands	Soporte para bicicletas	Range-vélo	4	$39,591
26	26	Bike Racks	Portabicicletas	Porte-vélo	4	$39,360
25	25	Vests	Camiseta	Veste	3	$35,687
23	23	Socks	Calcetines	Chaussettes	3	$5,106.32
22	22	Shorts	Pantalones cortos	Cuissards	3	$71,319.81
21	21	Jerseys	Jersey	Maillot	3	$172,950.68
20	20	Gloves	Guantes	Gants	3	$35,020.7
19	19	Caps	Gorra	Casquette	3	$19,688.1
3	3	Touring Bikes	Bicicleta de paseo	Vélo de randonnée	1	$3,844,801.05
2	2	Road Bikes	Bicicleta de carretera	Vélo de route	1	$14,520,584.0363
1	1	Mountain Bikes	Bicicleta de montaña	VTT	1	$9,952,759.5644

FIGURE 33-1

Now that you have your data and expressions in place, you can start looking at laying out your report. There are a number of areas that you can work with in a Pivot Table, as you can see in Figure 33-2. We'll give you a tour of the major features.

1. **Slicers Vertical and Slicers Horizontal:** The slicers enable you to apply a filter, or "slice," across your entire report. For instance, for a sales report by region you could use a product category slice to see performance for different product mixes quickly.

2. **Report Filter:** This will add columns to the report, but not to the pivot table itself. These columns will act as a filter based on the values you select.

3. **Column Labels and Row Labels (Horizontal and Vertical Axes):** These boxes control your column labels and what data goes on which axis.

4. **Data Values:** This is where you will drop your numeric values and DAX measures once you know what your report is focused on.

Drag and drop the data elements into the grids as shown in Figure 33-3. This will give you a good basis for your report. Once you have a good foundation, you can make your report even better for your users.

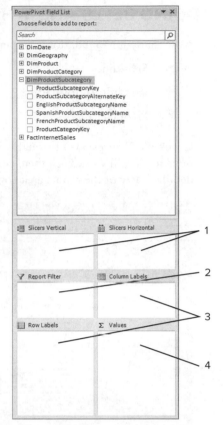

FIGURE 33-2

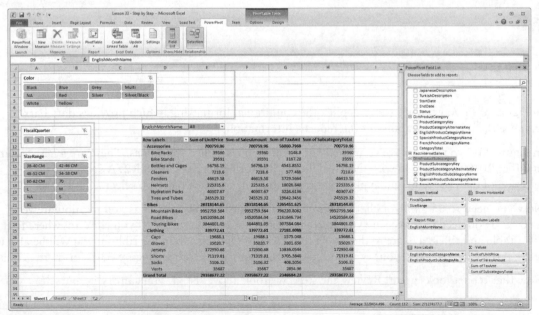

FIGURE 33-3

ADDING BELLS AND WHISTLES

Now that your foundation is in place, look at adding in the following visualization components:

➤ Sparklines

➤ Conditional formatting

➤ Pivot chart

Check out Figures 33-4 through 33-6 for the places in the ribbon in which to configure these components. You'll work with them yourself in a few minutes. See Figures 33-4, 33-5, and 33-6 for a detailed view of the report as it comes together.

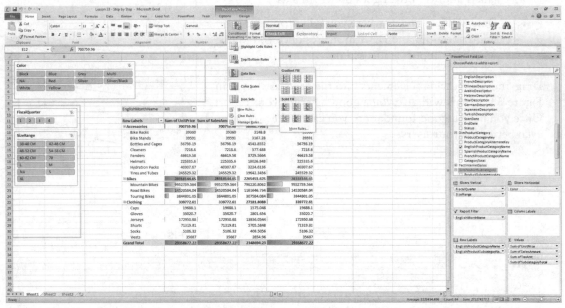

FIGURE 33-4

In Figure 33-4 you can see we've applied the conditional formatting, which provides data bars to enhance the quick view ability of the report's information.

In Figure 33-5 you can see we've applied our trending lines, called sparklines. These are a new feature in Office 2010 to match up with the capability in Reporting Services 2008 R2. A sparkline takes a selection of data to trend and applies that trend to a line for each row you select.

Now you need to add a pivot chart. This chart will adjust automatically as you manipulate your report, so you need to make sure you create it from the same pivot table. If you click anywhere in the pivot table and then navigate to the PivotTable Tools ⇨ Options tab in the ribbon, you will be able to select Pivot Chart, choose your type, and then size it for the report. See Figure 33-6 for more details.

Now that report looks great! Review the steps we took above. Next, you can try it yourself.

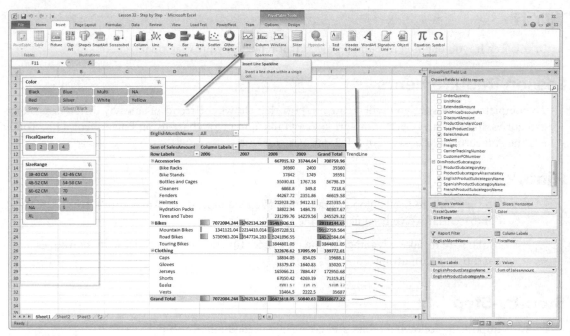

FIGURE 33-5

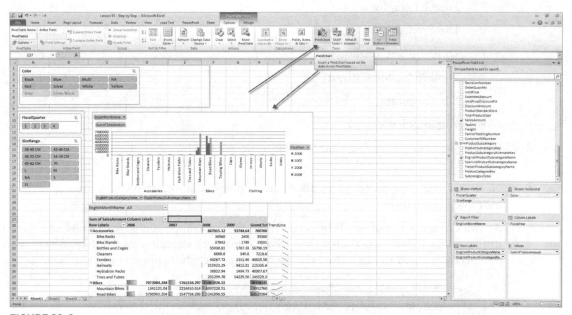

FIGURE 33-6

TRY IT

In this Try It, you're going to build a PowerPivot report of your very own.

Lesson Requirements

To complete this lesson, you will create a report that shows the trend of sales by different product categories and subcategories both with a PivotTable and pivot chart using PowerPivot data. You will use the Adventureworks DW 2008 R2 database for this.

Hints

➤ You're going to need a good data source. We recommend the AdventureWorks2008DW R2 database that we've been using in the past lessons.

➤ Make sure to take advantage of the new slicer functionality as well as the sparklines and conditional formatting.

Step-by-Step

1. Import the following tables and create any needed relationships.

   ➤ DimDate

   ➤ DimGeography

   ➤ DimProduct

   ➤ DimProductCategory

   ➤ DimProductSubCategory

   ➤ DimCustomer

   ➤ FactInternetSales

2. Choose the data points you want to put in your report. Our recommendations are shown in Figure 33-7.

3. Now that your data points are in place, add a column for your sparklines. See Figure 33-8 for more information.

   As you can see, to create sparklines you select the data range you wish to trend and then the display range for the actual lines themselves. It is pretty straightforward. Experiment with the formatting and layout features in the ribbon to see which options you like best.

 Lesson 29 talks about working with sparklines in more detail.

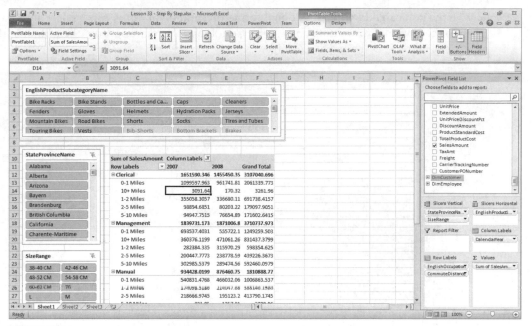

FIGURE 33-7

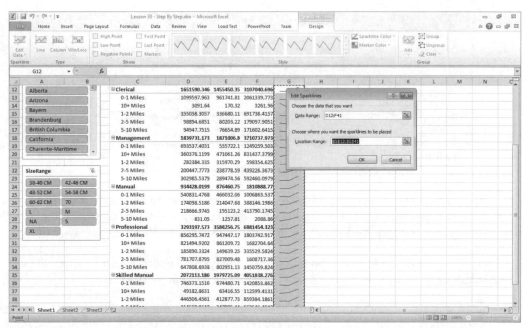

FIGURE 33-8

4. Now you can add your conditional formatting and pivot chart. First, select your data range for conditional formatting and choose Conditional Formatting from the ribbon at the top. See Figure 33-9 if you have trouble.

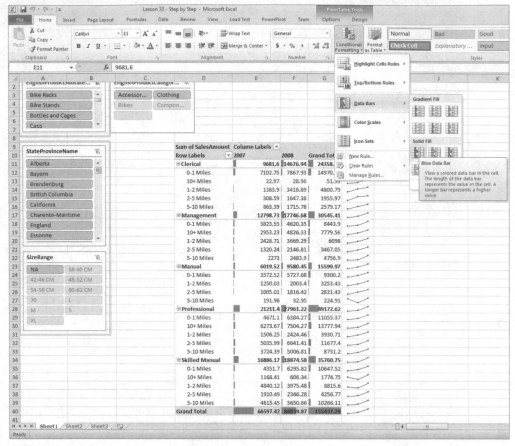

FIGURE 33-9

5. Next, apply a nice pivot chart to make the data more appealing for your users. Remember that you need to click in the PivotTable and then go up to the Options tab under PivotTable Tools and pick the kind of chart you want. See Figure 33-10 if you have trouble.

Congratulations! You have just built your first PowerPivot report. If you followed these steps, it should look something like the report in Figure 33-11. Great job!

 Please select Lesson 33 on the DVD to view the video that accompanies this lesson.

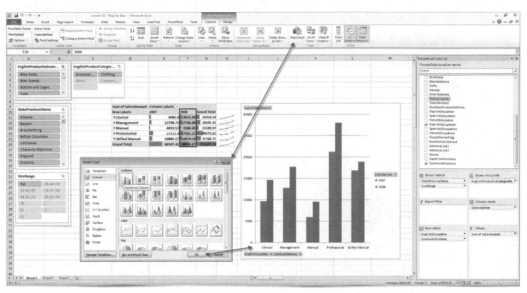

FIGURE 33-10

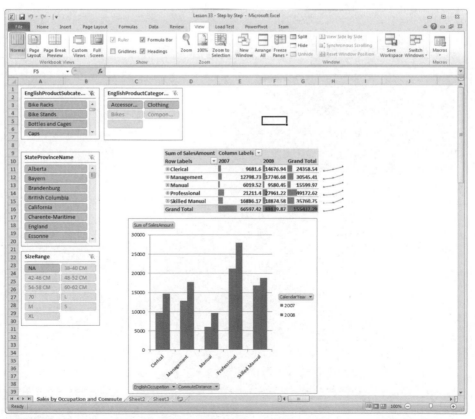

FIGURE 33-11

34

Data Mining in Excel

Now that you've modeled, loaded, and analyzed your data in a cube, you can apply some of the data mining concepts discussed in Lesson 19. One of the best ways to apply these is through the data mining add-in for Excel. This lesson explains what the add-in does, how it works, and how you can use it to jump start your data mining in a very short time.

You'll remember from Lesson 19 that data mining allows you to find patterns, influencers and combinations in our data, among other things. In order to do this you need a large flat data set or analysis services cube (that will flatten the data for you on the fly). For this lesson you'll use the sample data set from the SQL Server data mining add-in, but more on that in a minute.

GETTING READY FOR EXCEL DATA MINING

First, you want to make sure you have a couple of things handy.

1. Excel 2007 installed on your computer

2. Analysis Services Instance somewhere in your environment

3. Data Mining Add-In install executable downloaded to your machine

The add-ins install executable should be downloaded from `http://www.SQLServerDataMining.com`. This Microsoft site focuses specifically on data mining offerings. Once the add-in is downloaded, you will need to configure it.

Installing the Data Mining Add-Ins for Excel 2007

When you first run the data mining add-in, you accept the license terms and input your user information as usual in a Microsoft Office installation. Then, as seen in Figure 34-1, you choose which items you want to install. By default, only two of the four are selected, but you'll also want to include at least the data mining client for Excel. You can also choose the location of the install, but these files are very small and do not generally affect any particular drive from a space perspective.

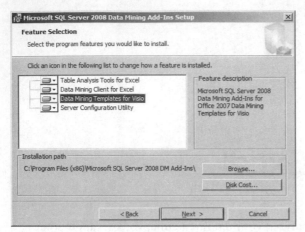

FIGURE 34-1

Next, you let the install do its work. This is a very straightforward install program and should take approximately 30 to 120 seconds to complete on your computer. You will know it completed successfully when you see a dialog like Figure 34-2.

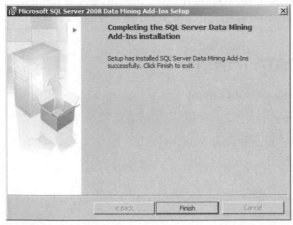

FIGURE 34-2

Configuring the Data Mining Add-Ins for Excel 2007

Now that the add-in is installed, you need to configure it. Depending on your version of Windows, the shortcut for the Server Configuration Utility should be located right off the Start menu under Microsoft SQL 2008 Data Mining Add-ins, as shown in Figure 34-3.

After accepting the introduction in the wizard, you will point the wizard to the server where you have Analysis Services installed and configured. See Figure 34-4.

FIGURE 34-3

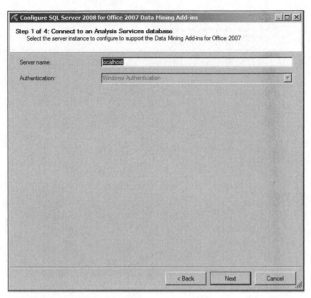

FIGURE 34-4

The wizard is going to make sure you have the appropriate levels of access and configuration to create temporary mining models to process the data coming from Excel. See Figure 34-5.

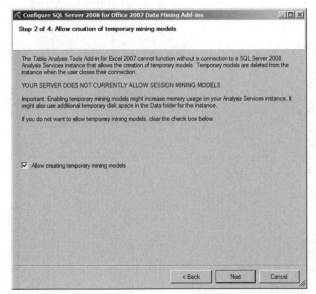

FIGURE 34-5

The next to last step in configuring the Data Mining Add-ins is to provide the wizard with the name of a new Analysis Service Database that it can use for managing the mining model processing. By default, the name is DMAddinsDB, but you can change it to something else, like in Figure 34-6.

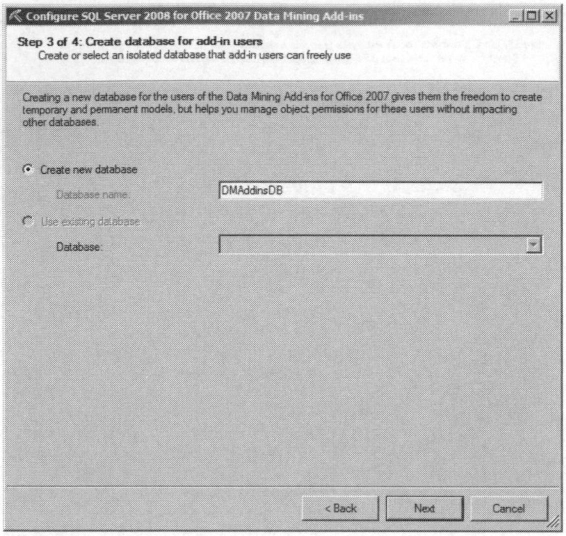

FIGURE 34-6

The very last step is to give the add-ins' users the correct permissions on the Analysis Services instance. Users of the add-ins will need administrative permissions to create and destroy objects in the database created in the previous step. Add those users here before you finish the wizard. If they are already administrators on the entire Analysis Services instance, they do not need to be explicitly added here. For more details, see Figure 34-7.

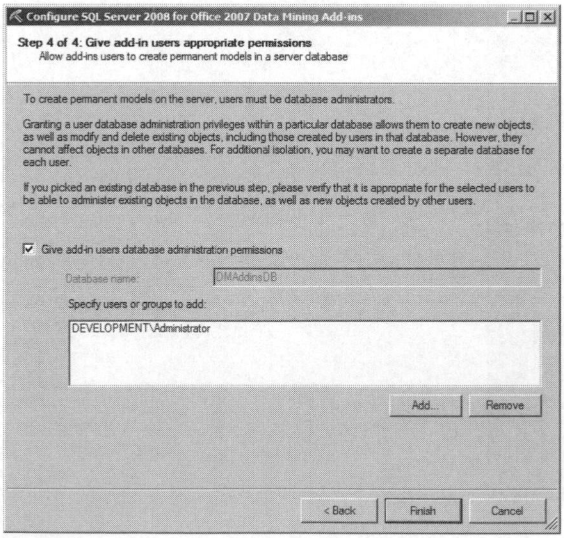

FIGURE 34-7

Once you see all green checkmarks and successes, your add-ins are configured and ready to use. The confirmation will look like Figure 34-8.

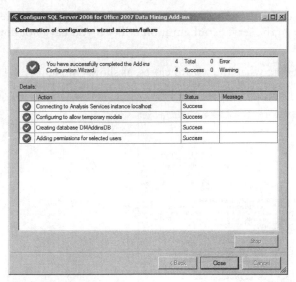

FIGURE 34-8

EXPLORING THE DATA MINING ADD-INS

Once you have installed and configured the add-ins, you can open Excel 2007. The dialog in Figure 34-9 will open right away and prompt you for some final configuration. It also gives you an introduction to the different types of analysis you can do with the add-in.

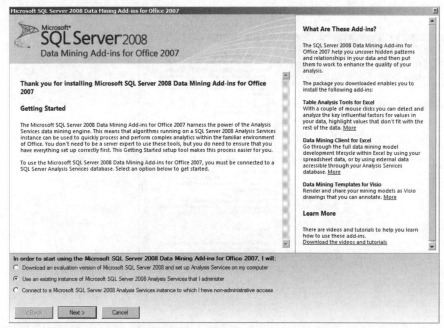

FIGURE 34-9

You need to choose the middle option to connect to an Analysis Services instance that you administer. Excel will prompt you, as in Figure 34-10, to run the server configuration utility if you have not done so already. You have because you're prepared!

You now have the option to open a test table of data when the wizard closes, as shown in Figure 34-11. That is exactly what you are going to do.

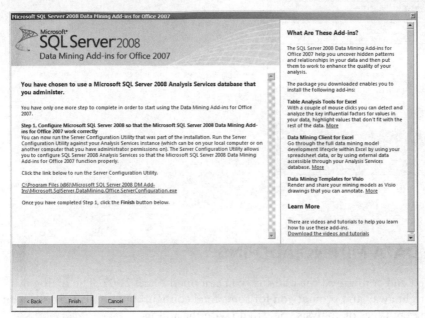

FIGURE 34-10

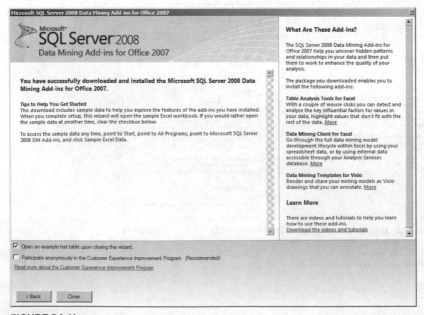

FIGURE 34-11

That shortcut will open up the DMAddins_SampleData.xlsx spreadsheet that was installed along with the add-ins. See Figure 34-12. This spreadsheet is the main artifact you'll continue to work with in this lesson. The introduction tab walks you through the different types of analysis you can work on in this example data set with the new add-ins you just installed.

SQL Server 2008 Data Mining Addins for Office 2007 Sample Data

This file contains data sets suitable for experimenting with the Data Mining Addins. The data contained is extracted from the Adventure Works sample database that is included with SQL Server 2008. Please note that although the tools will find patterns, the data are artificially generated and the patterns have been artificially simulated by the data set designers. While attempts have been made to make the patterns seem as realistic as possible when discovered by the data mining algorithms, they should not be considered to be representative of patterns in the real world and merely serve as an example of the types of results one would receive using real data.

Page	Description
Table Analysis Tools Sample	Data suitable for experimenting with most of the Table Analysis Tools, excepting Forecast and Fill From Example.
Forecasting	Data for use with the Forecast Table Analysis Tool or the Forecast Model task in the Data Mining ribbon.
Fill From Example	Data for use with the Fill From Example Table Analysis Tool.
Source Data	Source data for training most of the Data Mining ribbon models.
Training Data	Training data split from the Source Data page using the default settings of the Partition Data Wizard.
Testing Data	Testing data split from the Source Data page using the default settings of the Partition Data Wizard.
New Customers	A set of customer data that can be used with the Query Data task on the Data Mining ribbon after models have been created.
Associate and Shopping Basket	Market Basket data for use with the Associate task on the Data Mining ribbon and the Shopping Basket Analysis Table Analysis tool.

FIGURE 34-12

You will also notice in Figure 34-12 that the spreadsheet has a tab for each type of analysis you can do. If you select the Table Analysis Tools Sample tab and click anywhere in the tool, you'll see the Ribbon has another section called Table Tools, highlighted in yellow. On the Analyze portion of the Table Tools, you find all the user-friendly data mining tools that Excel has to offer to you now with the add-ins. The arrows in Figure 34-13 show you the options and the box highlights the utilities on the Ribbon.

You're now ready to explore data mining in Excel 2007. First things first — some analysis in this tab to get you started.

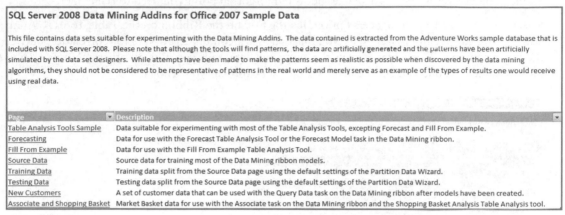

FIGURE 34-13

ANALYZING KEY INFLUENCERS IN EXCEL

Keeping in mind that data mining requires a large flat data set, this spreadsheet has one here for you. The only caveat is that you need to format it as a table in Excel. This is what triggers the "table" analysis tools. This is a simple, but often forgotten point you need to remember.

Select the Analyze Key Influencers option. It's the first on the Ribbon on the Table Tools ⇨ Analyze Tab. As you can see in Figure 34-14, you must choose a column to analyze for correlation between the other columns. This wizard walks through your data, tells you how all other columns relate and may influence the one you choose here. Select Occupation as your choice.

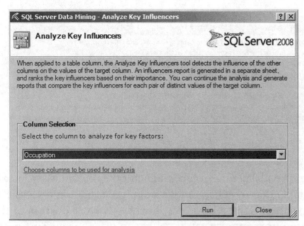

FIGURE 34-14

Next, choose the columns to analyze in the hyperlink at the bottom of Figure 34-14. You want to see all the columns the first time. You will see a dialog that shows the Analyze Key Influencers progress as it processes data as shown in Figure 34-15.

FIGURE 34-15

Once this finishes, in the background, you'll see a main report that shows relative impact between different data combinations in your columns. You also get a dialog to generate a specific report to compare two specific values in your chosen column to the other columns for influencers. See Figure 34-16.

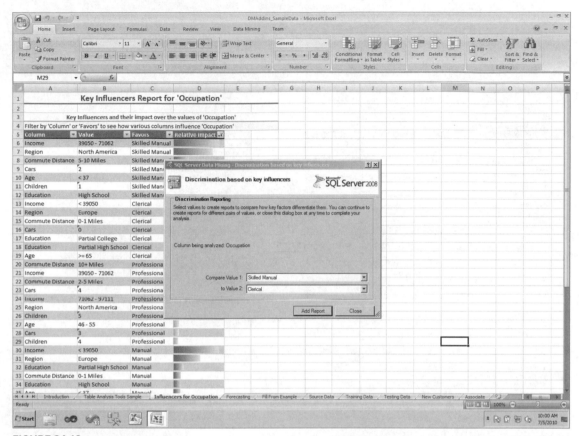

FIGURE 34-16

For example, if you knew your two most common occupations were Skilled Manual and Professional, you could eliminate those and generate a special report by choosing them in the dialog and selecting Add Report. This adds the report in the background and you can continue to add custom pairs as many times as you need to get the analysis you require. Now review the report generated in Figure 34-17.

You can see in the report generated by the add-ins what data points will favor one occupation over another. You can use this immediately to improve marketing targeting, to lower costs due to duplicate efforts, and to send more strategic messages in your communication with customers. Let's break down this report so you can see what each column is doing.

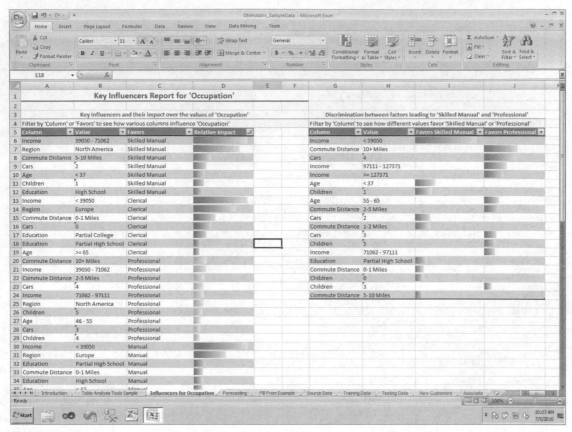

FIGURE 34-17

Before breaking down this report, you need to have a little more information. You've probably already noticed that these reports generate a new tab called Influencers for Occupation and the reports themselves are formatted as Excel tables. An *influencer* is defined as something that contributes to the column you are analyzing. These tabs are great because not only can you perform filtering and formula based analysis on influencers after running this initial report, but you can also use influencers as a data mining source if they have enough data for accurate assessments. No special tricks there — it's all basic Excel functionality for the sorting and filtering.

➤ **Column:** This tells you which column in the data you are looking at. These can repeat because the add-in is looking for patterns that favor one category over the other. You'll see some of these repeat because things like commute distance may favor one or the other in relative ranges.

➤ **Value:** This column tells you the values or ranges of values for which the column is favoring one category over the other. Value combines directly with Column to give you the actual influencer. i.e. Age of 55-65 or Commute Distance of 2-5 Miles.

➤ **Favors Skilled Manual:** This column displays a relative impact data bar. This data bar's length and darkness demonstrate the impact the influencer on that line in the report has on Skilled Manual. The longer and darker it is, the more impact it has.

➤ **Favors Professional:** This column displays a relative impact data bar. This data bar's length and darkness demonstrates the impact the influencer on that line in the report has on Professional. The longer and darker it is, the more impact it has.

Now you're going to build an influencers report in Excel 2007 using the data mining add-ins in the Try It section that follows.

TRY IT

In this Try It section you're going to build an influencers report that categorizes bicycle buyers by education.

Lesson Requirements

You will create a report in Excel 2007 that uses the sample data from the DMAddins_SampleData Spreadsheet and categorizes the main influencers for bicycle buying between different levels of buyer education. To do this, use the following hints.

Hints

➤ Make sure to install and configure the add-ins before you begin.

➤ Use the Table Analysis Tools Sample Tab for your source data.

➤ Make sure to click in the table to expose the options you need.

Step-by-Step

1. Open the Sample Spreadsheet. If you have already closed out the wizard, you can access it directly from the start menu as in Figure 34-18.

2. Because you're going to analyze for key influencers, select the tab for Table Analysis Tools Sample and then click in the table. See Figure 34-19.

3. This exposes the Table Tools portion of the Ribbon as shown in Figure 34-13 earlier in the lesson. Make sure you select the Analyze tab under Table Tools.

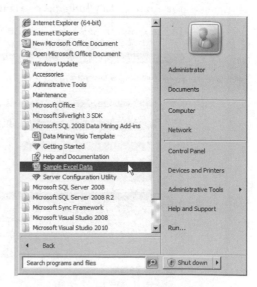

FIGURE 34-18

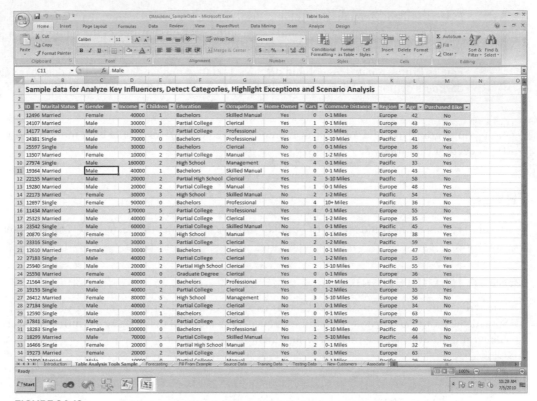

FIGURE 34-19

4. Click the first option, Analyze Key Influencers, on the left end of the Ribbon. This brings up the Analyze Key Influencers wizard for you to choose your options.

5. In the Column Selection area on the wizard, select Education, as shown in Figure 34-20.

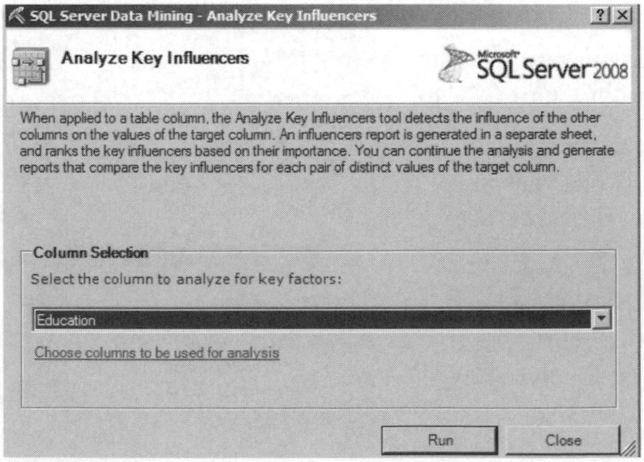

FIGURE 34-20

6. Because you don't want to analyze every column for this report, click the "Choose columns to be used for analysis" hyperlink at the bottom of the wizard. You should see the dialog in Figure 34-21.

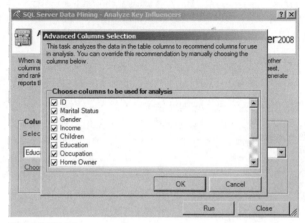

FIGURE 34-21

7. Because we don't care about ID and Home Owner in this fictional report, deselect the checkbox next to these columns to eliminate them from analysis. Click OK.

8. Click Run in the wizard to generate the report. The results are shown in Figure 34-22.

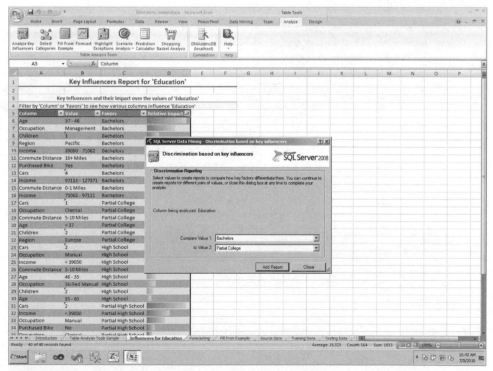

FIGURE 34-22

9. Select which two education levels you want to analyze. For this example, select Bachelors and Graduate Degree as the two options.

10. Click Add Report to add the main influencers report to the spreadsheet.

11. Cut and paste the report from below the first table to the top so it lines up next to the first table. See Figure 34-23 for an example.

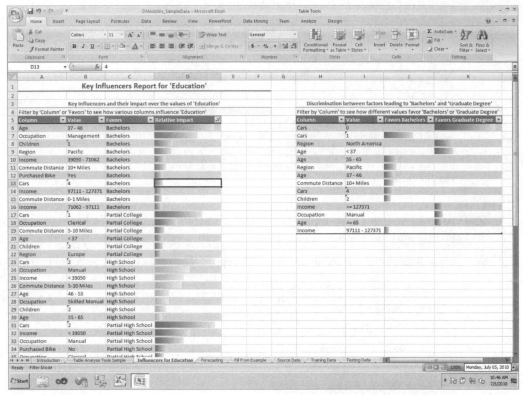

FIGURE 34-23

12. Filter the main influencers report so that only Commute Distance, Income, and Occupation are showing. See the results in Figure 34-24.

Discrimination between factors leading to 'Bachelors' and 'Graduate Degree'			
Filter by 'Column' to see how different values favor 'Bachelors' or 'Graduate Degree'			
Column	Value	Favors Bachelors	Favors Graduate Degree
Commute Distance	10+ Miles		
Income	>= 127371		
Occupation	Manual		
Income	97111 - 127371		

FIGURE 34-24

Congratulations! You just built your first report using data mining in Excel 2007!

 Please select Lesson 34 on the DVD to view the video that accompanies this lesson.

SECTION VI
SharePoint

35

Understanding SharePoint for Business Intelligence

Microsoft Office SharePoint Server (MOSS) is a highly successful tool that at its most basic level is a collaboration tool used for sharing ideas, documents, and business solutions. Many companies use SharePoint to cut the costs of developing an expensive internal intranet infrastructure, because of the many offerings it has and the fact that it is highly customizable. In this section of the book you will specifically learn how Business Intelligence and SharePoint work together to place the final bow on top of the present you have been wrapping in all the previous sections. You have learned how to create the back end of your BI solution using Integration Services and Analysis Services; now it is time to build the client-facing tool that will really get your end users to say, "Wow!"

The SharePoint client interface is a web interface that can easily be accessed through a variety of web browsers. In fact, with the SharePoint 2010 web browser, compatibility has been expanded. When building a BI solution in SharePoint you will start by creating sites that are essentially ASP.NET web applications. Any site content data is stored in a SQL Server database that is created upon installation of SharePoint. When creating sites, you will find an assortment of templates including the Business Intelligence Center template, shown in Figure 35-1, which can easily be used to display analytic tools like dashboards, KPIs, and reports.

SharePoint has several identities and can play different roles for a company depending on whom you ask. It is best known as a collaboration tool, a platform for sharing files and ideas, and because of that has been underestimated when it comes to its BI capabilities. With SharePoint 2007 and the now highly revamped SharePoint 2010, any notions that BI and SharePoint do not go hand in hand should be put to rest. The ever-increasing set of integrated features propels SharePoint to the front of the line as an enterprise analytics and collaboration platform. The goal is not only to be able to develop the analytics, but to share them and use them as a team, which is where SharePoint really helps take BI to the next level.

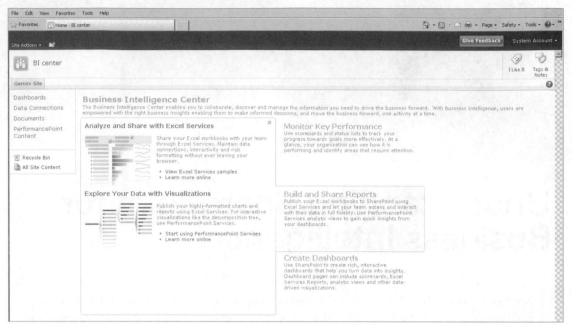

FIGURE 35-1

You may already know that BI projects have a very high failure rate; you may even have experienced this type of failure firsthand. There are many reasons BI projects fail but several of them can be avoided if you successfully implement a tool like SharePoint company-wide. Business Intelligence solutions are often not adopted because they are not easy enough to use. So what can you do to make it easier for users to access and understand the data you are trying to provide? SharePoint has many integrated features, which we will talk about in this section of the book, that allow users who are already comfortable using Microsoft Office tools like Excel to have a centralized location to get the information they need.

Your goal is to determine which of these integrated features help in actually solving your business problems. For example, if you have a need for an executive dashboard with KPIs (key performance indicators), Performance Point will be the tool to help build the dashboard, as Figure 35-2 shows. If you have hundreds of Reporting Services reports but they are not easily found by users, Reporting Services integration with SharePoint will expose your reports to a wider audience.

By first clearly identifying the problem, you can then easily determine which SharePoint BI tools can help in solving it. Remember that a determining factor in your solution's being accepted by the whole company is how easy it is for your users to access and understand the data presented. In Table 35-1 you will find each of the SharePoint BI features and a very general explanation of its benefits.

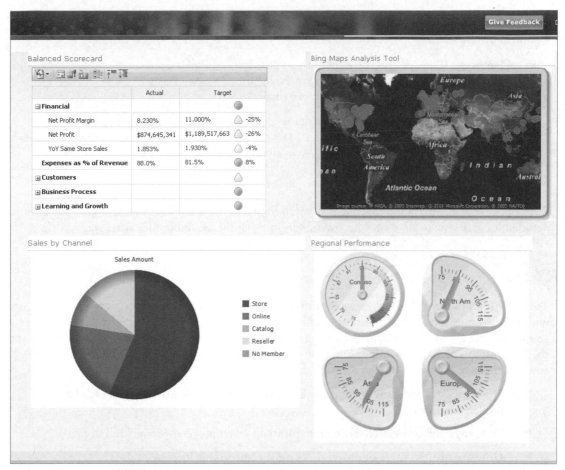

FIGURE 35-2

TABLE 35-1

SHAREPOINT BI FEATURE	BUSINESS PROBLEM	BENEFIT OR FUNCTION
Performance Point Integration	Executives want dashboard with KPIs and a glimpse of company performance at a glance.	Builds KPIs and dashboards inside SharePoint. Gives an overall snapshot of business with the ability to drill through easily to detailed data.
Power Pivot Integration (SharePoint 2010 only)	Users want OLAP functionality and query performance with any data source in Excel.	Gives users self-service BI. Can process millions of rows in memory from within Excel.

TABLE 35–1 *(continued)*

SHAREPOINT BI FEATURE	BUSINESS PROBLEM	BENEFIT OR FUNCTION
Excel Services Integration	You want to share the same Excel report you have built with a group of people.	Builds Excel functionality directly into SharePoint.
Reporting Services Integration	Reports have been developed: now they need to be made available to an entire company.	Shares the reports you develop in SharePoint. This allows your reports to be seen by a wider audience.

Each of the lessons following this one is devoted to one of these features and will give you a more detailed look at how to develop your own solution using the available BI feature set.

TRY IT

Your Try It section for this lesson is a bit different. Throughout the book you have been challenged with hands-on lessons to make sure you understand the lessons you're reading and technologies you're reading about. For this lesson, your goal should be to keep in mind how SharePoint fits into the BI solution you have developed and how each piece helps solve the puzzle. For instance, ask yourself these questions as you go through the rest of this book:

➤ How does my company share thoughts and ideas now, and are they successfully implemented?

➤ Does my company effectively communicate to all employees, foreign and domestic?

➤ How are my end users or power users most comfortable looking at data?

➤ How can I ensure that the KPIs, dashboards, and reports I spend valuable time designing actually get used effectively?

If you can keep these questions in the back of your mind while reading the rest of this book, they can truly help you make decisions about how SharePoint can take your BI solution to the next level.

 Please select Lesson 35 on the DVD to view the video that accompanies this lesson.

36

Deploying and Using Reporting Services in SharePoint 2010

Reporting Services integration with SharePoint is something that has been around for several versions of the tool at this point. The process of configuring the integration has become less and less problematic with each version. There has been a major effort to simplify the integration of tools with SharePoint in the 2010 release of the product. In this lesson you will walk through the configuration and deployment steps needed to integrate Reporting Services with SharePoint 2010.

You may have noticed while stepping through the SQL Server installer that, if you included Reporting Services as part of the installation, the installer asked whether you would like to install in SharePoint-integrated mode. Selecting "Install the SharePoint integrated mode default configuration," seen in Figure 36-1, will save you the trouble of manually converting the report server databases, which are created with every installation of Reporting Services, to be in SharePoint-integrated mode.

If you have previously installed Reporting Services in native mode, without SharePoint integration, then you must manually make the switch to integrate the two products. To start the process of manually converting from native mode to integrated mode, open the Reporting Services Configuration Manager and connect to the instance of Reporting Services you wish to change. Ensure the service is started and then select the Database page, shown in Figure 36-2.

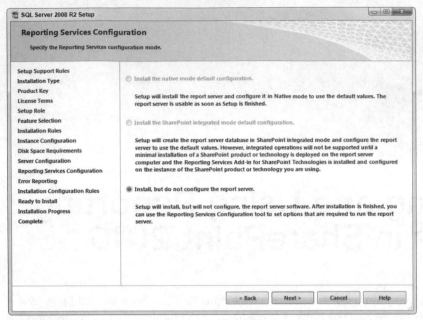

FIGURE 36-1

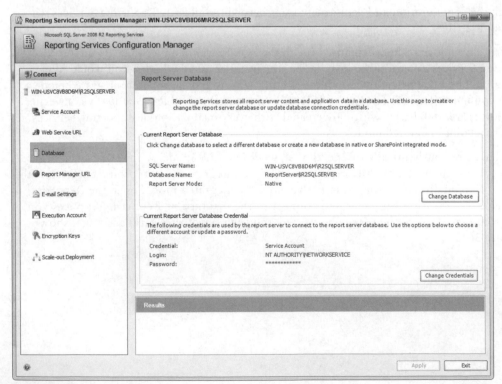

FIGURE 36-2

Click the Change Database button, which will open the Report Server Database Configuration Wizard. Select "Create a new report server database," and then click Next. Choose the database engine instance on which you wish to create the new integrated report server database, and then click Next. Figure 36-3 shows that you must switch the Report Server Mode property from Native Mode to SharePoint Integrated Mode, and then click Next. Complete the rest of the wizard using the defaults.

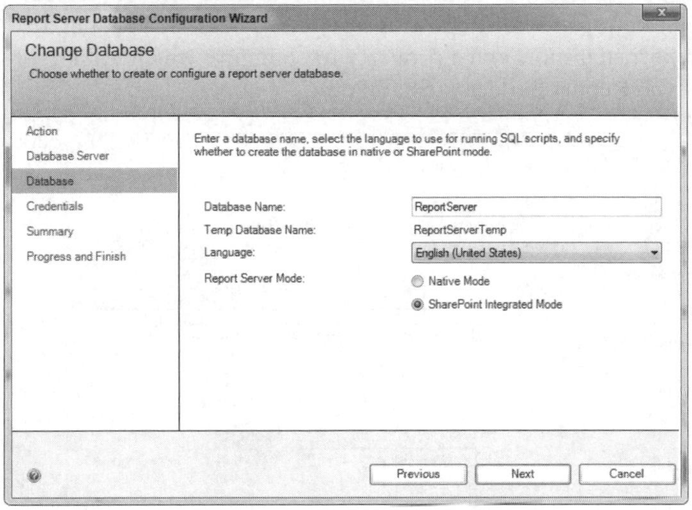

FIGURE 36-3

You have now configured Reporting Services to work in SharePoint-integrated mode, and if you attempt to view reports using the Report Manager you will receive the following error:

```
This operation is not supported on a report server that is configured to run in
SharePoint integrated mode. (rsOperationNotSupportedSharePointMode)
```

There are a few more steps to do on the SharePoint side to complete the integration. First, download and install the Reporting Services add-in for Microsoft SharePoint Technologies 2010. Go to the Microsoft download site (www.microsoft.com/downloads) and search for **SharePoint 2010 Reporting Services add-in** to ensure you get the most up-to-date version. After downloading the add-in, run the installer, in which you will be able to specify whether you will be deploying to a SharePoint farm or a stand-alone instance of SharePoint.

With the add-in installation complete, open your SharePoint site and select Site Actions ➪ Site Settings. Under the Site Collection Administration section, click "Site collection features." Ensure that Report Server Integration Feature is activated, as shown in Figure 36-4.

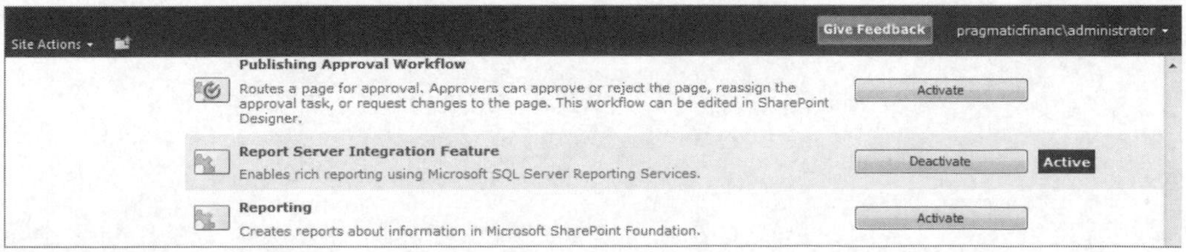

FIGURE 36-4

With the service activated, you can now configure the feature by clicking General Application Settings. Look for the Reporting Services section: if this section is missing, the add-in did not properly install or the feature did not get activated as detailed in the previous paragraph. Select Reporting Services Integration and specify the report server site in the Report Server Web Service URL (`http://servername/reportserver`), shown in Figure 36-5. You will also need to set up security credentials before you click OK. You then have the option to configure the "Set server" defaults to change some of the default options set for Reporting Services. These include, but are not limited to, a property to limit report snapshots and a property to configure which version of Report Builder launches when you click Report Builder in SharePoint.

Central Administration ▸ Reporting Services Integration

Warning: this page is not encrypted for secure communication. User names, passwords, and any other information will be sent in clear text. For more info

Use this page to configure integration settings for SQL Server Reporting Services.

	OK	Cancel

Report Server Web Service URL
Specify the URL of the report server instance that you want to integrate with this SharePoint environment.

The Report Server service will be restarted once the service account has been granted access successfully.

`http://pragmaticfinancial:8080/reportserver`

Authentication Mode
Specify the authentication mode that is used by the SharePoint site or farm.

Windows Authentication ▾

Credentials
Specify the credentials of a user who is a member of the Administrator group on the computer that hosts the report server.

To re-provision the existing integration between this SharePoint environment and SQL Server Reporting Services, specify the credentials of a user who is a member of the Administrators group on the computer that hosts the report server.

User Name:
dknight

Password:
••••••••••••

Activate the Reporting Services Feature
Specifies the site collection or collections in which the Reporting Services feature is activated.

⦿ Activate feature in all existing site collections
○ Activate feature in specified site collections

	OK	Cancel

FIGURE 36-5

Now that you have completed the configuration needed to integrate Reporting Services and SharePoint, you can start deploying reports. Deploying to SharePoint is a lot like deploying to the regular report server. When you have opened Business Intelligence Development Studio (BIDS) you will right-click the Report Server project and select Properties. In the Deployment section, shown in Figure 36-6, you will first point the TargetServerURL property to the SharePoint URL. Then you will point the four properties labeled Target above this one to the appropriate library to which you wish to deploy. Once you have finished configuring, right-click the project, and, this time, select Deploy.

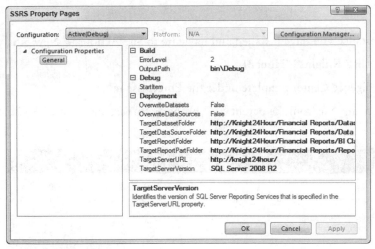

FIGURE 36-6

Once your reports complete deployment, you can navigate to the SharePoint library to which you just chose to deploy and select the report to view it in SharePoint. Now that you have learned how to configure SharePoint for integration with Reporting Services, try it by deploying your own report in the next section.

TRY IT

In this Try It, you will learn how to create a new site in SharePoint 2010. You will create a document library that will store your reports. Finally, you will set up BIDS to deploy reports to your SharePoint instance.

Lesson Requirements

You should already have SharePoint installed and started. We're assuming you followed the steps listed earlier in the lesson to configure SharePoint and Reporting Services integration.

Hints

➤ Create a new site using the Business Intelligence Center template and call it **Knights24HourBI**.

➤ Create a new document library to store your reports.

➤ Use BIDS to deploy a report to your new SharePoint site.

Step-by-Step

1. Open the SharePoint instance you have installed and navigate to Site Actions ⇨ New Site.

2. Name the site title and URL **Knights24HourBI**.

3. Select the Business Intelligence Center template under the Enterprise tab.

4. Change the "Use the top link bar from the parent site" property to Yes, and then click Create, as shown in Figure 36-7.

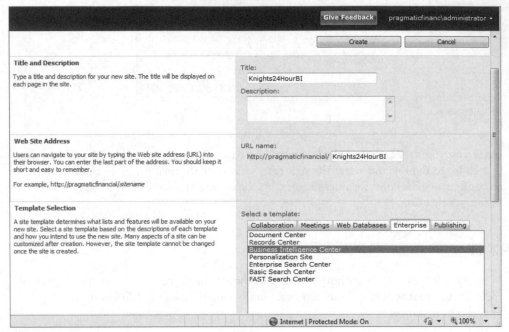

FIGURE 36-7

5. After the site is created, click Documents in the navigation pane.

6. Click Create and select Document Library.

7. Give the Document Library the name **Reports**, then click Create as shown in Figure 36-8. Figure 36-8 may look different if you do not have Silverlight installed.

8. Open BIDS and find any report that was developed previously in this book, or one of your own.

9. Right-click the report project and select Properties.

10. Make the changes to the following properties (Table 36-1), replacing *yourservername* with your actual SharePoint Server URL (Figure 36-9).

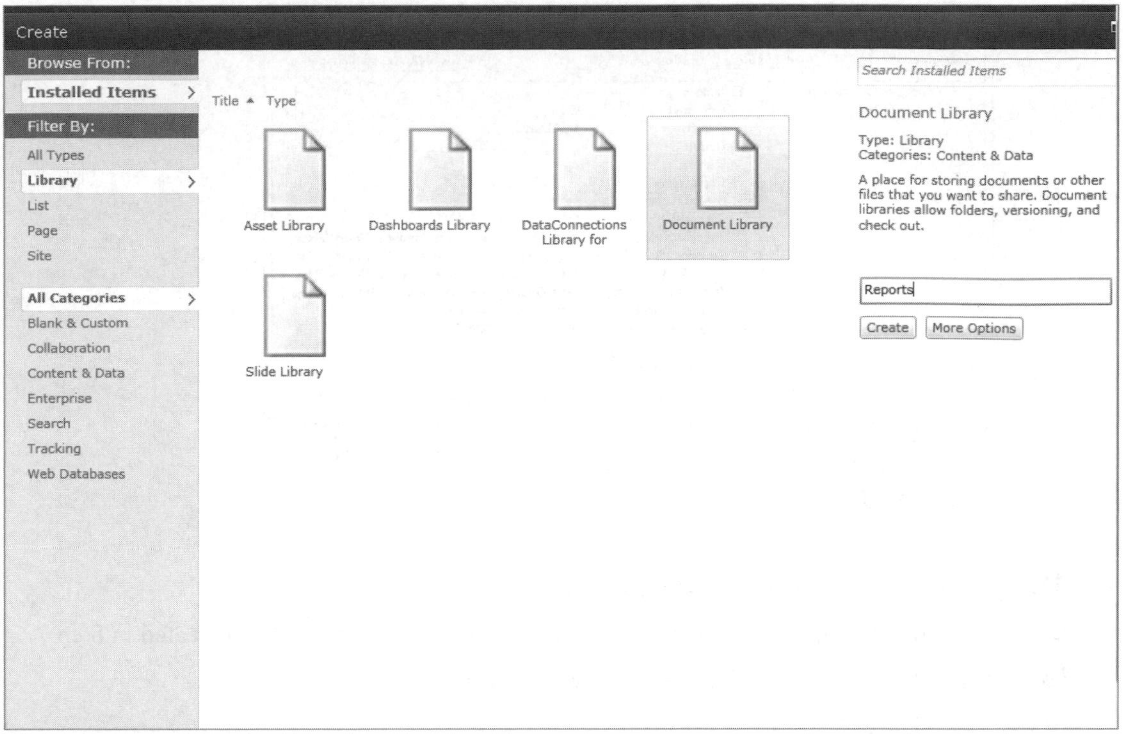

FIGURE 36-8

TABLE 36-1

PROPERTY	VALUE
TargetDatasetFolder	http://*yourservername*/Knights24HourBI/Reports/Datasets
TargetDataSourceFolder	http://*yourservername*/Knights24HourBI/Reports/Data Sources
TargetReportFolder	http://*yourservername*/Knights24HourBI/Reports
TargetReportPartFolder	http://*yourservername*/Knights24HourBI/Reports/Report Parts
TargetServerURL	http://*yourservername*/

Click OK when the setting changes are complete.

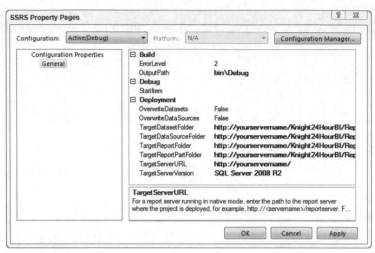

FIGURE 36-9

11. Right-click the report project again, but, this time, click Deploy.

12. Once the deployment completes, open the Document Library that you created in Step 7.

13. Click the report you just deployed to view it inside SharePoint.

Congratulations! You deployed your first report to SharePoint. You have taken your first step to experiencing Business Intelligence inside SharePoint.

 Please select Lesson 36 on the DVD to view the video that accompanies this lesson.

37

Building PerformancePoint Dashboards in SharePoint 2010

PerformancePoint is a tool that helps a business monitor and analyze its performance. It can help you understand company and regional goals across your entire organization. This way, there is a clear understanding of the strategy that your business is taking to reach its objectives. Taking this information on their company's strategies, employees can quickly adjust their work habits to align with the company's goals.

As a Business Intelligence developer, you will use PerformancePoint to design KPIs (key performance indicators), scorecards, reports, and dashboards so your business users can have a quick overview of how well their business is doing. Your business users can easily view what you have created from SharePoint 2010, which they are likely already used to opening every morning when they arrive at work.

PerformancePoint 2010 has come a long way since the previous version and is now fully integrated into SharePoint 2010. It no longer functions as a stand-alone server, as it did in PerformancePoint 2007. Because of this new integration, SharePoint serves as the repository for all things PerformancePoint. Data connections, KPIs, scorecards, reports, and dashboards are all stored on the SharePoint server. PerformancePoint acts like any other service in SharePoint server, which allows it to take advantage of many SharePoint features like scalability, collaboration, backup, and recovery.

One of the most interesting new features of PerformancePoint 2010 is the Decomposition Tree. Many of the chart types will allow you to right-click and view the Decomposition Tree, which allows you to see the driving forces behind the values you are viewing. Figure 37-1 shows a Decomposition Tree that displays the paths to how company sales occurred.

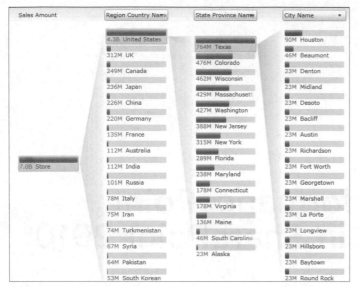

FIGURE 37-1

PerformancePoint can not only give you a high-level overview of a company's results but can also give you more detail with drill-up and drill-down, shown in Figure 37-2, that will go to the next level of a user-defined hierarchy. If you need even more detail, you can also select Show Details and get a grid view of the underlying data. This provides solutions to many different types of problems. Sometimes a broader view of the company is needed to gain an overall perspective of the business, while other times it is important to go to the lowest granularity to solve a problem.

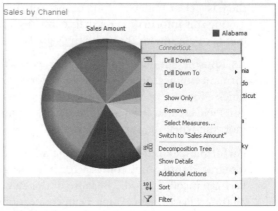

FIGURE 37-2

To create content using PerformancePoint, you will use the Dashboard Designer. If you have already created a Business Intelligence Center site as we did in the previous lesson, it's very simple to open the Dashboard Designer. Open the PerformancePoint Content Library and select Add new item. This will automatically install and open Dashboard Designer on your machine.

With the Dashboard Designer open you can create a connection to your data source. You'll connect to a previously created Analysis Services cube to take either already-built KPIs to just display their results, or build KPIs from the ground up using PerformancePoint. Figure 37-3 shows all the possible data sources you have in PerformancePoint.

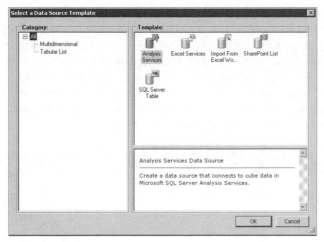

FIGURE 37-3

When you create a new connection to Analysis Services you choose the server, database, and cube, as shown in Figure 37-4. You can also specify the authentication you wish to use for the connection. You can pick Per-user Identity, which means each user's own account will be used to access the cube. Using this method requires that the domain administrator configure Kerberos delegation between PerformancePoint and the Analysis Services database. You can also pick Unattended Service Account, which requires its own set of extra configuration. Having an Unattended Service Account means one account is always responsible for displaying the content you develop.

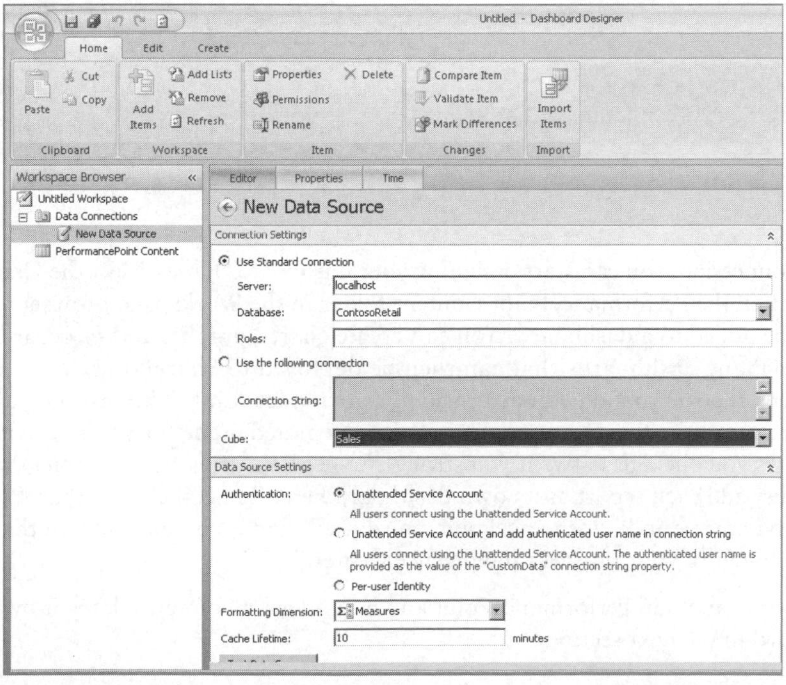

FIGURE 37-4

To use Unattended Service Account authentication you must navigate to the Central Administration site and click Manage Service Applications under the Application Management heading. Select Secure Store Service and click Generate New Key in the Edit ribbon on the page. You must give the new key a passphrase and then click OK. Next you need to configure PerformancePoint to use an account of your choice. Return to the Manage Service Applications section and select the PerformancePoint service. Choose PerformancePoint Service Application Settings and configure the Secure Store and Unattended Service Account, as shown in Figure 37-5. You will now be permitted to use the Unattended Service Account option when you return to the Dashboard Designer.

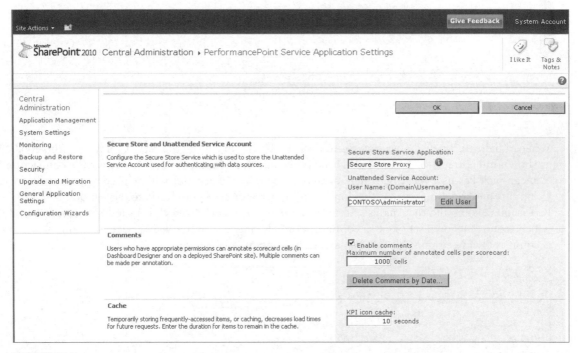

FIGURE 37-5

After creating a new data connection, you can start designing your dashboard. Either select the Create tab in the ribbon or right-click the PerformancePoint Content folder in the Workspace Browser to create new items that can be added to a dashboard. You can create charts, graphs, and scorecards, then place them on one or many dashboards that can then be deployed to SharePoint. You can also add Reporting Services reports to a dashboard inside PerformancePoint. The instance of Reporting Services does not even have to be set up in SharePoint integrated mode for you to use it in PerformancePoint. This gives you one alternative if you struggle to get Reporting Services integrated with SharePoint; you can just add each report as its own dashboard here. Remember that SharePoint is the repository for anything created in PerformancePoint, so you will find each item listed in the PerformancePoint Content folder of your Business Intelligence Center.

Now that you know what you can do in PerformancePoint and how to get it configured, try it by creating your own dashboard in the next section.

TRY IT

In this Try It, you will learn how to create a new dashboard using PerformancePoint 2010 and deploy it to SharePoint 2010. You will import an existing KPI from Analysis Services but display it in a scorecard and dashboard.

Lesson Requirements

Use the Dashboard Designer to create a dashboard that displays a revenue scorecard and analytic charts. This section assumes you followed the steps listed earlier in the lesson to be able to use the Unattended Service Account credentials.

Hints

➤ Deploy the completed Analysis Services database in the C:\Program Files\Microsoft SQL Server\100\Tools\Samples\AdventureWorks 2008R2 Analysis Services Project directory.

➤ Create a scorecard using the Internet Revenue KPI.

➤ Create an analytic chart showing sales amount by country and delivery date.

Step-by-Step

1. If you have not yet done so, deploy the completed Adventure Works cube that you receive when you download the sample database from www.codeplex.com. You will find the sample files to deploy in the C:\Program Files\Microsoft SQL Server\100\Tools\Samples\ AdventureWorks 2008R2 Analysis Services Project directory. If you need further assistance on deploying these files, review Section III of this book concerning Analysis Services.

2. Open the SharePoint site Knights24HourBI created in the previous lesson. If you are starting first on this lesson, just create a new site using the Business Intelligence Center template.

3. Select PerformancePoint Content from the Navigation pane on the left.

4. Click "Add new item." This will open the PerformancePoint Dashboard Designer.

5. Right-click Data Connections and select New Data Source.

6. Choose Analysis Services as the template and click OK.

7. Rename the connection **Adventure Works** and fill in the properties shown in Table 37-1. (See also Figure 37-6.)

TABLE 37-1

PROPERTY	VALUE
Server	localhost (or where you deployed the AdventureWorks cube to)
Database	Adventure Works DW 2008 R2
Cube	Adventure Works
Authentication	Unattended Service Account

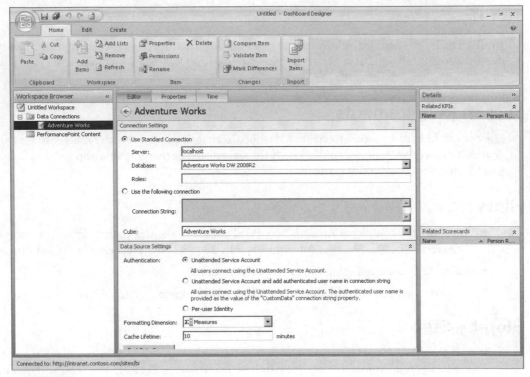

FIGURE 37-6

8. Right-click the new connection called Adventure Works in the Workspace Browser and hit Save.

9. Right-click the PerformancePoint Content folder and select New ⇨ Scorecard.

10. Select the Analysis Services template that will use an existing Analysis Services data source to create the scorecard and then click OK.

11. Choose the Adventure Works data source from the list of Data Connections and then click Next, as shown in Figure 37-7.

12. Select Import SQL Server Analysis Services KPI and click Next.

13. Check the Internet Revenue KPI and click Next, as shown in Figure 37-8.

14. Click Next to bypass the Add Measure Filters window without making any changes.

15. Click Next to bypass the Add Member Columns windows without making any changes. You can add measure filters and member columns at any time.

16. Click Finish to publish the KPI to the PerformancePoint Content folder.

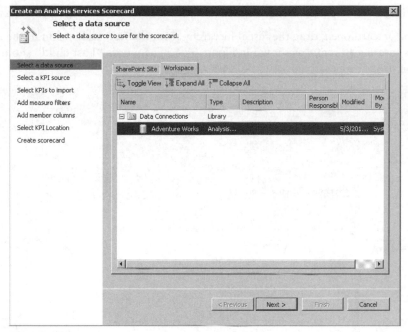

FIGURE 37-7

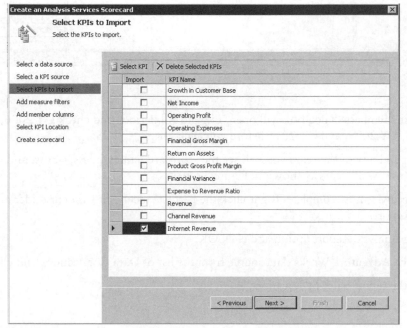

FIGURE 37-8

17. Rename the new scorecard **Internet Revenue Scorecard** in the Workspace Browser.

18. With the scorecard open, drag the Fiscal hierarchy from the Date dimension to the right of the words Internet Revenue as shown in Figure 37-9. The words "Last child" should appear before you drop the hierarchy.

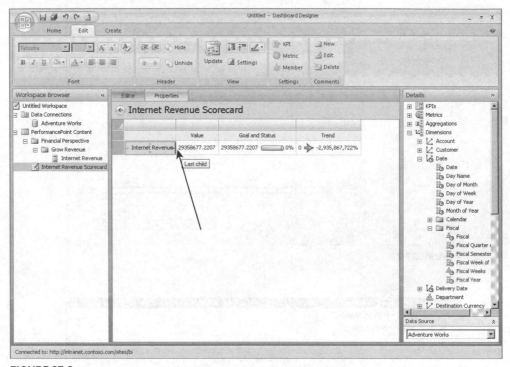

FIGURE 37-9

19. The Select Members dialog box will open. Expand All Periods and check CY 2006, CY 2007, CY 2008, CY 2009, and CY 2011 before you click OK.

20. If you expand any of the years you will see the scorecard values, goals, status, and trends expand to show all years as shown in Figure 37-10.

21. The scorecard is now complete. Right-click the PerformancePoint Content folder and select New ⇨ Report.

22. Select the Analytic Report option and click OK.

23. Choose the Adventure Works data source from the list of Data Connections and click Finish.

24. Rename the report **Sales by Location**.

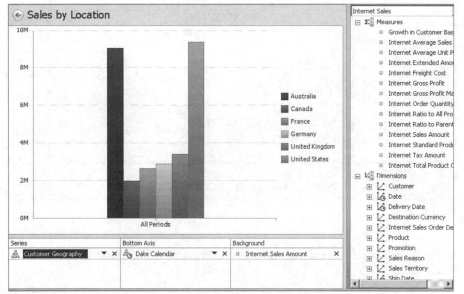

	Value	Goal and Status		Trend	
⊟ Internet Revenue			⊠		
⊞ FY 2006	7072084.2438	7072084.2438	0%	0 ⇒	-707,208,424%
⊟ FY 2007	5762134.2969	7779292.66818	-26%	-1 ⬇	576,213,530%
⊞ H1 FY 2007	2724632.9392	3593011.02226	-24%	-1 ⬇	272,463,394%
⊞ H2 FY 2007	3037501.3577	4186281.64592	-27%	-1 ⬇	303,750,236%
⊞ FY 2008	16473618.05	6338347.72659	160%	1 ⬆	1,647,361,705%
⊞ FY 2009	50840.63	18120979.855	-100%	-1 ⬇	5,084,163%
⊞ FY 2011		55924.693		-1 ⬇	

FIGURE 37-10

25. Drag Internet Sales Amount to the Background box, the Calendar hierarchy from the Date dimension to the Bottom Axis box, and the Geography hierarchy to the Series box from the Customer dimension.

26. You should have one bar on the bar chart now. Click the one bar and the chart will drill down to show all the children of the Geography hierarchy. Figure 37-11 is what the graph should look like after you click the single bar.

FIGURE 37-11

27. Right-click the PerformancePoint Content folder and select New ⇨ Dashboard.

28. Select the 2 Columns template and click OK.

29. Rename the dashboard **Internet Sales Dashboard**. Also, rename the page **Sales Dashboard**.

30. Drag the Internet Revenue Scorecard to the left column of the dashboard from the Details pane on the right of the Dashboard Designer.

31. Drag the Sales by Location report to the right column of the dashboard from the Details pane. Figure 37-12 shows the Dashboard Designer with Steps 28 through 30 completed.

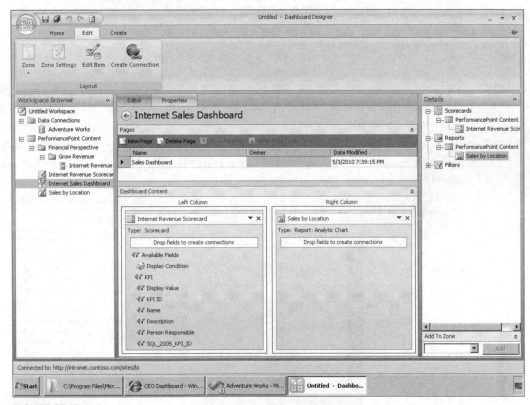

FIGURE 37-12

32. In the Workspace Browser, right-click the Internet Sales Dashboard and select Deploy to SharePoint.

Congratulations! You deployed your first PerformancePoint dashboard to SharePoint. This is a major step toward giving your business users an overview of the company's performance.

 Please select Lesson 37 on the DVD to view the video that accompanies this lesson.

38

Deploying and Using Excel Services

As you have noticed from the previous lessons on SharePoint, there are many integrated features that allow you to use stand-alone Microsoft products in a web environment. Excel Services is another feature that allows you to bring the capabilities of Excel into the web interface of SharePoint so you can view, edit, and share Excel documents in a collaborative environment. Most business users are familiar with and very comfortable building Excel workbooks, spreadsheets, and calculations. Finding the data your end users need could not be any easier than with the capabilities of Excel and SharePoint combined in Excel Services.

Excel Services allows you to view workbooks that are currently trapped in a shared folder by exposing them on a web interface. Users will no longer need a direct connection to the Analysis Services to view pivot tables and charts that are created either. Using a trusted connection, Excel Services gives wider access to already created pivot tables that have been created from cubes.

The Excel Services architecture has three components: Excel Calculation Services, Excel Web Access, and Excel Web Services. The Excel Calculation Service (ECS) is the engine of Excel Services, which updates data from external data sources, runs calculations on Excel sheets and loads the Excel document itself. Excel Web Access (EWA) is where the user actually interacts with the Excel workbook through a web application. Excel Web Services (EWS) is a web service hosted by SharePoint Services that allows developers to build a custom application based on an Excel workbook.

The management tools for Excel Services can be found on the SharePoint 2010 Central Administration site. Select Manage service application from the Application Management section. Click the service called ExcelServiceApp1 to see the administrator options, shown in Figure 38-1.

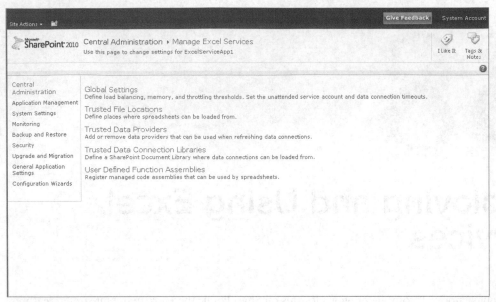

FIGURE 38-1

From the Manage Excel Services page you can define the trusted file locations, trusted data providers and trusted data connection libraries. A trusted file location can be a Microsoft SharePoint Foundation location, network file share, or web folder in which Excel Services is permitted to open workbooks. Creating a Microsoft SharePoint Foundation trusted location with `http://` as the address and checking "Children trusted," as shown in Figure 38-2, enables the entire SharePoint site as a trusted location.

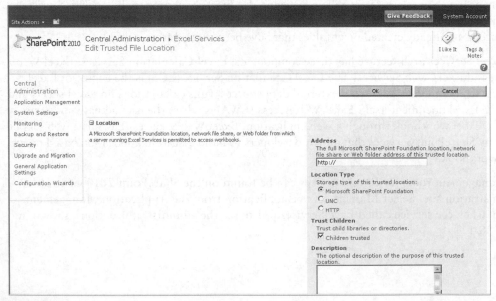

FIGURE 38-2

Trusted data providers are external databases that the Excel Calculation Service has been told are acceptable providers. Only data providers listed as trusted data providers can be processed in an Excel Services workbook inside SharePoint. The data providers provided by default are shown in Figure 38-3.

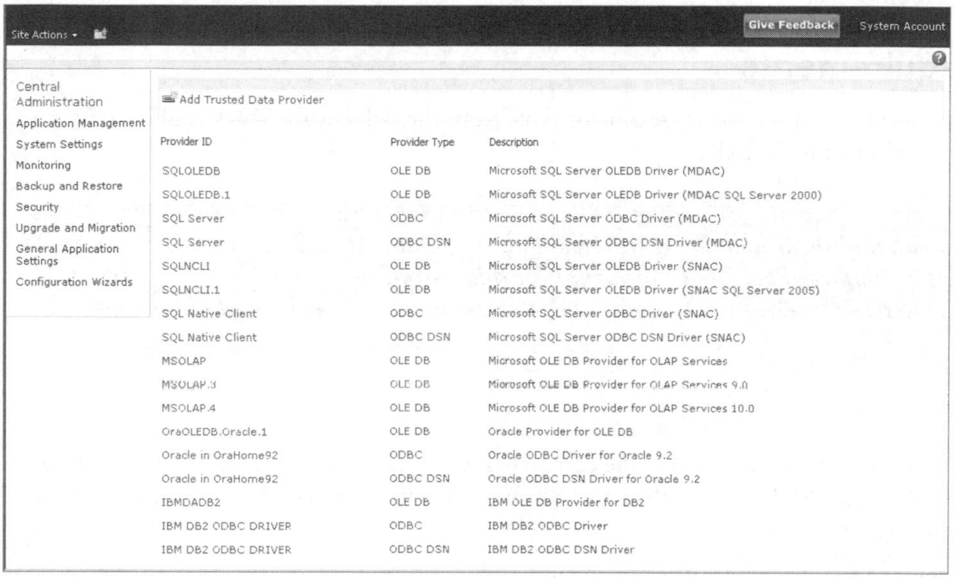

FIGURE 38-3

Trusted data connection libraries are SharePoint document libraries that store Office data connection files. If you choose to, you can configure Excel Services to use .odc files instead of embedded connections. You may recognize this file extension from Lesson 31, in which you browsed the cube in Excel. Any time you create a new data connection inside Excel, Excel creates and saves this .odc file, as shown in Figure 38-4. The default configuration uses embedded connection string storage, but you can save these files to SharePoint, if you prefer.

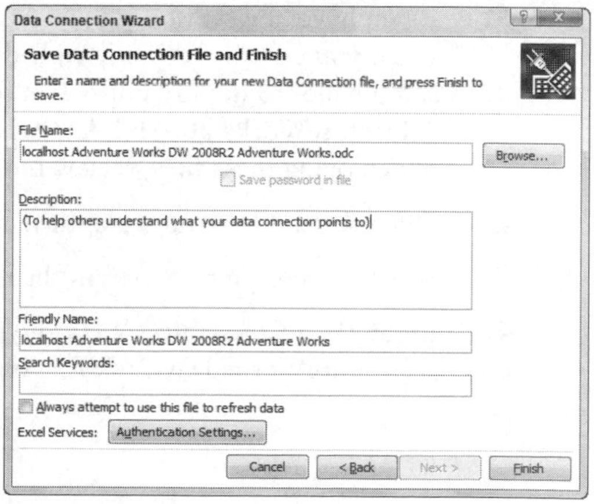

Also found in the SharePoint Central Administration site is the Global Settings page, which allows you to handle security, memory usage, and timeouts. If you need to add any custom code assemblies for calculations, you can do so in the User Defined Function Assemblies page.

Now that you have learned about the benefits and architecture of Excel Services with SharePoint, try it in the next section by creating a workbook and deploying it to SharePoint.

FIGURE 38-4

TRY IT

In this Try It, you will learn how to create a new Excel report using Excel 2010 and deploy it to SharePoint 2010. With Excel Services you will be able to interact with a workbook inside SharePoint as if it were still in Excel.

Lesson Requirements

In this lesson, use Excel 2010 to create a pivot table from the Adventure Works cube, and then deploy that Excel sheet to SharePoint.

 You can find the download associated with this lesson at www.wrox.com. *It contains a completed version of the Try It for this lesson.*

Hints

➤ If you have not already, deploy the completed Analysis Service database in the C:\Program Files\Microsoft SQL Server\100\Tools\Samples\AdventureWorks 2008R2 Analysis Services Project directory.

➤ Connect to the AdventureWorks cube in Excel.

➤ Create a pivot chart and table that show Internet sales, with the Calendar hierarchy from the Date dimension on the rows and the Sales Territory hierarchy from the Sales Territory dimension on the columns.

Step-by-Step

1. If you have not yet done so, deploy the completed AdventureWorks cube that you receive when you download the sample database from www.codeplex.com. You will find the sample files to deploy in the C:\Program Files\Microsoft SQL Server\100\Tools\Samples\ AdventureWorks 2008R2 Analysis Services Project directory. If you need further assistance in deploying these files, review the Analysis Services section (Section III) of this book.

2. Open Excel 2010 and select the Data tab.

3. Select From Other Sources in the ribbon and pick From Analysis Services.

4. In the Data Connection Wizard type the name of the server to which you deployed the AdventureWorks DW 2008R2 Analysis Services database. Click Next.

5. Select Adventure Works DW 2008R2 from the database drop-down list and click the AdventureWorks cube. Click Next.

6. Click Finish to confirm the data connection and start the pivot table. Note that Excel Services is set by default to Windows Authentication when you click the Authentication Settings button.

7. In the Import Data dialog box choose PivotChart and PivotTable Report. Click OK.

8. In the PivotTable Field List pane change the "Show fields related to" drop-down box to Internet Sales.

9. Check the Internet Sales Amount measure to add it to the Values data box at the bottom right of your screen.

10. Find the date dimensions and drag the Calendar hierarchy into the Axis Fields data box.

11. Find the Sales Territory dimension and drag the Sales Territory hierarchy into the Legend Fields data box. Your screen should look like Figure 38-5 after you fit the chart on the screen.

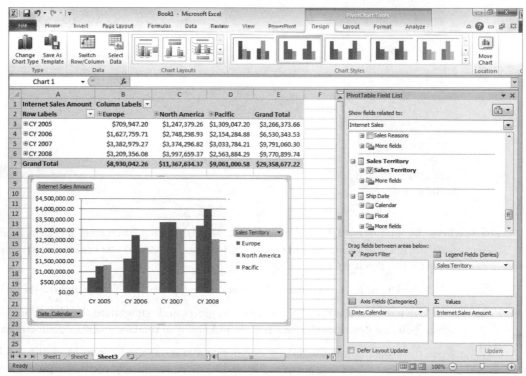

FIGURE 38-5

12. To deploy this Excel workbook to SharePoint use the File tab and click Share or Save & Send.

13. Pick Save to SharePoint and select "Browse for a location," as shown in Figure 38-6.

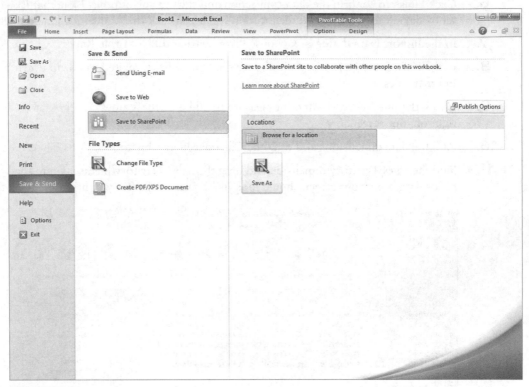

FIGURE 38-6

14. Type the SharePoint URL for the Knights24HourBI that you created in the previous lesson for the folder location. If you are starting first on this lesson, just create a new site using the Business Intelligence Center template.

15. Select the Documents document library and save the workbook as **Knights24HourBI.xlsx**.

16. With the workbook saved, open Internet Explorer and navigate to the SharePoint site to which you just deployed the file. You should find it in the Documents document library.

17. Open the workbook in SharePoint and notice that it has the look and feel of Excel but is built into SharePoint, as shown in Figure 38-7. You can interact with the pivot table just as you would in Excel and drill down deeper into each hierarchy.

Congratulations! You just deployed your first Excel workbook to SharePoint. Now you can share all current and future workbooks with the rest of your company.

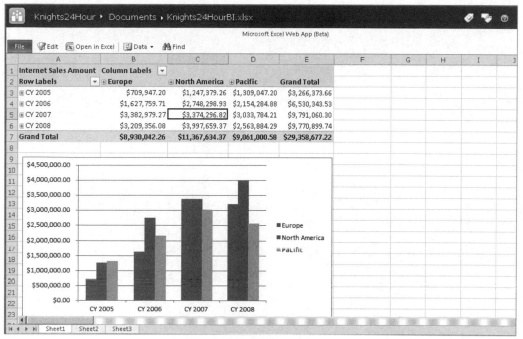

FIGURE 38-7

 Please select Lesson 38 on the DVD to view the video that accompanies this lesson.

39

Deploying and Using PowerPivot in SharePoint

In Lesson 33 you learned how PowerPivot can load massive amounts of data into Excel and then users can create reports that process all within a system's memory. This new technology may change how we think about Business Intelligence projects. PowerPivot gives end users much of the same functionality that Analysis Services gives them in Excel, with the addition of slicers, which were discussed in Lesson 33. For large enterprise data warehouse projects, it makes sense to go through the process of designing an Analysis Services cube, but for small departmental projects, PowerPivot fits perfectly.

Adding PowerPivot reports to SharePoint can be a lengthy process, but the payoff can be impressive to end users. For example, SharePoint 2010 has new web parts for PowerPivot that can be used to display PowerPivot documents. Figure 39-1 shows the PowerPivot Gallery and the carousel effect it has, which gives you a way to preview each document before opening it. In this lesson you will walk through the steps needed to configure SharePoint and PowerPivot to work together, before creating a PowerPivot Gallery for your users.

The process for installing and configuring the PowerPivot integration with SharePoint begins with the installation of both SQL Server 2008 R2 and SharePoint 2010. When installing, you must ensure that you choose to install SharePoint as a Server Farm instead of a Standalone instance (see Figure 39-2). Standalone installations are not supported for PowerPivot. It is also important not to run the configuration wizard until after SQL Server is installed. When installing SharePoint, uncheck the option at the end of the installation to run the SharePoint Product and Technologies Configuration Wizard immediately.

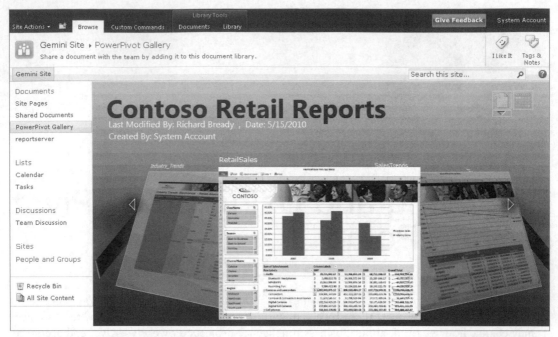

FIGURE 39-1

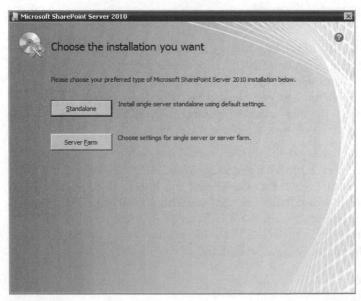

FIGURE 39-2

Next you must run the installation for SQL Server 2008 R2 to install SQL Server PowerPivot for SharePoint, as shown in Figure 39-3. SharePoint uses Analysis Services as a shared service to provide the in-memory processing that PowerPivot requires.

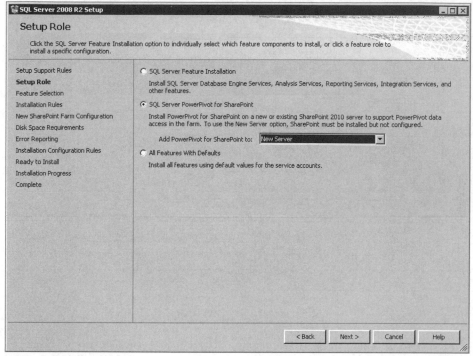

FIGURE 39-3

To configure this new instance, you must provide a domain account that will be used to run the Central Administration service and to access the configuration database. Setup will not permit any built-in or regular Windows accounts, so ensure that you can provide the needed domain account. You will also need to create a passphrase that will be used when you add a new application server, as shown in Figure 39-4. Lastly, you must specify a port number for the Central Administration web application. Setup automatically generates a valid number, but you can manually override that number here. During the installation SQL Server runs the SharePoint Products and Technologies Configuration in the background, so, upon completion, SharePoint will be ready as well.

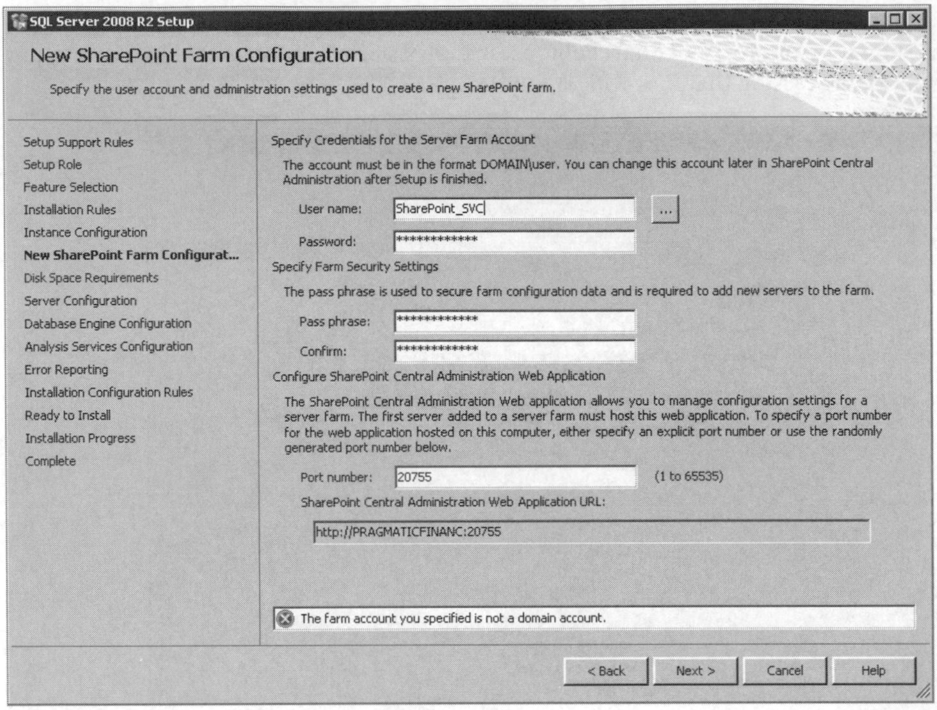

FIGURE 39-4

To confirm the successful installation, open SharePoint 2010 Central Administration and select "Manage farm features" under the System Settings heading. Verify that the PowerPivot integration feature is set to active. Return to the Central Administration main site, and visit the "Manage services on server" page under System Settings. Check that SQL Server Analysis Services and SQL Server PowerPivot System Service have started. Lastly, in the Application Management section of the Central Administration site, select "Manage service applications." Open the Default PowerPivot Service Application to configure the services and provide an account for unattended data refresh. To test that PowerPivot is correctly configured, deploy some reports you create to SharePoint.

Now that you have learned how to set up the integration between PowerPivot and SharePoint, try it in the next section by deploying to a PowerPivot Gallery in SharePoint.

TRY IT

In this Try It you will create a new PowerPivot Gallery in SharePoint 2010. Then, with Excel 2010, you will create a set of PowerPivot reports and deploy them to the PowerPivot Gallery.

Lesson Requirements

Use Excel 2010 to create a PowerPivot table from the AdventureWorks cube. Then deploy it to SharePoint in the PowerPivot Gallery.

 You can find the download associated with this lesson at www.wrox.com.

Hints

➤ Download the PowerPivot add-in for Excel.

➤ Download the AdventureWorks sample databases.

➤ Connect to the AdventureWorksDW2008 R2 database in PowerPivot.

➤ Create a PivotTable and PivotChart using Internet Sales and Years. Also add a slicer using the category name.

➤ Deploy the completed document to the SharePoint PowerPivot Gallery.

Step-by-Step

1. If you have not yet done so, download the AdventureWorks sample databases from www .codeplex.com.

2. If you have not yet done so, download the PowerPivot add-in for Excel. (Lesson 32 walks you through this step.)

3. Open Excel 2010 and select the PowerPivot tab.

4. Click PowerPivot Window in the ribbon on the PowerPivot tab. This will open PowerPivot for Excel.

5. In the PowerPivot for Excel ribbon, click the From Database drop-down list and select From SQL Server.

6. Enter **localhost,** or the name of the server the AdventureWorks databases are on, for the server name.

7. Select AdventureWorksDW2008 R2 from the "Database name" drop-down list; then click Next. Steps 6 and 7 are shown completed in Figure 39-5.

8. Leave the default "Select from a list of tables and view to choose the data to import"; then click Next.

FIGURE 39-5

9. Select the following tables before hitting Next:
- ➤ FactInternetSales
- ➤ DimDate
- ➤ DimProduct
- ➤ DimProductSubcategory
- ➤ DimProductCategory
- ➤ DimSalesTerritory

10. When all tables are successfully imported, your screen should look like Figure 39-6. After all tables are imported click Close.

11. In the PowerPivot for Excel ribbon, select the PivotTable drop-down list and select Chart and Table (Vertical). Click OK when you are asked to create a new worksheet.

12. With the PivotTable selected go to the PowerPivot Field List and select the following fields (Table 39-1) from their corresponding tables.

13. With the PivotChart selected go to the PowerPivot Field List again and select the following fields (Table 39-2) from their corresponding tables. (Note that the vertical slicer carries over to this chart. Do not remove it.)

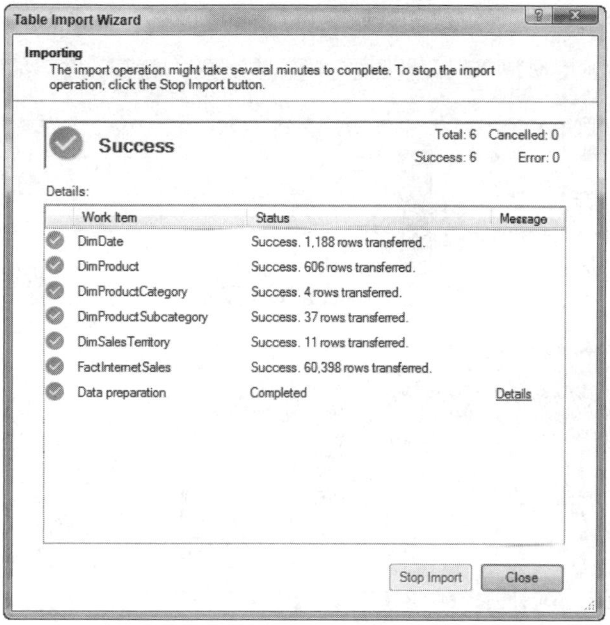

FIGURE 39-6

TABLE 39-1

LOCATION	TABLE	FIELD
Row Labels	DimDate	CalendarYear CalendarQuarter
Values	FactInternetSales	OrderQuantity
Column Labels	DimProductCategory	EnglishProductCategoryName
Slicers Vertical	DimProductCategory	EnglishProductCategoryName

TABLE 39-2

LOCATION	TABLE	FIELD
Legend Fields (Series)	DimDate	CalendarYear
Values	FactInternetSales	OrderQuantity
Axis Fields (Categories)	DimProductCategory	EnglishProductCategoryName

When these fields are added your screen should look like Figure 39-7.

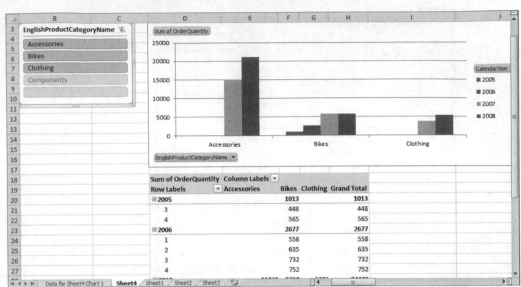

FIGURE 39-7

14. Open SharePoint and create a new site called **Knights24HourPowerPivot** that uses the PowerPivot Site template.

15. Return to Excel and select the File tab; then click Share or Save & Send.

16. Pick Save to SharePoint and select Browse for a location.

17. Navigate to the PowerPivot Gallery document library and save the file as **Knights24HourPowerPivot**, as shown in Figure 39-8.

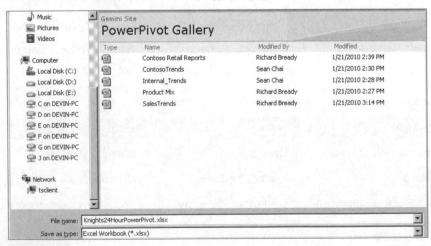

FIGURE 39-8

18. Return to the SharePoint site and select the PowerPivot Gallery. You will see a document carousel that will allow you to flip through the documents. Figure 39-9 shows the document in the gallery.

FIGURE 39-9

19. Continue to build more PowerPivot documents and deploy them to the same location to load the carousel.

Congratulations! You have deployed your first PowerPivot workbook to SharePoint.

 Please select Lesson 39 on the DVD to view the video that accompanies this lesson.

40

Managing SharePoint Business Intelligence

In the previous lessons of this section of the book, you learned how each Business Intelligence tool built into SharePoint is configured and then used to provide solutions to your end users. In this lesson, you will walk through some of the management tools available to monitor your Business Intelligence solutions.

The SharePoint 2010 Central Administration site is where these management tools are available. If you go to the Central Administration site and select General Application Settings, you will find two sections for managing Business Intelligence, shown in Figure 40-1. Notice that although there is a Reporting Services section here it does not help with managing day-to-day usage. The purpose of this section, which was discussed in Lesson 36, is to configure Reporting Services integration with SharePoint. The section that you should focus on from a management perspective is the PowerPivot section.

FIGURE 40-1

The PowerPivot Management Dashboard enables you to monitor PowerPivot usage, failures, and general server health. The first graph on the top of the page, Infrastructure — Server Health, initially shows the query response time by day for your PowerPivot reports. Figure 40-2 shows October 10 with a longer-than-expected query run time. You can easily toggle among Query Response Times, Average Instance Memory, and Average Instance CPU views in this report to see all relevant server health information.

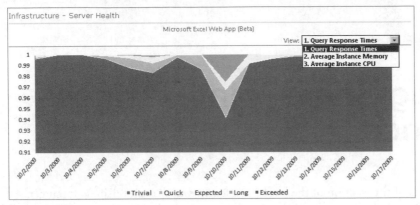

FIGURE 40-2

Below this chart you will find Workbook Activity — Chart. This chart displays the number of users using a workbook and also the number of queries on each workbook, as shown in Figure 40-3. Pressing the play button will animate the chart so that it shows changes in user habits over time and how the importance of different workbooks changes. Each dot on the chart represents a workbook, and, if you select a dot, it will give you statistics on the selected item. To the right of Workbook Activity — Chart you will find Workbook Activity — List, which displays a grid view of the reports monitored in the chart.

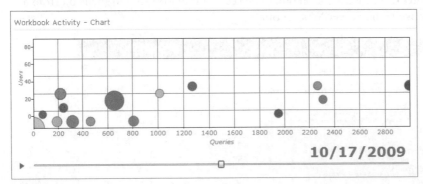

FIGURE 40-3

You can then monitor the time it takes to refresh data on these reports by using the Data Refresh — Recent Activity view. This list shows the most recent updates to report data and how long the data took to update. Figure 40-4 shows the most recently updated reports, the dates they were updated, and how many seconds the data took to update. Any failures in data refreshes can be found to the right of this list in the Data Refresh — Recent Failures list.

Managing Reporting Services in SharePoint is fairly simple. You learned how to deploy reports to SharePoint in Lesson 36, and managing them is not very difficult. With a report stored on SharePoint, things like subscriptions are handled much as they would be on the Report Manager. With SQL Server R2, SharePoint and the Report Manager are even more similar. To set up a subscription, select the report and click Subscribe. Follow the same steps you learned in Lesson 28 on deploying and administering SSRS to complete the subscription.

Data Refresh - Recent Activity		▾
Workbook	**End Time**	**Duration (seconds)**
OperationsForecast.xlsx	5/24/2010 4:01:23 AM	1
AsiaForecast.xlsx	5/24/2010 4:01:23 AM	0
DanJumpForecasts.xlsx	5/24/2010 4:01:23 AM	0
industrybikesAccess.xlsx	5/24/2010 4:01:23 AM	0
SalesTerritoryAnalysis.xlsx	5/24/2010 4:01:23 AM	0
industrybikesAccess.xlsx	4/8/2010 10:44:27	0

FIGURE 40-4

TRY IT

Your Try It section for this lesson is a bit different. Throughout the book you have been challenged with hands-on lessons to make sure you understand the technologies we're covering. For this lesson, your goal should be to keep in mind how your Business Intelligence solution is being used in SharePoint. For instance, ask yourself these questions as you work on your own SharePoint project:

➤   Is the hardware I am currently using able to handle the number of users I need to access my PowerPivot reports, Reporting Services reports, and PerformancePoint dashboards?

➤   Have I given adequate access to my users in the places they need it?

➤   Are my reports easy to find for the users who require them?

➤   If there is a failure during a data refresh, where do I go to find out when it occurred and on what report?

If you can keep these questions in the back of your mind while working on developing your SharePoint BI solution, they can truly help you make the right decisions for your end users.

 Please select Lesson 40 on the DVD to view the video that accompanies this lesson.

APPENDIX

APPENDIX

What's on the DVD?

This appendix provides you with information on the contents of the DVD that accompanies this book. For the latest and greatest information, please refer to the ReadMe file located at the root of the DVD. Here is what you will find in this appendix:

➤ System Requirements

➤ Using the DVD

➤ What's on the DVD

➤ Troubleshooting

SYSTEM REQUIREMENTS

Make sure that your computer meets the minimum system requirements listed in this section. If your computer doesn't match up to most of these requirements, you may have a problem using the contents of the DVD.

➤ PC running Windows XP, Windows Vista, Windows 7, or later

➤ An Internet connection

➤ At least 512MB of RAM

➤ A DVD-ROM drive

USING THE DVD

To access the content from the DVD, follow these steps.

1. Insert the DVD into your computer's DVD-ROM drive. The license agreement appears.

2. Read through the license agreement, and then click the Accept button if you want to use the DVD.

   The DVD interface appears. Simply select the lesson number for the video you want to view.

*The interface won't launch if you have AutoRun disabled. In that case, click Start ⇨ Run (For Windows Vista or Windows 7, Start ⇨ All Programs ⇨ Accessories ⇨ Run). In the dialog box that appears, type **D:\Start.exe**. (Replace D with the proper letter if your DVD drive uses a different letter. If you don't know the letter, see how your DVD drive is listed under My Computer.) Click OK.*

WHAT'S ON THE DVD

This DVD is the most exciting part of this book for the author team. With this DVD you can listen to five geeks who love Business Intelligence work through the lessons you've worked with throughout the book. Because we believe strongly in the value of video training, this DVD contains hours of instructional video. At the end of most lessons in the book, you will find a reference to an instructional video on the DVD that accompanies that lesson. In that video, one of us will walk you through the content and examples contained in that lesson. All you need to do is play the DVD and select the lesson you want to watch.

TROUBLESHOOTING

If you have difficulty installing or using any of the materials on the companion DVD, try the following solutions:

➤ **Reboot if necessary.** As with many troubleshooting situations, it may make sense to reboot your machine to reset any faults in your environment.

➤ **Turn off any anti-virus software that you may have running.** Installers sometimes mimic virus activity and can make your computer incorrectly believe that it is being infected by a virus. (Be sure to turn the anti-virus software back on later.)

➤ **Close all running programs.** The more programs you're running, the less memory is available to other programs. Installers also typically update files and programs; if you keep other programs running, installation may not work properly.

➤ **Reference the ReadMe.** Please refer to the ReadMe file located at the root of the DVD for the latest product information at the time of publication.

CUSTOMER CARE

If you have trouble with the DVD, please call the Wiley Product Technical Support phone number at (800) 762-2974. Outside the United States, call 1 (317) 572-3994. You can also contact Wiley Product Technical Support at `http://support.wiley.com`. John Wiley & Sons will provide technical support only for installation and other general quality control items. For technical support on the applications themselves, consult the program's vendor or author.

To place additional orders or to request information about other Wiley products, please call (877) 762-2974.

INDEX

INDEX

C

WILEY PUBLISHING, INC.
END-USER LICENSE AGREEMENT